Neil Marlow
oct? 1993.

Theories and concepts of politics

This new textbook offers social science students an exciting introduction to social and political theory. It asks the questions at the heart of contemporary political debate — Why should the individual obey the law? Do people have a right to welfare? Is equality all that feminists aim for? What does it mean to be Green? — and explains the meaning of the concepts that we use to answer them.

Each chapter discusses a particular concept or theoretical issue. Topics covered include freedom, citizenship and rights, social justice and equality, constitutionalism and democracy, political obligation, power, violence and revolution, feminism, environmentalism, realism and international relations, and welfare. Referring to current political debates to illustrate their argument, the authors show how people of different political or theoretical persuasions view each of these concepts or issues in often dramatically different (and frequently flawed) ways. They offer original solutions of their own as to how these interpretative disputes might be resolved.

This book will be essential reading for students of political and social theory.

Richard Bellamy is Professor of Politics at the University of East Anglia.

D1325031

Theories and concepts of politics
An introduction

edited by
Richard Bellamy

Manchester University Press
Manchester and New York
Distributed exclusively in the USA and Canada by St Martin's Press

Published by Manchester University Press
Oxford Road, Manchester M13 9PL, UK
and Room 400, 175 Fifth Avenue,
New York, NY 10010, USA

Distributed exclusively in the USA and Canada
by St Martin's Press, Inc.,
175 Fifth Avenue, New York, NY 10010, USA

British Library Cataloguing-in-Publication Data
A catalogue record for this book is available from the British Library

Library of Congress Cataloging-in-Publication Data
Theories and concepts of politics / edited by Richard Bellamy.
    p. cm.
  Includes index.
  ISBN 0-7190-3655-0. – ISBN 0-7190-3656-9 (pbk.)
  1. Political science. 2. Political science – Philosophy.
I. Bellamy, Richard (Richard Paul)
JA.T495   1993
320 – dc20   93-9872   CIP

ISBN 0 7190 3655 0 *hardback*
ISBN 0 7190 3656 9 *paperback*

Typeset in Great Britain
by Williams Graphics, Llanddulas, North Wales

Printed in Great Britain
by Bell & Bain Limited, Glasgow

Contents

Notes on contributors

Zenon Bańkowski is a Reader in the Centre for Criminology and the Social and Philosophical Study of Law in the University of Edinburgh. Among other works, he is the author with J. McManus and N. Mullin of *Lay Justice?* (1987) and the editor, with Neil MacCormick, of *Enlightenment, Rights and Revolution: Essays in Legal and Social Philosophy* (1989).

Barry Barnes was a Professor of Sociology and Director of the Science Studies Unit at the University of Edinburgh. He is now Professor of Sociology at the University of Exeter. His many publications include *Scientific Knowledge and Sociological Theory* (1974), *Interests and the Growth of Knowledge* (1977), *T. S. Kuhn and Social Science* (1982) and *The Nature of Power* (1988).

Richard Bellamy was a Lecturer in the Politics Department at the University of Edinburgh from 1988–1992. He is now Professor of Politics at the University of East Anglia. He is the author of *Modern Italian Social Theory* (1987), *Liberalism and Modern Society* (1992) and, with Darrow Schecter, *Gramsci and the Italian State* (1993). He has edited *Liberalism and Recent Legal and Social Philosophy* (1989) and *Victorian Liberalism: Nineteenth Century Political Thought and Practice* (1990).

Beverley Brown is a Senior Lecturer in the Centre for Criminology and the Social and Philosophical Study of Law at the University of Edinburgh. She was editor of the feminist journal *m/f* and has published numerous articles on feminist theory, pornography, and women and the law.

Martin Clark is a Reader in the Politics Department of the University of Edinburgh. His publications include *Antonio Gramsci and the Revolution that Failed* (1977), *Modern Italy 1871–1982*

(1984) and the modern (1847–1975) section of M. Guidetti (Ed.), *Storia dei Sardi e della Sardegna*, Vol. 4 (1990). Since 1988 he has taught a course on the politics of the environment.

Lisa Dominguez is a Lecturer in the Politics Department of the University of Edinburgh. She is the co-editor, with Malcolm Anderson, of *Cultural Policy in Western Europe.*

Richard Gunn is a Lecturer in the Politics Department of the University of Edinburgh. Amongst his recent publications is 'Against Historical Materialism' in Werner Bonefeld, Richard Gunn and Kosmas Psychopedis (Eds.), *Open Marxism* (1992).

John Holmwood is a Lecturer in the Department of Sociology of the University of Edinburgh. He is the author, with A. Stewart, of *Explanation and Social Theory* (1991).

Alison Jeffries was a Lecturer in the Politics Department of the University of Edinburgh from 1988–1990. She is currently a Tutorial Fellow in Politics at Magdalene College, Oxford. She has just completed her D. Phil. on the conception of freedom in contemporary political argument.

Neil MacCormick is Regius Professor of Public Law and the Law of Nature and Nations at the University of Edinburgh. His publications include *Legal Reasoning and Legal Theory* (1978), *Legal Right and Social Democracy* (1982) and, as editor with Zenon Bańkowski, *Enlightenment, Rights and Revolution: Essays in Legal and Social Philosophy* (1989).

Michael A. Menlowe is a Lecturer in the Department of Philosophy at Edinburgh University. He is the author of various articles on legal and moral philosophy and the editor, with Eric Matthews, of *Philosophy and Health Care* (1992).

Acknowledgements

This book was conceived as a collaborative effort between colleagues at the University of Edinburgh. Other commitments and shifting personnel has meant that not all of those engaged in teaching social and political theory have been able to be involved. In this regard, I am particularly grateful to Paul Smart and his successor Leo MacCarthy for the support they offered me as editor at the beginning and final stages respectively of this project. As one of those who has subsequently moved on since the completion of this book, I would also like to thank all of those at Edinburgh − including, but not only, the contributors to this volume − for having made my period at the university so intellectually enjoyable and fruitful. I dedicate the book to them and Malcolm Anderson in particular.

1 *Richard Bellamy*

Introduction: The demise and rise of political theory

In a famous introduction to a collection of articles on *Philosophy, Politics and Society* published in 1956, the editor, Peter Laslett, lamented the 'death' of political philosophy in the English speaking world:

> It is one of the assumptions of intellectual life in our country that there should be amongst us men whom we think of as political philosophers. Philosophers themselves, and sensitive to philosophic change, they are to concern themselves with political and social relationships at the widest possible level of generality. They are to apply the methods and the conclusions of contemporary thought to the evidence of the contemporary situation. For three hundred years of our history there have been such men writing in English, from the early seventeenth to the twentieth centuries, from Hobbes to Bosanquet. Today, it would seem, we have them no longer. The tradition has been broken and our assumption is misplaced, unless it is looked on as a belief in the possibility that the tradition is about to be resumed. For the moment, anyway, political philosophy is dead. (Laslett, 1956, p. vii)

In this introduction I shall briefly trace the demise and rise of Anglo-American political philosophy with the aim of providing a brief overview of the contemporary scene. As we shall see, although theorising about politics is much healthier in the 1990s than it was in the 1950s, it is no longer the confident enterprise of the great tradition bemoaned by Laslett. Neither the 'methods' nor the 'conclusions' of contemporary thought appear to provide the secure guides for today's political philosophers that Laslett suggested they offered their predecessors.

Laslett had no doubt who political philosophy's murderers were: 'the Logical Positivists did it' (Laslett, 1956, p. ix). Their refusal to allow the meaningfulness of any statement that was not either definitional (analytical) or empirical (synthetic), meant that prescriptive political theorising was, following the Humean injunction, committed to the flames as containing 'nothing but sophistry and illusion' (Hume, 1975, p. 165). In consequence, a neat division of labour occurred between philosophers and social scientists. The first group analysed political concepts in a formal manner, supposedly without introducing either empirical evidence or evaluative presuppositions. The second group sought to develop a new type of political theory which would enable them to classify and assess empirical data and formulate law-like generalisations concerning human behaviour. In both cases, the professionalisation of the two disciplines within the universities greatly aided this process. Political philosophy of the kind mourned by Laslett became a somewhat amateurish affair, its practitioners within academia being driven to historical studies in an effort to revive, and give scholarly prestige to, an activity which was denied contemporary relevance (e.g. Berlin, 1962; Strauss, 1959; Voeglin, 1952 and Wolin, 1960).

Of the two approaches, conceptual analysis has proved the more resilient, and in its recent uses not totally barren.[1] Philosophers such as T. D. Weldon (Weldon, 1953), Margaret MacDonald (MacDonald, 1951), and other members of the linguistic school, maintained that questions like 'Why should I obey *any* law or support *any* government?' were meaningless in the same way as questions like 'Am I deluded when I see things?' Sensible questions of a more limited kind, like 'Why should I obey the Conscription Act?', did not require philosophers to answer them. Their role merely consisted in revealing the 'worthless logical grounds' of putative answers to questions of the first kind, and in clarifying the 'meaning of terms' employed in answers to questions of the second kind. Their aim, in the words of Felix Oppenheim, was 'to provide basic political concepts with explications acceptable to anyone regardless of his normative or ideological commitments so that the truth or falsity of statements in which these concepts thus defined occur will depend exclusively on inter-subjectively ascertainable evidence' (Oppenheim, 1973, p. 56).

This task proved more difficult than they thought. Its coherence as a 'neutral' activity depended upon being able to separate the definition of concepts from considerations of their worth and practical realisation. Some of the difficulties of this approach are analysed by Alison Jeffries in her chapter on freedom (Chapter 2). According to the linguistic school, we could resolve the problem of whether a person was free or not by asking whether their situation conformed to the state conventionally denoted by the term 'free'. However, the assumption of an 'unequivocal' 'ordinary use of language' is inappropriate. Take Weinstein's use of the linguistic method to analyse the nineteenth century conception of freedom. Commenting on T. H. Green's 'positive' definition (Weinstein, 1965, p. 151), he argued that to say someone who lacks the resources to read books was unfree to read them was a misuse of the term. What was really meant was that the individual was unable to read them. If the distinction between being free to do something and being able to do something was eroded, he claimed, then there would be no words left to refer to the case of someone who was legally prohibited from reading. However, as Jeffries shows, the debate over different views of freedom cuts deeper than a discussion over correct usage. A person who regards the practical ability to perform an act to be included in the term freedom is articulating a different moral principle and vision of society from someone who wishes to restrict the term to its narrow negative sense of a lack of legal or physical impediments. Both senses can be employed without manifest absurdity. Resolving a dispute over the preferred meaning of freedom is not analogous to establishing whether, for example, 'crown' in a given context means a piece of royal head gear, a silver coin, or the top of someone's head. In this instance, the objects referred to, and hence their senses, are clearly distinct and no value judgements are involved in employing one rather than the others. To say the king gave his vassal a crown and not specify it was a coin would simply be misleading. In contrast, to describe a people as unfree on account of their poverty rather than their tyrannical ruler is not to employ words incorrectly but to refer to a particular set of political commitments. Within that context the statement is perfectly intelligible, and to challenge it will involve engaging in substantive arguments about the likely practical and moral consequences of adopting such a view.

The value-dependency of political concepts introduces a dimension of relativity or contestability into theorising about politics which undermines not only the project of linguistic analysis but equally that of positivist political science (Connolly, 1974; Gallie, 1956). This point informs the discussions of power and realism in international relations by Barry Barnes (Chapter 9) and Lisa

Dominguez (Chapter 10) respectively. Political scientists, such as
Seymour Lipset, Harold Lasswell and David Easton, drew a sharp
distinction between normative and empirical political theory. Whilst
accepting that, in Easton's words, 'we cannot shed our values in the
way we remove our coats' (Easton, 1953, p.225), they maintained
that:

> facts and values are logically heterogeneous. The factual aspect of a
> proposition refers to a part of reality; hence it can be tested by reference to
> the facts. In this way we check its truth. The moral aspect of a proposition,
> however, expresses only the emotional response of an individual to a state
> of real or presumed facts. It indicates whether and the extent to which an
> individual desires a particular state of affairs to exist. Although we can
> say that the aspect of a proposition can be true or false, it is meaningless
> to characterise the value aspect of a proposition in this way. (Easton, 1953,
> p.221)

Since, on this view, values 'can ultimately be reduced to emotional
responses conditioned by the individual's total life-experiences',
there was little point in engaging in reasoned argument about them.
'Normative' theory needed to be replaced by 'empirical' theories
which established correlations between the observable phenomena
of political life on the model of the natural sciences. Whilst these
political scientists generally admitted that this aim was yet to be
achieved, they were optimistic 'that the next hundred years will see
an unprecedented development in this field' (Hull, 1943).

The plausibility of this enterprise rested on a behaviourist
epistemology and the assumption that, in the developed democracies
of the West at least, ideological disputes were at an end. The
positivist thesis, however, soon came under attack from analytical
philosophers awakened to the implications of the value-laden
nature of language by the later writings of Ludwig Wittgenstein.
Peter Winch's book *The Idea of a Social Science* played a highly
original and important role in this respect. Winch disputed the
view that human behaviour could be adequately described without
reference to the intentions, motives and reasons of the actors
involved. Winch claimed that social behaviour entailed the acceptance
and following of rules. The act of voting could not be reduced to a
set of physical movements; rather, it was constituted by a set of
beliefs about the ways political decisions should be made. The formal
procedures of voting embodied what Wittgenstein called a 'form of

life' which gave them meaning (Wittgenstein, 1952, p. 226). The observer could only distinguish between a fair and a rigged election, or understand why participants regarded voting as a better way of arriving at collectively binding decisions than, say, deferring to a priest's expert analysis of the intestines of a goat, by grasping the 'forms of rationality' involved. Winch took this argument to the extreme of maintaining not simply moral relativism but cognitive relativism as well: in other words, the perception that knowledge is relative, not absolute. The rationality of the social scientist was itself rule-governed and parochial. Thus, to cite Winch's example, we could understand the witchcraft beliefs of the Azande, but we could not explain or criticise them (Winch, 1958). Alasdair MacIntyre, in an influential review of Winch's book (MacIntyre, 1971, Ch. 19), significantly modified this thesis to allow at least the possibility of asking whether the believer in witchcraft, for example, was a rational credent. Yet, even with the proviso that attention to the self-understandings of the agents involved does not rule out empirical questions about the factors influencing a given set of beliefs, the aspirations of political science are considerably weakened by Winch's criticisms.

These arguments were powerfully restated in a series of articles by Charles Taylor (1985, Part I) and MacIntyre (1971, Part II; 1981, Chs. 7–8). They make three main criticisms of the purported value-neutrality and scientific pretensions of the positivist project. First, they point out how the explanatory framework adopted by a political scientist has what Taylor calls a 'value slope'. A given framework draws on a particular view of human needs and potentialities which limit the range of acceptable political possibilities and implicitly point to certain policies or arrangements as better than others at satisfying the requirements of citizens.

Second, they argue that choosing between frameworks cannot be made on empirical grounds alone. For a given body of evidence can be frequently accommodated by alternative theories without proving decisive for any one of them. The success of general law-like explanations in the natural sciences depends upon the possibility of explaining all material changes from the first three minutes onwards according to the same concepts and processes. Human beings, however, adopt divergent and often disproportionate conceptual schemes, which in turn define the sort of people they conceive themselves to be and restrict the types of acts they perform. It is a function of this diversity that almost any complex political event will be the subject of numerous rival accounts of comparable plausibility. Moreover, disagreement over how to explain these events will run parallel with a broad consensus about their 'outside' detail, like the time and place they occurred. What differs are the 'inner' motivations of the participants and the difficulty of bringing all of them under a single covering law or set of laws.

Finally, the aspiring political scientist's problems are compounded by the openness of human affairs. The determining factors can be multiplied almost endlessly. Momentous political events have been attributed to causes ranging from the length of Cleopatra's nose to the invention of the wheel. It would be impossible to account for occurrences such as these in advance. Mark Anthony's aesthetic sense belongs to an unknown chemistry; his meeting with Cleopatra was a chance encounter. Similarly, prior to the existence of the wheel it would be impossible to imagine its influence on future events, since one could not predict its impact without actually inventing it. Thus, human life is constantly bound up with individual preferences, contingency and conceptual innovations which radically change the patterns of our lives. These interactions are so complex and un-planned that to provide a scheme capable of taking all of these into account plainly defies our ingenuity. This problem need have nothing to do with the sheer scale of the enterprise – though I cannot imagine how this hurdle could be overcome – the difficulties arise from the impossibility of guessing the moves both of ourselves and others, given a potentially infinite number of variables. Contingency, linked with our ability constantly to change the conceptual framework within which we view and interpret events and our responses, makes the search for constant factors a seemingly endless and futile task.

Of course, political life does not appear to us in as anarchistic and disjointed a manner as the above account suggests. Interaction with others assumes that we all *do* have a reasonable insight into what other people intend by their words and actions, built upon numerous, largely unconscious, shared meanings. Our lives gain coherence and comprehensibility through engaging in various practices which co-ordinate our actions with those of others. Both MacIntyre and Taylor have elaborated upon Wittgenstein's notion of a 'form of life' as embodied in rule-governed practices, largely with reference to the theories of Aristotle and Hegel respectively (MacIntyre, 1981; Taylor, 1979). However, they are haunted by the absence of a modern ethical community, or *Sittlichkeit*, and the impossibility in the complex, multicultural, transnational societies of today of recreating such a communal life in anything like its Hegelian or Aristotelian form. Both have become severe critics of modernity, in MacIntyre's case full of pessimism about the new dark ages and hoping for a new St Bernard to restore a return to order in a few isolated communities.

The central political problem as they see it concerns finding a viable theory of obligation capable of providing morally and practically compelling reasons for co-operation between the diverse groups and members of the modern world. How, in other words, can one end social antagonism without denying plurality? In Chapters 8 and 12, Michael Menlowe and Richard Gunn respectively discuss a number of the difficulties encountered by some of the contemporary answers to this question. According to MacIntyre, Taylor and their fellow 'communitarians', the essential problem lies in the fact that an account of political obligation requires a shared sense of the common good for its coherence. They believe that the individualistic approach of most recent theories ultimately proves self-defeating. For these theories promote an atomistic and egoistic ethos that undermines the social bonds uniting us. In their view, mutual self-interest cannot replace shared values as a secure basis for politics. As a result, they question the adequacy of the two main schools that currently dominate contemporary Anglo-American political thinking: utilitarianism and neo-Kantianism. I shall briefly outline these two schools of thought before returning to the criticisms of Taylor, MacIntyre and others.

Neither particularly new, utilitarianism and neo-Kantian liberalism nevertheless form the bulk of the so-called revival of political theory since the late 1960s. Both schools involve, albeit in different ways, an appeal to equality (Kymlicka, 1990). This feature originates in turn from a weakening of the traditional claims of political philosophy. For instead of founding a view of the good polity upon a particular conception of truth or goodness, contemporary political philosophers have attempted to formulate a theory of political justice capable of acceptance by people holding differing views of the good and the true. For these thinkers, the basis of a state's legitimacy rests not in its promotion of any particular way of life so much as in its showing equal concern and respect for each person's pursuit of whatever way of life he or she may choose. Unlike most of the political philosophers of the past, such as Plato, Locke or Hegel, therefore,

the main contemporary theorists purport to justify their preferred
political principles without reference to a wider metaphysical system
claiming to provide objective grounds for their validity.[2]

Utilitarianism (and, to an extent, the various forms of rational
choice theory which have been spawned by it) derives its plausibility
partly from its epistemological appeal as a 'scientific' theory of
ethics, partly from its providing a convenient ideological counterpart
to capitalist market rationality. Utilitarians respond to the problem
of an increasingly individualistic and morally diverse society by
offering a practical criterion of decision-making that purports not
to make potentially contestable judgements about the worth of the
various values and preferences people might hold. Utilitarians merely
seek to maximise human utility whilst giving equal weight in their
calculations to the utility of each individual as he or she conceives
it. Historically, definitions of what counts as human utility have
varied from simple happiness, be it from the enjoyment of beer or
books, to informed preferences, again either for activities of a crude
or more sophisticated nature. Regardless of the definition adopted,
however, utilitarians generally take the wants, preferences or pleasures
of the individuals concerned as given and firmly rooted. There is no
space here to go into all the refinements various philosophers have
given the theory (for a review of the recent literature see Sen and
Williams, 1982). Suffice it to say that these have usually served to
define the notion of utility in ways that make utilitarian calculations
practically impossible, without escaping the main objections to the
theory: namely, the narrowness of the model of human agency it
presupposes and its insensitivity to the diversity of human goods.
Both objections are related in turn to the central difficulty that
utilitarians have of combining their egalitarian commitment to weigh
human interests equally with their injunction to maximise human
welfare.

In spite of the ingenuity of its modern practitioners, such as Derek
Parfit (1984), the continued elaboration of utilitarian ethics has
necessarily gone hand in hand with the denial of any valid notion
of personal identity as an 'internally' constituted entity. Good
utilitarians are supposed to spend their time calculating the effects
on overall utility (however defined) of the various courses of action
available to them. Consequently, they must treat those constitutive
commitments – to family, particular causes and attachments – that
largely define who we are, as of no more worth or significance than

the commitments or preferences of other people. Their actions must always be determined by their impact on the satisfactions of others. This is a consideration that leaves them with little room to structure their own lives in terms of the kind of person they would like to be. They will always be at the service of other people's welfare, a psychologically problematic and morally undesirable attitude. For similar reasons, good utilitarians may also find themselves giving equal weight to preferences or interests that fail to show equal concern and respect. Within a racist society, for example, a policy of white supremacy might be deemed to maximise overall utility. Although more sophisticated forms of utilitarianism manage to exclude some kinds of illegitimate preferences from utilitarian calculations, the general problem raised by each person having an equal claim on our actions and resources remains. (These sort of criticisms are made by both communitarians, e.g. Taylor, 1985, Ch. 9, and neo-Kantian liberals, e.g. Rawls, 1971, p. 27.)

The fact that the maximisation and distribution of goods continues to be the principal concern of governments will undoubtedly ensure utilitarianism a long and healthy future. Indeed, as long as capitalist systems remain confident of providing sufficient abundance for all, its ascendence seems unassailable. But once people begin to point to the losers in such a system, then its values start to be challenged. The belief that all actors are rational goal maximisers, whose utilities can be grouped together, appears increasingly implausible and potentially intolerant of our plurality and distinctness. Some readers may find this criticism odd, given that utilitarian reasoning has proved particularly popular amongst economists concerned with issues of scarcity and welfare. However, when a general level of prosperity allowing most people to pursue their chosen way of life can no longer be assumed, then the utilitarian desire to maximise the general welfare inevitably results in using some as means to the happiness of all and so fails to treat everybody as ends in themselves. It is little wonder then that, a few radical iconoclasts apart (e.g. Singer, 1980), contemporary utilitarians have been preoccupied with revising the theory in ways that prevent inferences that might offend conventional moral sensibilities concerning the rights of individuals against the incursions of others.

The blossoming of neo-Kantian liberal theories of justice in the 1970s and 1980s was in part a response to a growing dissatisfaction with utilitarian theories within an increasingly adverse economic climate. Additional motivation came from the false use of utilitarian reasoning to justify certain American military tactics in Vietnam, such as saturation bombing and the use of napalm, on the grounds that the massacre of innocent lives was legitimate if it prevented notionally greater losses in the future. In contrast to utilitarians, these neo-Kantian theorists maintain that equal concern and respect is best shown by ensuring that each person has an equal right to a fair share, rather than that everyone should simply have an equal voice in determining how shares should be divided. However, in order to treat the various projects and beliefs of different people in an even-handed manner, they seek to separate the principles of right and justice which serve to regulate social behaviour from any particular view of what is good for human beings. For these thinkers, the laws and institutions comprising what John Rawls has called the 'basic structure of society' should aim to be 'neutral' between conceptions of the good. They set out, therefore, to devise a set of rules capable of providing the framework for a fair system of coexistence and co-operation between a plurality of agents and agencies pursuing a variety of ends. The aim, in Rawls' words, is to 'bring together in one scheme all individual perspectives and arrive together at regulative principles that can be affirmed by everyone as he lives by them, each from his own point of view' (Rawls, 1971, p. 587). To achieve this purpose, such rules had to be framed in abstract and universalisable terms so as not to be biased towards any particular goals or ways of life. This sort of thinking inspires arguments for a written constitution and a bill of rights, and is explored and defended by Neil MacCormick in his chapter (Chapter 6).

In spite of agreement on the general approach, however, theorists within the liberal school differ considerably over which principles of rights and justice best promote equality of respect. This debate is examined by Zenon Bankowski in Chapter 4. On the one hand, New Right liberals, such as Nozick (1974) and Hayek (1960), regard all redistributive policies as incompatible with each individual having an equal right to pursue his or her good in his or her own way. All attempts to plan the distribution of goods and services within society involve imposing the planners's conception of the good on others and are necessarily coercive as a result. Only the free market respects the diversity of human purposes and the individual's liberty to pursue them on equal terms. On the other hand, social democratic liberals, such as Rawls (1971) and Dworkin (1977), believe that state action to secure social justice is essential to the liberal project of showing equal concern and respect, and maintain that this policy can be pursued in a neutral manner.

Many of the issues involved in the debate between these two liberal groupings are explored by Richard Bellamy (Chapter 3), Alison Jeffries (Chapter 2) and John Holmwood (Chapter 5). We argue that, the protestations of neutrality made by these theorists notwithstanding, their different policy preferences reflect the often hidden and far from neutral assumptions within their writings about the operation of certain social processes, the character of human motivation, and the nature of our moral responsibilities towards others. This observation brings us back to the criticisms of liberalism by Taylor, MacIntyre and others, such as Michael Sandel (1982) and Michael Walzer (1983), who argue from not dissimilar premises. These critics contend that the ideological diversity within the liberal camp reflects the emptiness of the neutralist approach. They claim that political principles cannot be arrived at by reasoning which abstracts from the concrete circumstances of human existence. Rather, our theories of justice arise out of the ways of life of the community within which we live. As a result, there are no universal conceptions of justice capable of gaining the assent of all; there are only the rules that regulate and orientate the various particular forms of life embodied in different kinds of communities.

This view has been reinforced by recent theorists of postmodernism, such as Richard Rorty, who similarly argue that there can be no 'Archimedian point' from which we can stand outside all specific contexts and evaluate political systems or mediate between conflicting values (Rorty, 1989). The plurality of heterogeneous claims to knowledge generated by different political cultures undermines the ability of the political philosopher to claim a privileged epistemological status. The role of the political philosopher, according to this school of thought, is no longer the Platonic one of rising above the immediate concerns and attitudes of ordinary men and women and fashioning an objective and universal standpoint *sub specie aeternitatis*, as Rawls believes (Rawls, 1971, p. 587). Rather, the political philosopher must simply aim 'to interpret to one's fellow citizens the world of meanings that we share' (Walzer, 1983, p. xv).

The communitarian approach has two main difficulties: it appears to endorse a conservative relativism that prevents criticism of existing social arrangements, and it seems to assume that we share a world of meanings. To take this last difficulty first, not only communitarians but also liberals can probably be criticised for assuming that the basic unit of the individual's political allegience is a fairly homogenous nation-state. However, this focus ignores the various forces within and outside states that have contributed to a redrawing of the boundaries of the political. The labour, women's and ethnic minorities movements, for example, have sought to redefine the identity of the modern citizen and to challenge the implicit or explicit assumption that the political agent is necessarily a white, middle class male. Beverley Brown explores this topic in her chapter on feminism (Chapter 7), in which she criticises liberal conceptions of equality, and so does John Holmwood in his analysis of the impact of considerations of gender on welfare policies (Chapter 5). Similarly, developments linked with the process of globalisation, such as the growing interconnectedness resulting from a world economic system, new technology and the changing character and pattern of military conduct, raise parallel problems in the international arena about the appropriate scope and nature of the political good. For example, caring for the environment, as Martin Clark's chapter shows (Chapter 11), entails a modification of traditional conceptions of justice to include not only entities other than humans but also those living outside the borders of any given political community.

The absence of a common framework of meaning and value adds to worries about the relativism of the communitarian position. Even where shared values and understandings exist, we would wish to be able to question those practices or widely held views we feel are wrong. After all, public opinion can be misguided or unreliable in a variety of ways. People are not uncommonly misinformed, prejudiced or self-deluded, their views as much the product of socialisation and various forms of indoctrination as reasoned argument. Oppression, for example, is often accompanied by the acquiescence of the oppressed as a result of their acceptance of their tormentors' ideological justification of their actions. Walzer's contention that 'a given society is just if its substantive life is lived ... in a way faithful to the shared understandings of the members' (Walzer, 1983, p. 313) potentially legitimises extremely coercive regimes, therefore.

The dangers of this total denial of any critical perspective increase rather than diminish within pluralist societies containing no common morality. The relativist argument provides no basis for the toleration of other societies that often motivates communitarian arguments of this kind (e.g. Walzer, 1983, p. 314). If X seeks to impose his or her life style on Y, on the grounds that this is necessary for its fulfilment, then Y can only restrain X by appealing to some principle beyond their respective subjective ideals, such as a doctrine of equality of respect. Even this notion will contain some idea of what makes human life worthy of our concern – otherwise why bother at all? Complete scepticism about any foundations for truth or morality leads not to tolerance but to the struggle between opposed ideologies in which might is right.

Political debate too often degenerates into the mere assertion of ill-thought-out and unjustified prejudices. Surely we expect political theorists to do better than this? Neither this introduction nor the individual chapters can hope to provide a full answer to the epistemological and empirical problems that confront any systematic attempt to construct a political philosophy today. However, most of the contributors agree upon the direction in which we should move in order to bring some coherence back to the enterprise of theorising about politics. This path lies in overcoming the split between the normative and the empirical study of politics brought about by logical positivism. Since our political values cannot be separated from our understanding of the political reality around us, an adequate political theory must seek to integrate the philosophical analysis of the concepts we use to think about politics with the empirical investigation of political processes and social structures. Both elements are inevitably bound up in any coherent political opinion. Whilst this approach may not yield the grand all-encompassing theories of the past, it does enable the normative–empirical assumptions of rival political views to be outlined and, to the extent that they lack logical coherence or factual basis, opens then up to criticism as well. To a large extent, political theory is an interdisciplinary endeavour, therefore, as the range of disciplines represented by the contributors to this volume testifies. It combines a historical sensitivity to the traditions and values that inform any political culture, a philosophical analysis of the concepts we use, a sociological awareness of the societal conditions constraining human action, and a concern with the enabling and constraining nature of different legal and institutional structures.[3] Such a programme may not yield totally uncontestable objective truths about politics, but it will at least provide theories worthy of our respect and attention and prevent political dialogue degenerating into the expression of mere subjective opinions between which no discussion is possible. If this volume makes some small contribution towards this goal, then my colleagues and I will be more than happy.

Notes

1   The following discussion draws on the analysis of this movement by Bernstein, 1976, Part III, Miller, 1983 and Plant, 1991, Ch. 1.

2   This statement is not true of utilitarianism when it is conceived as a comprehensive morality as opposed to a political morality, concerned simply with the nature of social and political institutions rather than the whole of our personal conduct. My remarks are intended to refer to the narrower conception.

3   In many respects this programme has been best realised by those adopting the contextualist approach to the history of political thought advocated by Quentin Skinner and others. This suggests that the tasks of contemporary political theorists are not so different from those of past thinkers as is often thought. For a discussion of the methodological issues involved in Skinner's work, see Tully, 1988.

References

Berlin, I. (1962), 'Does Political Philosophy Still Exist?' in P. Laslett and W. G. Runciman (Eds.), *Philosophy, Politics and Society*, Series 2, Oxford: Blackwell, 1–33.

Bernstein, R. J. (1976), *The Restructuring of Social and Political Theory*, London: Methuen.

Connolly, W. E. (1974), *The Terms of Political Discourse*, Oxford: Blackwell.

Dworkin, R. (1977), *Taking Rights Seriously*, London: Duckworth.

Easton, D. (1953), *The Political System*, New York: Alfred A. Knopf.

Gallie, W. B. (1956), 'Essentially Contested Concepts', *Proceedings of the Aristotelian Society*, 56: 167–98.

Hayek, F. (1960), *The Constitution of Liberty*, London: Routledge & Kegan Paul.

Hull, C. (1943), *Principles of Behaviour*, New York: Appleton-Century-Crofts.

Hume, D. (1975), *An Enquiry Concerning Human Understanding*, L. A. Selby-Bigge (Ed.), 3rd ed., Oxford: Oxford University Press.

Kymlicka W. (1990), *Contemporary Political Philosophy*, Oxford: Oxford University Press.

Laslett, P. (1956), 'Introduction' in P. Laslett (Ed.), *Philosophy, Politics and Society*, Series I, Oxford: Blackwell.

MacDonald, M. (1951), 'The Language of Political Theory' in A. Flew (Ed.), *Logic and Language*, First Series, Oxford: Blackwell.

MacIntyre, A. (1971), *Against the Self-Images of the Age*, London: Duckworth.

MacIntyre, A. (1981), *After Virtue: A Study in Moral Theory*, London: Duckworth.

Miller, D. (1983), 'Linguistic Philosophy and Political Philosophy' in D. Miller and L. Siedentop (Ed.), *The Nature of Political Theory*, Oxford: Oxford University Press.

Nozick, R. (1974), *Anarchy, State and Utopia*, Oxford: Blackwell.

Oppenheim, F. (1973), 'Facts and Values in Politics', *Political Theory*, 1: 54–68.

Parfit, D. (1984), *Reasons and Persons*, Oxford: Oxford University Press.

Plant, R. (1991), *Modern Political Thought*, Oxford: Blackwell.

Rawls, J. (1971), *A Theory of Justice*, Oxford: Oxford University Press.

Rorty, R. (1989), *Contingency, Irony and Solidarity*, Cambridge: Cambridge University Press.

Sandel, M. (1982), *Liberalism and the Limits of Justice*, Cambridge: Cambridge University Press.

Sen, A.K. and Williams, B. (Eds.) (1982), *Utilitarianism and Beyond*, Cambridge: Cambridge University Press.

Singer, P. (1980), *Practical Ethics*, New York: Cambridge University Press.

Strauss, L. (1959), *What is Political Philosophy?*, Glencoe Ill.: Free Press.

Taylor, C. (1979), *Hegel and Modern Society*, Cambridge: Cambridge University Press.

Taylor, C. (1985), *Philosophical Papers 2: Philosophy and the Human Sciences*, Cambridge: Cambridge University Press.

Tully, J. (1988) (Ed.), *Meaning and Context: Quentin Skinner and his Critics*, Cambridge: Polity.

Voegelin, E. (1952), *The New Science of Politics*, Chicago: Chicago University Press.

Waltzer, M. (1983), *Spheres of Justice: A Defence of Pluralism and Equality*, Oxford: Martin Robertson.

Weinstein, W.L. (1965), 'The Concept of Liberty in Nineteenth Century British Political Thought', *Political Studies*, 13: 145–62.

Weldon, T.D. (1953), *The Vocabulary of Politics*, Harmondsworth: Penguin.

Winch, P. (1958), *The Idea of a Social Science*, London: Routledge & Kegan Paul.

Wittgenstein, L. (1952), *Philosophical Investigations*, Oxford: Blackwell.

Wolin, S. (1960), *Politics and Vision*, London: Allen & Unwin.

2 *Alison Jeffries*

Freedom

Introduction

The concept of freedom is a central one in the value systems of most contemporary societies. Regimes of many types use as a source of legitimation the claim that the political systems over which they preside enhance freedom. However, perhaps because of its importance, the definition of this term is deeply disputed. Political theorists have remarked upon the diversity of understandings of freedom and attempted to analyse and clarify the term in order to provide a method of adjudicating between competing meanings. Such theoretical treatment can alert us to important features of the way freedom is used and understood in politics. But we will see that no attempts to determine the 'best' definition (or even the more limited project of pointing to 'better' and 'worse' definitions) of freedom are likely to be successful. These attempts fail because 'freedom' can be understood in the context of many different ideological systems and consequently is used with a variety of competing, and incompatible, meanings.

This chapter will begin with an examination of perhaps the most influential analytic approach to the understanding of freedom, the distinction between positive and negative freedom. The discussion will make familiar the vocabulary used by political theorists in their studies of freedom. At the same time, some of the limitations of the abstract analytic approach can be enumerated. To remedy these problems, it will be suggested that it is helpful to look at two particular theories of freedom current in contemporary British politics. Finally, the implications of these studies for the understanding of freedom in particular, and for the practice of political theory in general, will be reflected upon.

Positive and negative freedom

Many theorists accept the claim that each political concept such as freedom, justice or democracy has several different *conceptions* – different interpretations or understandings of its characteristics (Rawls, 1973, p. 5). It is frequently argued that there are two major conceptions of freedom: positive and negative. The distinction between positive and negative freedom was elucidated most famously by Sir Isaiah Berlin (1982, pp. 118–72). His definition, put at its simplest, is that negative freedom is the absence of intentionally constructed barriers to our actions (p. 122). It is violated whenever some person or group places an obstacle in the way of our achieving a specific goal (or when they would do so, should we try to achieve such a goal). We are more free in this sense if, for example, there are no restrictions on the availability of books in shops and libraries, than if there are laws banning certain titles or limiting their supply. Positive freedom is defined as the achievement of self-mastery (p. 131). It exists when we are able to be fully ourselves and to realise our goals and potentials, and it is enlarged when we are able to take more conscious control over the circumstances of our lives and become better equipped to make choices. For example, educated people are more free in this sense than are the uneducated, and people who can vote have more freedom than those who cannot, even if the legal system under which the two groups live is otherwise identical (that is, even if their negative freedoms are exactly the same).

The splitting of the concept of freedom into its negative and positive aspects helps us to understand some of the complex features of the term as it is used in different contexts. It is a helpful analytic tool. For example, the negative definition of freedom – that one is free when one would not be prevented from carrying out an action by an obstacle placed in one's way by some person or group – reminds us that questions of freedom do not arise whenever we cannot do something, but only when the barrier to our action is caused by human actions. However, it should be noted (as does Berlin) that determining when a barrier to action can be said to be socially determined is in itself a matter of dispute (Berlin, 1982, pp. 122–3). In a primitive society, an old person who is prevented by cataracts from seeing and so from carrying out a variety of activities, straightforwardly suffers from an inability to act which does not affect his or her freedom to perform those actions. In a rich, developed society, it is arguable that the failure to provide cataract operations for those in need of them amounts to a social decision to prolong a person's blindness, and so amounts to a cause of unfreedom. This conclusion rests on a particular view of the way societies function and of our obligations to one another. Hence, the negative concept of freedom does not in itself rule out the recognition of freedom (and unfreedom) arising from social organisation. But it does force us to explain the mechanism by which we believe that a person's inability to act in a certain way is actually caused by the actions of others, such that it can reasonably be described as a source of unfreedom. Giving attention to these details can be a useful exercise that prevents the sloppy bandying around of the concept of freedom as a general term of approbation.

Berlin's analysis also points to some potential problems for the theorist, since the enlargement of positive freedom may involve the restriction of negative freedom. An example here is compulsory education for children and young people. Children are clearly denied the negative freedom to use their time as they desire because they are forced to go to school. On the other hand, it is widely believed that as the result of receiving education these children will grow up to be more free in the positive sense because they will have acquired a greater ability to make choices for themselves and developed more of the skills necessary to organise their lives to achieve their own goals.

The analysis of positive and negative is often taken further and used as the basis for a prescriptive argument about the superiority of one of the two conceptions of freedom. As we shall see, this can be problematical. Many theorists, following Berlin, argue that negative freedom is a superior conception. They claim that positive freedom, attractive as it may be, can slide into its own absurd opposite, a legitimation of totalitarianism. For it may entail the belief that some actions are only performed by those not in full control of their own choices – those who are not 'masters' of their own lives (Berlin, 1982, pp. 133–4). For example, it might be said that if a woman were truly free and self-determining she would not choose to marry and keep house for a man. If she does this willingly, she is suffering from false consciousness. To make her free we may have, in the first instance, to deny her certain options, or even to 're-educate' her so that she recognises that her preference for the domestic role is not her own but arose because of the process of socialisation to which she was subject. She must, that is, be forced to be free.

Berlin would insist, however, that such 'corrective' action clearly involves a violation of negative freedom, and the imposition of some other person's view of the world on the woman in question. It is arrogant to assume that a particular choice, because it is not a choice that we might make, would only be made by someone who is somehow not in control of their own life. It is far better, he says, to recognise the loss of (negative) freedom involved whenever we are made to act in a certain way against our will, or prevented from doing something that we would like to do. He maintains that to disguise this loss by claiming it increases total (positive) freedom provides a licence for almost limitless coercion by ruthless dictators claiming to make us more free. However, he argues that we must also recognise that there may be competing values that can rightly, in certain contexts, outweigh the value of freedom (pp. 167–72). For example, in the interests of equality, perhaps, all girls should be taught the principles of feminism, or all men forced to take courses in housework. It is the stuff of politics to decide which values should take priority and when.

Against this view, many advocates of positive freedom would claim that there is no necessary connection between the recognition that freedom requires self-mastery, and the imposition of any particular pattern of behaviour. Indeed, many advocates of positive freedom may believe that to force someone to be free is in itself a violation of the principle of self-mastery. In the case of the willing housewife, for example, it might be argued that the enlargement of freedom for women requires the state to open women's centres, to publicise the alternative possibilities for women, to provide easy access to education and employment for female returners, to provide cheap good quality child-care, and to ensure that the expectation that women should perform domestic duties is not enshrined in educational material or institutionalised through the tax-benefit system. It might be claimed that our housewife is living a highly circumscribed and hence unfree life because of the self-perception that was drummed into her during her upbringing, and because she lacks the knowledge and skills necessary to choose a different course of action. However, the response should be to provide a great deal of information and many incentives and opportunities for change, while leaving the responsibility for acting on these to the individual so that her negative freedom is not affected. It could then be assumed that anyone who chose the role of housewife was doing so because she wanted to and was, therefore, not unfree.

Positive libertarians in their turn accuse negative theorists of holding an absurd position that leads to claims that individuals are free who clearly enjoy no autonomy at all. Positive theorists of freedom point out that on the negative view one would have to say that a person was free if they lived in a world where there were no external limitations to their actions, but where they had been deliberately brainwashed to act only in certain ways. They would never choose to do anything that the controller of the brainwashing did not wish them to. The only way out of this absurd position is to say that to be free it must be possible to show that a person's 'wants' are in some sense his or her own. Once one has granted this argument, then it is hard to distinguish the negative view of freedom from the revised positive view described in the previous paragraph.

Those theorists who consider positive conceptions of freedom to be valid have still, however, to answer a different objection. Critics of positive liberty claim that it confuses freedom with omnipotence. They suggest that if we are to admit into the definition of freedom the suggestion that to be free we must enjoy self-mastery then, for as long as there are any barriers to our self-fulfilment that could possibly be removed, we are not free. Freedom would, therefore, require the expenditure of unlimited resources on overcoming our limitations and expanding our capacity to do things. Such a conclusion, it is claimed, is obviously absurd since it would be more-or-less impossible for us ever to explore all possible avenues of achievement and, hence, freedom would be unattainable except for a person who was omnipotent.

Against this, however, it can be argued that a similar absurd conclusion would result if it was insisted that a person be freed of all possible barriers to their negative freedom. To make an individual negatively free to the extent that no person or group could, by their action or inaction, impede the first individual's negative freedom would require massive intervention into the activities of all others in society. This would make a nonsense of the idea that a society could value the achievement of negative freedom by all of its members.

In fact, in determining what is necessary before we describe a person as free we must implicitly or explicitly make reference to the interests and goals of free individuals. Some things matter to freedom and others do not. Not all limitations, therefore, are considered to be limits to freedom. For example, a system based on enshrining the negative freedom of all individuals to make use of their property and the income from the application of their talents necessarily also limits the negative freedom of others to make use of these goods. One cannot, therefore, claim with many classical liberals, that private property based market systems are compatible with freedom because they do not infringe negative liberty. One must, rather, invoke a moralised version of freedom, where the negative freedom of the property owner is given priority over the freedom of the unpropertied (Cohen, 1979, pp. 11–12).

The inescapable fact that some negative freedoms are more important than others, even to advocates of the negative conception of freedom, forms the basis of Charles Taylor's criticism of negative liberty. He has pointed out that if we insist that negative freedom should be taken as the only acceptable definition of freedom, then we are left unable to distinguish between the political significance of different negative freedoms (except in terms of other values) (Taylor, 1985, pp. 217–20). We might be forced to admit that a poor but authoritarian state, such as Albania under the communist regime, which lacks the huge body of law concerning, for example, the conduct of business, consumer safety, and the regulation of traffic, typical of modern liberal societies, is more free than somewhere like the United States. Communist Albania had few laws but they affected matters of great personal and political significance: what one could say, where one could live, and so on. America, on the other hand, has more laws on its books, but nevertheless it allows individuals relatively unimpeded action in the areas of expression of opinion and does not normally regulate its citizens' movements within and outside of the state. It becomes absurd if we have to dress up in terms of other values, such as justice or equality, our intuition that the United States is the system that those of us imbued with broadly liberal ideological perceptions believe to be the more free. Clearly, therefore, the judgement of whether people (or political systems) are more or less free cannot be made simply by adding up negative freedoms, but actually rests on an implicit theory about the set of liberties (positive and negative) that are significant to political freedom.

We may conclude that Berlin's account of positive and negative freedom, while helpful analytically, is limited in scope. If we start to use his analysis to argue for the superiority of one version of freedom over another we run into problems. As we have seen, without some respect for unimpeded action for the individual, positive freedom can collapse into tyranny. Without some assurance that we are in control of our own choices, negative freedom is not enough for us to describe a person as free. However, it is not a solution to say that subject to the condition that individuals are in control of their own minds, those individuals are free when left to make un-impeded choices about the course of their lives. For this immediately raises the questions 'what is it to have self-determination?', 'when am I in control?', 'what counts as a barrier to my action?' A further problem with both positive and negative liberty that we have seen is that we need to give some account of the freedoms that matter to us as free people living in a free society. The advocacy of a pure and unlimited form of either positive or negative freedom is doomed to collapse into absurdity.

In practice, most conceptions of freedom that are employed in political argument contain both positive and negative elements. It is the particular description of negative and positive freedoms, and the resulting view of the balance between them necessary to describe an individual as free, that lies at the root of the dispute over the meaning of freedom. These two issues are resolved differently in competing ideological systems. The resulting understandings of the term freedom cannot be discovered by philosophical investigation. For a theorist to comment on the meaning of freedom, it is necessary for her or him to examine the way the term is actually used in political debate.

Two theories of freedom

The overarching difficulty that has been highlighted in the account of positive and negative freedom is their inability to make much sense of our claim that a person can be more or less free, and their lack of contribution to the widely shared desire to assess how, and in what respects, a state can be said to enhance freedom or deny it to its citizens. It has also been made clear that political theorists can only understand freedom by looking at the term's location in the ideologies that shape political debate. This point can be made more clearly by looking at some examples, drawn from British political discourse, of the way in which the term is used.

A view of freedom from the British right
With the election of Mrs Thatcher to the Conservative leadership in 1976 came a new emphasis on Conservative freedom. Many commentators labelled this focus 'Thatcherism' (Hall, 1979), but arguably it was simply the restatement, albeit in strident terms, of themes already present in Conservative thinking, and which continue to inform Conservative views of what it is to be free. Much was heard then about the need for individual independence, of the pernicious influence of the 'nanny state', and of the essential relationship between property and freedom. Britain was said to be losing its freedom, and its citizens were rapidly becoming enslaved (Ferns, nd). Far from this being empty rhetoric, a rallying cry for the party faithful, it will be argued here that Thatcher espoused a clear and relatively coherent conception of freedom. It is this right-wing conception that will now be examined.

The free person, according to many on the right, is someone who is self-reliant, independent and not constrained by rules and regulations imposed upon him (as we shall see, with this school of thought the individual is most comfortably thought of as male) by the State. In particular, the welfare state is believed to be the source of much unfreedom. It directly limits what people can do, hemming them in by a nagging nannying insistence on doing what is best for them or for their children, directly controlling the choices of those who are welfare recipients, and also forcing all tax-payers to support a system of benefits and services whether or not they believe that system to be an appropriate use of their money (O'Gorman, 1986, p. 233; Thatcher, 1989, pp. 7–17).

The rules and regulations, generally castigated as 'red tape', that surround the welfare state constitute limitations on negative freedom. However, this is not the only objection to what the right calls 'welfarism'. Mrs Thatcher herself was insistent that the existence of a welfare state is enervating both for recipients and, perhaps less crucially, for all the rest of the population. Welfare recipients become dependent and beholden to the providers of money and services. They cease to think for themselves or to use their initiative to get themselves out of difficult situations. They lose their capacity for independence and become 'moral cripples', mere shadows of free, independent individuals (Thatcher, 1989, p. 55; Seldon, 1975, p. 46). The welfare state, therefore, destroys freedom by first destroying free people. Thus, within an apparent claim for the priority of negative freedom, leaving people to get on with their own lives unencumbered by the state, is found a conception of positive freedom, an idea that a person who is nannied ceases to have the capacity for self-mastery.[1]

It is not just welfare recipients that are affected in this way. Others are also diminished because the incentives to take care of oneself are tempered by the knowledge that there is always the state to fall back on. Another consideration is that the social mechanisms for dealing with need without calling in the state – voluntary service and neighbourly help – are themselves undermined by the existence of state-provided welfare. This erosion of community spirit means that once the state enters into the sphere of welfare provision it will find itself in an ever-increasing spiral of intervention as the whole edifice of the free society is gradually stripped away. It was for this reason that at one point Thatcher's team started talking about 'active citizenship' (Hurd, 1989, p. 20; Carvel, 1990, p. 3). That is, it was desirable to restore voluntary networks for caring if the state was to be withdrawn from the provision of welfare. This idea was also an ancillary element in the Conservative Governments' attraction to the policy of community care.

Of course, a key element in the Conservative objection to the provision of state services is that it distorts the pattern of property ownership (Mount, 1984). Property is vital to the view of freedom that is currently under discussion. Firstly, property ownership – which can be taken broadly to also include the ownership of income from property and labour – provides the individual with a sphere within which he may act as he pleases. What he does with his property is his own affair. How he chooses to spend his money – what goods and services he purchases and what type of life he makes for himself and his family using his own means – are similarly entirely his own affair (Howell, 1981, p. 18).

More generally, the existence of property ownership allows the exercise of free choices by, on the one hand, enabling markets to function and, through the operation of supply and demand, produce the goods and services that people want, and, on the other hand, ensuring that some people have the resources to live their lives insulated from the preferences of others (Joseph, 1975a; Thatcher, 1989, p. 23).[2] If property is in private hands, there is the possibility of, for example, the publication of minority viewpoints, or the opportunity for those who do not conform to majority views of the good life to purchase their own space and conduct their own affairs according to their own preferences (Lewis, n.d., pp. 44–8; Joseph and Sumption, 1979, p. 56).

However, the respect for property, and for the market, is not motivated purely by the view that one is most free when left to act without interference. It also reflects the view that the free person – the self-directed individual – is most likely to thrive where there are incentives to individual achievement and where the responsibilities of the self-reliant individual are obvious. Clearly, markets are preferred not just for their operational efficiency, but more especially for their effect on the moral character of citizens (Thatcher, 1989, p. 90; Griffiths, 1983). This background assumption was especially clear in the discussion of the merits of 'popular capitalism' (Letwin and Letwin, 1986; Redwood, 1988).

Freedom, therefore, is more than the absence of intervention. The free person has a certain sort of character which has to be sustained by institutions. This aspect of the theory can be developed further. One clear problem for any theory of political freedom that focuses on the interplay of individual property-owning agents is that the wants and needs of these agents can clash. How are these clashes to be resolved without undermining freedom? Are such disputes only soluble with reference to other values? The Conservative answer to this question seems to be in the negative. There are ways of harmonising the lives of individuals without damaging freedom. Indeed, freedom itself is defined with reference to the principles upon which the free society is founded.

The most important principles are contained within the dual commitments to the rule of law and to tradition. The rule of law is a phrase that describes the principles that all are equally subject to the law, that the law is general in its provisions (not aimed at particular individuals), and that those provisions are known and certain in effect.[3] If these principles pertain the individual is able to plan his life, something which is itself a major source of his freedom to achieve his goals. He is also enabled to protect his property and go about his lawful business without interference.

However, the link between freedom and the rule of law is more than just instrumental. It is closely bound up with the definition of free individuals. What is of importance here is the common law (Joseph, 1975b, p. 5; Jones, 1989, p. 57). The common law is that body of principles that have developed over time and in response to particular disputes. It is judge-made law, where the judges are charged with applying known and certain principles (case law), and with elucidating principles to be applied to new sorts of problems in a way that best fits with the principles that already pertain. This law has developed organically and in accordance with the understandings of right and wrong that are current in society. This evolutionary process means that, in theory, common law always follows popular understandings.

This ensures that such law is closely associated with freedom. The free person, the Conservative argues, is someone who is able to live according to what Hayek called his 'legitimate expectations' (Hayek, 1982, vol. I, p. 98; vol. II, pp. 37 and 93–6). Free people do not live in a vacuum. They have perceptions of what they ought to be allowed to do, and it is the violation of these perceptions that constitutes unfreedom. Organically developed law, therefore, cannot offend freedom but rather entrenches it by enshrining legitimate expectations and upholding the practices that have evolved to protect individual autonomy, notably the institution of property. It is for this reason that the Conservative Party in the 1970s was strident in its rejection of the ever-escalating quantity of new statutes which were intended to transform the legal system and replace the common law with a new and imposed system of regulation (Johnson, 1978, p. 3; Boyson, 1978, p. 163).

Similarly, traditions are important to the organisation of a free society. Traditional practices help to regulate private life. They ensure that the behaviour that is essential to free life – self-reliance, law-abidingness, honesty, caring for one's family – are all perpetuated. Without these principles the state would have to intervene all the time. In consequence, the attempts of liberals to overturn moral taboos by, for example, relaxing the laws on divorce, abortion and homosexuality, are fundamentally misconceived (Dawson, 1984, p. 48; Crowther, 1973, p. 19). Such reforms would not only destabilise the moral systems that sustain social order and hence the freedom that is associated with the fulfilment of legitimate expectations, but also undermine the capacity of individuals for freedom. Here the Conservative view assumes a psychological model of human personality whereby all people require some certainty about the limits and boundaries of behaviour if they are to be able to be self-defining and in control of their personalities (Letwin, 1978, p. 59). To remove the limitations of tradition and culture on the way we conceive of ourselves and on what we understand to be right or wrong is not to free us, it is to leave us anomic – out of control – and fundamentally incapable of being free. The free person is not, therefore, a libertine (Utley, 1970; Chaudet, n.d., p. 15; Crowther, 1983, p. 42; Ashworth, 1972, p. 10; Phillips, 1988, pp. 39–40 and 46–9). He is a highly self-disciplined individual, who defines himself in respect of, and respects fully, social norms and expectations. Certain institutions acquire a great deal of significance in this account of the free person and the free society. We have already noted the importance of voluntary organisations to provide for the needy, and so obviate the need for state intervention. The church also acquires significance as the arbiter of traditional moral rectitude – hence the particular obloquy reserved for radical clerics by Conservatives (Utley, 1989, p. 211). But most important of all, is the family.

The family is the institution within which a great number of aspects of the Conservative view of freedom come together. It is largely because of responsibilities to the family that individuals are motivated to take control of their own lives and to develop a determined independence. Property has even more value if the person acquiring it knows that it can be passed on to younger members of the family. It is within the family that the values necessary to freedom are transmitted, respect for the law and convention, and personal habits that are conducive to a free life. Finally, families take responsibility for many of the caring functions that would otherwise fall to the interventionist state. Indeed, families form an alternative source of authority to that of the state (Mount, 1982).

The family is clearly of central importance to the theory, therefore. This can leave women in an odd position. On the one hand, the language of individual freedom employed by Conservatives is gender-neutral. Indeed, many Conservatives speak of women having the equal right to participate within the marketplace, which is the location of much of the activity of the free person. However, it is also vital that the family is sustained, and women are perceived to have a key role in this respect (Morrison, 1978, pp. 73–5). It would seem that often the individual about which the theory is centred is assumed to be the male head of household. Tellingly, a Freedom Association[4] publication of 1978, just one year before Mrs Thatcher entered office, spoke of 'the citizen and his wife' (Gouriet, 1978, p. 33). It was unsurprising, therefore, that the first Conservative administration toyed with the Family Policy Group, which sought ways to enshrine the traditional roles of woman (Dean, 1983). The problem of how women fit into Conservative thinking on freedom in the modern world where traditional roles cannot be taken for granted is a difficult one, and one which has not yet been resolved.

Thus, the British right holds a quite distinctive view of freedom. This view endorses the value of property and celebrates the market in which property in goods and services is exchanged according to the freely chosen preferences of free men and women. However, this account of freedom also involves a quite complex understanding of the nature of the free individual and the relationship of that individual to the state and social institutions. The theory of freedom which results can only be fully understood when examined in the wider context of Conservative ideology. One cannot deduce the theory from any single statement about freedom. Such statements could have several different meanings, depending on the way they fit into an overall pattern of ideas. This multi-faceted view of freedom comprises a bundle of negative and positive freedoms combined in a distinctive way and constituting an overall picture of what it is to be free. It is based on a particular and controversial understanding of human nature and social life. In consequence, to dispute the Conservative version of freedom is also to challenge the whole edifice of Conservative thinking and to substitute another distinct account of the self and society. It is to one such alternative account of what it is to be free that I will now turn.

A left-wing variant of freedom

The British left has a quite different understanding of freedom. Many of those on the left would endorse the same general definition of what it is to be free as the Conservatives: namely, that to be free is to live one's own life in one's own way. It is to be autonomous and self-determining, not subject to arbitrary limitations on one's life, not made to tolerate or accommodate oneself to the interference of others, and not affected by coercive interventions in one's life. However, those on the left feel a deep unease that the guarantee of a certain set of negative liberties, particularly in the economic sphere, will help to achieve and entrench this ideal. Nor do thinkers of the left accept the notion that the establishment of the free person and the free society requires the sort of social and moral universe that right-wing theorists believe to be necessary to those goals.

On the contrary, these thinkers take a quite different view of what it is to be subject to coercion. Beginning with the New Liberal theorists of the late nineteenth century (Freeden, 1978), the British left has asked whether it is meaningful to regard as free a person who dare not leave his or her job for fear of starvation, someone who cannot speak out on issues relating to their working life or even on matters of more general import which might be of interest to his or her employers for fear of losing a job, or somebody who is similarly beholden to landlords, money lenders or providers of the charity upon which he or she is dependent (Labour Party, 1988, p. 3; Gould, 1985, p. 211; Titmuss, 1970, p. 270; Kinnock, 1986, p. 7).

Interestingly, so far the position described is quite compatible with Berlin's account of negative freedom. What have been described are barriers to freedom – if people act in certain ways they know that they will precipitate consequences that are so unpleasant that they dare not act. But they are barriers that those on the right do not acknowledge since they believe that such economic limitations do not serve as checks to action which are appropriately considered coercive. (For the right there are alternative providers of work and housing, and by diligent application and self-disciplined work it is possible to extract oneself from circumstances which one finds unappealing.) Berlin himself suggested that what is counted as a barrier to freedom would vary within different social and economic theories.

However, the left goes beyond viewing such economic considerations as checks on one's negative freedom, and argues further that they actually prevent people from acquiring or exercising the capacity for free life. If one is bowed down by material circumstances, one will come to see all aspects of life as controlled by others, so that it is not worth trying to make choices. People will both lose the habit of freedom and, more fundamentally, they will not develop as agents with the capacity to make choices. They will be subservient, frightened and limited human beings, in no way describable as free people (Bevan, 1978, p. 62).

To counter this source of unfreedom, the left has incorporated in its view of freedom the idea that free people are those who have a world view in which they are able to see themselves as effective and self-determining. Free people are aware of their own needs and capacities, and have sufficient information and skills to make reasoned choices about the way their lives should go. A free society will be comprised of vibrant, dynamic individuals, who are able to harness their abilities and to take opportunities for personal growth because they are autonomous and self-directing. People who have had such opportunities will not tolerate tyranny or petty coercion; they will insist on organising their own communities and on maintaining the institutions that are necessary to their freedom.

To achieve this highly desirable state of being, it is necessary to do more than remove barriers to action. Three fields of activity are central. The first of these is education. Education must be freely provided, and there must be constant access to it for adults to acquire skills that they did not have the opportunity or the will to acquire when young. This education, while giving people the skills necessary to make their own way in the world, is not simple training. It must also be aimed at developing the capacity for critical thought and reflection to equip people to take control of their own lives, and to free them from vulnerability to manipulation and demagogy from political agitators (Barratt Brown, 1972, pp. 139–40).

Secondly, political participation is necessary for freedom. People must be able to affect the legal and social environment within which they live if they are to be free and self-determining. This understanding of democracy differs from the view of the right, which sees democratic participation as simply an imperfect technique for ensuring that governments do not start to usurp power and interfere with the private activities of free individuals. A particular feature of the left's view is that it is unacceptable for a whole aspect of adult life – what happens to one at work – not to be subject to personal control. Thus, many on the left argue that workplace democracy (Kendall, 1976, p. 3; Green, 1986, pp. 49–62; Coates, 1971, pp. 197–202) or co-operatives (Shuller, 1985, chs. 4–7; Hattersley, 1987, pp. 198–202; Labour Party, 1980b; Benn, 1980, pp. 60–70 and 158–60) are vital in a free society, both because of the direct effect of being able to affect the things that happen to one, and because of the indirect educative effect of discussing problems, resolving differences in ways that are non-dictatorial, and making decisions effective. Both of these effects are vital to the creation and sustenance of the free society.

Finally, freedom requires that economic circumstances be such that people are not bowed down by want and by fear for survival, nor must they be excluded from full social life because they lack the means to participate (Field, 1987, p. 227; Kinnock, 1986, p. 3). People who cannot afford to make use of local amenities, who cannot afford newspapers or television, who cannot travel to visit museums or art galleries, will come to see themselves as marginal, will regard social and political institutions as irrelevant to them, and will, as a result, live highly constrained and diminished lives, without access to political power or social influence (Whitehead, 1984, p. 113). They will, therefore, be unfree.

Government action is necessary to enact these conditions. The state, therefore, is central to freedom (Plant, 1988, p. 1). However, it should not be strongly directive. Free individuals must have the ability to shape the course of their lives and not be circumscribed by rules and regulations designed to institute the good society. Indeed, over the years the British left has demonstrated a consistent fear of the stultifying effects of bureaucracy (Gwyn, 1971, pp. 384–402) and has shown concern that too much emphasis on state intervention (in the economy, for example) will lead to a loss of awareness that the purpose of state planning in all areas of life is to increase human freedom (Wright, 1979, p. 51; Crossman, 1965, p. 30). The left has also been clear that unless individuals are able to criticise the state and to give expression to their individual characteristics without fear of punishment, freedom will not flourish. As such, the left has been strong in its support for civil liberties (Hattersley, 1987, pp. 102–3; Benn, 1979, p. 2).

This account of freedom clearly arises from a particular view of the individual (the self), and of society. The self to be freed is not taken as given; the free agent has, rather, to be created and nurtured by the environment. The attempt to enshrine freedom by 'rolling back the state', therefore, is doomed to failure because one would also roll back the conditions that make possible the emergence of free, self-directing individuals. Furthermore, one would leave individuals subject to untrammelled power such as that enjoyed by private monopolies etc. (Gould, 1985, pp. 14–16 and Ch. 5; Tawney, 1953, pp. 87–9; Benn, 1982a, p. 42). Free people do not come together and create social institutions and the state, therefore, but rather the social institutions and the state may create free individuals.

Those on the left who have come to see freedom as the highest form of human existence consider this view to be one that developed through the enlightenment, the reformation and the experience of the unfolding of democracy since the ending of feudalism. That is to say, the value given to freedom is itself an historical product, but no less important for that since it is now so intimately bound up with our identity as human individuals (Gould, 1985, pp. 25–9).

This political value has such significance that to be legitimate a state must direct itself to the provision of the conditions of freedom (Hattersley, 1987, p. 102). If it does not do so, the state loses the right to rule. Furthermore, the only condition under which all members of a social group will feel obliged to accept allegiance to the state is that the state treats all equally.[5] Freedom and equality are, therefore, compatible (Radice, 1989, pp. 63–5; Gould, 1985, p. 35; Hattersley, 1987, p. 129). In consequence, the key point about a free society is that it must ensure the provision of equal freedom (Attlee, 1954, p. 267; Gould, 1985, pp. 11–12; Benn, 1982a, p. xii; Hattersley, 1987, p. 130). This provision, the left argues, is palpably not what is achieved under the right-wing view of freedom.

This last point gives rise to the problematic issue of what is to be done about behaviour that might limit the freedom of others. Some argue, for example, that pornography can lead to attitudes to women which greatly restrict their opportunities to develop as free, self-directing individuals. Accordingly, some on the left insist that in this case there should be some intervention by the state to further the goal of the provision of equal freedom for all. Likewise, the free choice to buy goods and services that might affect the ability of others to enjoy equal freedom – for example, the acquisition for one's child of educational advantage and ultimately access to a privileged and powerful elite through the purchase of private education – may be considered incompatible with life in a free society (Hattersley, 1987, pp. 115 and 145–7; Field, 1987, pp. 116–78). Therefore, some limits may be placed on activity in the name of the liberal goal of equal freedom for all (Labour Party, 1980a, p. 31).

However, many on the left find restricting choice uncomfortable, and prefer to deal with the issue by providing counterweights to the undesirable influences that remove their impact, rather than forbidding the activities. Such counterweights could involve endorsing and furthering a positive and equal role for women, for example, and providing an extremely well funded state educational system and ensuring that higher education and training is provided according to merit. Some believe that a more lasting solution will only be found when education succeeds in persuading people to adopt a common, socialistic value system, so that they do not wish to act in ways that would limit the equal freedom of other citizens (Crossmann, 1951, p. 7; Benn, 1982b, p. 132).

In summary, the left considers that freedom is only achievable within a social, political, and economic framework which must be sustained by an active and interventionist state. Freedom is not synonymous with individualism, the free unimpeded actions of self-interested individuals. Instead, the creation of people who enjoy the fullest self-direction, personal distinctiveness, and the richest development of skills and capacities to fulfil the life plans and desires of free individuals, requires collective provision and state activity. The stress of the left is on the creation and sustaining of individuality – with the recognition that individual life takes its meaning from its location within a group – rather than individualism. Individuality is both the result and thereafter the guarantor of institutions which have as their purpose the establishment of freedom. As with the right, freedom and social organisation are inextricably linked but the world view and the understanding of what this implies is quite different and largely incompatible with the right's view of what is necessary to a free life.

The ideology of freedom
What are the implications of the discussion of these two theories for the analytic approaches to freedom considered at the beginning of this chapter?

Firstly, it is clearly not helpful to label theories of the left as theories of positive freedom. And it is far from complete to describe the British right as endorsing principles of negative freedom. The left believes that many choices must be made by individuals who are not interfered with in the making of those choices. Indeed, many of its proposals are intended to widen the realm within which individuals are able to exercise unimpeded choice as, for example, with workplace democracy. The right, on the other hand, is concerned not just with leaving people to lead their own lives with as few barriers to free choice as possible. Those who endorse this view of freedom believe that freedom itself requires that there is a stable moral and legal framework so that the free agent is able to survive. So, like the left, with its focus on education and the development of talent, the right is concerned with establishing the conditions for freedom. These conditions are themselves a part of what is meant when we talk about free people or when we consider whether a political system is one that provides a favourable climate for the flourishing of freedom. Simply labelling theories of freedom as positive or negative fails to capture this highly important aspect of the understanding of political freedom.

The inadequacy of Berlin's categories of positive and negative freedom in the classification of the two views of freedom discussed probably results from the fact that, as do most analytic theorists, he sought to resolve problems of meaning and definition in abstraction. Analytic theorists focus on the immediate linguistic context of sentences containing, in this case, freedom, rather than on the ideological contexts of the statements. The inadequacy of this approach can be shown very clearly by looking at what seems initially to be a very plausible analysis of freedom, that of MacCallum. He suggests that all meaningful uses of the term freedom conform to the following formula: 'x is (is not) free from y to do (not do, become, not become)' (MacCallum, 1972, p. 176).

However, for someone on the right to state that 'people cannot be free in a permissive society' is not simply to claim that 'x is not free from pornography to live a life uncontaminated by obscenity', or even 'x is not free from the chaos caused by loose morals to live in a stable society'. The statement is far more complex, resting on an underlying theory of human agency and the nature of the relationship between the individual and society. Out of this theory springs a belief that the free agent cannot actually be sustained in a society that does not provide a firm framework of expectations and a responsible, non-hedonistic pattern of behaviour. This cannot be discovered by analysis of the sentence 'people cannot be free in a permissive society'. It requires nothing less than a full investigation of the whole system of ideas that makes this statement meaningful. Our two examples, in the briefest way, sketched the results of the attempt to do precisely this. We should now reflect more directly on what these examples tell us about the nature of political freedom and about how we, as theorists, might go about studying such questions.

The two examples given in the last section outlined alternative versions of what it is to be a free person and to live in a free society, each of which is grounded in a different view of self and society. These, of course, are only two of many possible variants. Furthermore, they have been described at a high level of generality. If we narrowed our focus we would find more precise sub-theories, with slightly different nuances and implications, existing within each of these general theories of freedom. However, broad though our account has been, it has served to demonstrate that 'freedom' as a political value is located in and surrounded by different patterns of ideas.

Included within this pattern are a number of positive and negative freedoms, or, to put it another way, the understanding of freedom in general (the free person or the free society) includes a commitment to many particular freedoms or liberties that are themselves captured by different theories of freedom. I am not claiming, therefore, that these overarching theories of freedom constitute the only meaning of freedom in political contexts. However, it is necessary to distinguish what we might call 'freedom in general' from specific freedoms. Specific freedoms – freedom from want, freedom to use and dispose of property – gain their significance for human freedom in general from their location in an overall pattern of political values. It is to a discussion of these patterns that I shall now turn.

The patterning of ideas such as that which has been identified in each of our two examples, and the distinctive world view that is enshrined by the patterns, can be labelled as ideology. Ideologies do not have to be grand theories that are then applied to society. The term ideology can also be applied to the distinctive and consistent world views that inform everyday thinking about politics (Freeden, 1986, pp. 3–5).

These competing world views mean that we cannot finally adjudicate between the two views of freedom discussed. We can try to persuade one side of the superiority of the world view of the other side, but ultimately there are no logically coercive arguments which will force holders of one of the views to accept the other. The irreducible nature of the dispute between the competing conceptions of the term is what causes political theorists to label the term essentially contestable (Gallie, 1964; Connolly, 1983, pp. 14ff; Gray, 1977, 1978 and 1983). It should be noted that the two contestants share much. They agree that individuals, to be free, must be able to give expression to their personality, to make life choices for themselves, and to control their own circumstances. It is clear that they are talking about the same value, therefore. However, what they think these characteristics of freedom entail is not agreed, so that the political policies believed by the two sides to be necessary to ensure freedom differ substantially.

We can label the resulting theories of freedom substantive theories. They are accounts of the different conceptions of freedom that appear in political practice and which can be deduced from the study of political discourse. The way in which we have arrived at these accounts, by drawing together evidence about the ways in which

political actors speak about and understand freedom, carries implications for political theorists which are worth reflecting upon. This
chapter will conclude, therefore, with a brief consideration of this
approach for the way political theory is conducted.

Conclusion: The practice of political theory

The first thing that we might note is that political theorists sitting
in their offices reflecting in abstract on the nature of freedom will
not be able to come up with the substantive views of freedom that
have been described here. In fact what they will end up producing,
if they attempt to give prescriptive definitions of the term, are elegant
and codified versions of their own understandings of it. These will,
of course, be deeply ideological and will not be at all compelling to
those who hold different world views. If they attempt to describe a
variety of competing understandings of the term their descriptions
will be half-baked, drawn from their own memories and resting on
their imperfect understandings of the views of others, rather than
on careful study of the evidence. If they try to provide universal
definitions that all users of the term freedom will agree with, they
risk both the above pitfalls. Furthermore, the definitions they produce will be so bare as to be of no help in elucidating the problems
and issues that arise as we try to understand the different ways in
which political freedom is understood. Clearly, then, the theorist
would be helped in the attempt to understand freedom by a willingness
to get his or her hands dirty and actually to engage with the stuff
of politics.

The obvious response to the argument thus far is to ask whether
political theory can be any more than what one theorist has described
disparagingly as 'philology' (Miller, 1983, p. 51) — by which he meant
the careful transcription of the meanings that words can be taken
to have in everyday use. Is theory not, it is asked, downgraded to
nothing more than a cataloguing process? Furthermore, does it not
then lose any distinctive value as an activity? I would have thought
the answer to these questions is a resounding no.

Firstly, the careful elucidation and exploration of the links between
ideas, and the construction of accounts of the meanings which a
term such as freedom has in different ideological systems, are themselves tasks which require skills of the sort that a political theorist
can offer. It is not enough simply to list the different uses of a term.

For one thing, knowing what is meant by a given use of a term is far from obvious. The same sort of phrase may have quite different significances in different ideological systems. To list its meanings one must first try to work out where the utterance is to be placed in terms of its ideological significance. To build up a picture of the competing ideologies, it is necessary to consider how a term such as freedom is linked to ideas such as equality and justice, and to see how different political ideologies build up different portfolios of ideas which, taken together, give meaning to their view of political freedom. This enterprise would seem to provide an exciting source of activity for political theorists, and to be far from a dull compilation of lists of uses of the word freedom.

Secondly, the task of explaining and clarifying how and why terms come to have the importance that they have is a highly significant one. Without it, political theory fails to be able to explain to us the discourse of politics. Abstract theories may appear in debate, but often only in cases where they are taken up to bolster, or where they serve to refine and codify, principles and beliefs that are already in play. Certainly, the theories of political philosophers do not exhaust political thinking about a term such as freedom, and if we try to understand political argument about such an important political term only in the light of these highly refined theories we risk distorting our understanding of politics. For example, many theorists argued that what they called Thatcherism was inconsistent because it opposed the state in the economic sphere and embraced it in the moral sphere (Behrens, 1980, ch. 2; Durham, 1989, p. 64; Hoover and Plant, 1989, pp. 9–12; Levitas, 1986, p. 7). As we have seen, however, these attitudes to the state result from a coherent view of freedom and the view that they are contradictory results from the imposition of the categories of liberal political philosophers.

Thirdly, if we wish as theorists to prescribe, to make statements about what we believe to be the best theories of freedom, we need to be able to persuade our audience. We must be aware of the significance that a term already has for those who employ it. Michael Walzer has argued that the Jewish prophets did not bring down completely new ideas from Heaven (1987, pp. 71, 76–8 and 82–9). If they had, the people would not have been able to understand them because they would have lacked any comprehension of their significance. What the prophets did was to reorder the ideas that already existed, and in which people claimed to believe. This reordering forced them to rethink their attitudes on a whole range of issues. So, Walzer argues, if the political theorist wishes to persuade people of his or her argument, he or she must speak in language that they already understand and appeal in terms of values to which they are already attached. This exercise necessarily requires that we know what those values and understandings are. Hence, the empirical study of political discourse is a necessary background to the practice of prescriptive political theory.

Some political theorists might still argue that this is a more limited intellectual exercise than the analytic philosophical treatment of abstract terms. This conclusion seems doubtful, but in any case the study of the way terms are used, and the attempt to understand the ideas which inform political argument and affect public policy, are essential and exciting tasks which only political theorists are equipped to carry out.

Notes

1   This is a long-standing Conservative view (Cecil, 1910, p. 53; Benn, 1931, p. 154; Raison, 1964, p. 25; Mount, 1986, p. 13).

2   Perhaps the most eloquent proponent of this position is Hayek (1960, Part 1; 1978, pp. 232–40; 1982, Vol. II, Ch. 10). He has frequently been cited by prominent Conservatives.

3   The exemplary exposition of this view was that of Albert Venn Dicey (1885, pp. 187–96 and 202–3).

4   The Freedom Association is a right-wing 'think tank' which endorses a view of freedom which is compatible with the account offered here.

5   The argument on this point (Gould, 1985, p. 59; Labour Party, 1981; Benn, 1988, pp. 110–12; Heffer, 1985, pp. 149–51) seems to reflect that of Laski (1948, p. 93), who had a large influence on the development of contemporary British democratic socialist thought.

References

Ashworth, C. E. (1972), 'The Coming British Revolution', *Monday World*, Spring.

Attlee, C. R. (1954), *The Labour Party in Perspective*, extract in H. Pelling, *The Challenge of Socialism*, London: Adam and Charles Black.

Barratt Brown, M. (1972), 'Adult Education and the Liberal Tradition', in K. Coates (Ed.), *Essays in Socialist Humanism*, Nottingham: Spokesman Books.

Behrens, R. (1980), *The Conservative Party from Heath to Thatcher*, London: Saxon House.

Benn, E. J. (1931), *Account Rendered: 1900–1930*, London: Ernest Benn.

Benn, T. (1979), *Democracy and Human Rights*, London: Haldane Society.

Benn, T. (1980), *Arguments for Socialism*, Harmondsworth: Penguin.

Benn, T. (1982a), *Arguments for Democracy*, Harmondsworth: Penguin.

Benn, T. (1982b), *Parliament, People and Power: Agenda for a Free Society*, London: Verso.

Benn, T. (1988), *Fighting Back: Speaking Out for Socialism in the Eighties*, London: Hutchinson.

Berlin, I. (1982), 'Two Concepts of Liberty', in his *Four Essays on Liberty*, Oxford: Oxford University Press.

Bevan, A. (1978), *In Place of Fear*, London: Quartet.

Boyson, R. (1978), *Centre Forward: A Radical Conservative Programme*, London: Temple Smith.

Carvel, J. (1990), 'Tory Revives "Caring" Citizen Idea', *The Guardian*, 5/5.

Cecil, H. (1910), *Liberty and Authority*, London: Edward Arnold.

Chaudet, F. (n.d.), 'Free Enterprise, Instrument and Guarantee of Freedom', in Aims of Industry, *International Papers on the Revival of Freedom and Enterprise*, London: Aims of Industry.

Coates, K. (1971), *The Crisis of British Socialism*, Nottingham: Spokesman Books.

Cohen, G. (1979), 'Capitalism, Freedom and the Proletariat', in A. Ryan (Ed.), *The Idea of Freedom: Essays in Honour of Isaiah Berlin*, Oxford: Oxford University Press.

Connolly, W. (1983), *The Terms of Political Discourse*, 2nd ed., Oxford: Martin Robertson.

Crossman, R. H. S. (1951), *Socialist Values in a Changing Civilization*, London: Fabian Society, Tract 286.

Crossman, R. H. S. (1965), *Planning for Freedom*, London: Hamish Hamilton.

Crowther, I. (1973), 'How the Liberal Lost His Reason', *Monday World*, Spring.

Crowther, I. (1983), 'Mrs Thatcher's Idea of the Good Society', *Salisbury Review*, No. 3.

Dawson, G. (1984), 'Freedom, State and Tradition', *Salisbury Review*, No. 2.

Dean, M. (1983), 'Ministers Rethink Welfare State', *The Guardian*, 17/2.

Dicey, A. V. (1885), *Introduction to the Study of the Law of the Constitution*, 10th ed., Ed. E. C. S. Wade (1959), London: Macmillan.

Durham, M. (1989), 'The Right: The Conservative Party and Conservatism', in L. Tivey and A. Wright (Eds.), *Party Ideology in Britain*, London: Routledge.

Ferns, H. S. (n.d.), *Galloping Bureaucracy and Taxation: The Radicalism the Case Requires*, London: Aims of Industry.

Field, F. (1987), *Freedom and Wealth in a Socialist Future*, London: Constable.

Freeden, M. (1978), *The New Liberalism*, Oxford: Clarendon Press.

Freeden, M. (1986), *Liberalism Divided: A Study in British Political Thought 1914–1939*, Oxford: Clarendon Press.

Gallie, W. B. (1964), 'Essentially Contested Concepts', in his *Philosophy and the Historical Understanding*, London: Chatto and Windus.

Gould, B. (1985), *Socialism and Freedom*, London: Macmillan, pp. 11–12, 14–16, 25–9, 35, 59, 211.

Gouriet, G. (1978), 'Freedom and Enterprise', in K. D. Watkins (Ed.), *In Defence of Freedom*, London: Freedom Association, p. 33.

Gray, J. (1977), 'On the Contestability of Social and Political Concepts', *Political Theory*, 5.

Gray, J. (1978), 'On Liberty, Liberalism and Essential Contestability', *British Journal of Political Science*, 8.

Gray, J. (1983), 'Political Power, Social Theory, and Essential Contestability', in D. Miller and L. Siedentop, *The Nature of Political Theory*, Oxford: Oxford University Press.

Green, R. (1986), 'Freedom and Fairness at Work', in Coates (Ed.), *Freedom and Fairness*, Nottingham: Spokesman Books.

Griffiths, B. (1983), *The Moral Basis of the Market Economy*, London: Conservative Political Centre.

Gwyn, W. B. (1971), 'The Labour Party and the Threat of Bureaucracy', *Political Studies*.

Hall, S. (1979), 'The Great Moving Right Show', *Marxism Today*.

Hattersley, R. (1987), *Choose Freedom: The Future for Democratic Socialism*, London: Michael Joseph.

Hayek, F. (1960), *The Constitution of Liberty*, London: Routledge and Kegan Paul.

Hayek, F. (1978), 'The Pretence of Knowledge', in his *New Studies*, London: Routledge and Kegan Paul.

Hayek, F. (1982), *Law, Legislation and Liberty*, London: Routledge and Kegan Paul.

Heffer, E. (1985), *Labour's Future: Socialism or SDP Mark 2*, London: Verso.

Hoover, K. and Plant, R. (1989), *Conservative Capitalism*, London: Routledge.

Howell, D. (1981), *Freedom and Capital: Prospects of the Property Owning Democracy*, London: Conservative Political Centre.

Hurd, D. (1989), 'Freedom Will Flourish Where Citizens Accept Responsibility', *The Independent*, 13/9.

Johnson, P. (1978), *Britain's Own Road to Serfdom*, London: Conservative Political Centre.

Jones, K. (1989), *Right Turn: The Conservative Revolution in Education*, London: Hutchinson Radius.

Joseph, K. (1975a), 'The Economics of Freedom', in K. Joseph, A. Maude and I. Percival, *Freedom and Order*, London: Conservative Political Centre.

Joseph, K. (1975b), *Freedom Under the Law*, London: Conservative Political Centre.

Joseph K. and Sumption, J. (1979), *Equality*, London: John Murray.

Kendall, W. (1976), 'Why Workers Control', in D. Widgery (Ed.), *The Left in Britain*, Harmondsworth, Penguin.

Kinnock, N. (1986), *The Future of Socialism*, London: Fabian Society, Tract 509.

Labour Party (1980a), *Private Schools*, London: Labour Party.

Labour Party (1980b), *Workers Co-operatives*, London: Labour Party.

Labour Party (1981), *The Rights of Gay Men and Women*, London: Labour Party.

Labour Party (1988), *Democratic Socialist Aims and Values*, London: Labour Party.

Laski, H. J. (1948), *A Grammar of Politics*, 5th ed., London: George Allen and Unwin.

Letwin, S. R. (1978), 'On Conservative Individualism', in M. Cowling (Ed.), *Conservative Essays*, London: Cassell.

Letwin, S. R. and Letwin, O. (1986), *Every Adult A Share Owner*, London: Centre for Policy Studies.

Levitas, R. (1986), *The Ideology of the New Right*, Cambridge: Polity.

Lewis, R. (n.d.), *Neither Freedom Nor Enterprise*, London: Aims of Industry.

MacCallum, G. (1972), 'Negative and Positive Freedom', in P. Laslett, W. G. Runciman and Q. Skinner, *Philosophy, Politics and Society*, 4th Series, Oxford: Blackwell.

Miller, D. (1983), 'Linguistic Philosophy and Political Theory', in D. Miller and L. Siedentop, *The Nature of Political Theory*, Oxford: Oxford University Press.

Morrison (Lady Morrison of Lambeth) (1978), 'Freedom and the Family', in K. D. Watkins (Ed.), *In Defence of Freedom*, London: Freedom Association.

Mount, F. (1982), *The Subversive Family: An Alternative History of Love and Marriage*, London: Jonathan Cape.

Mount, F. (1984), *Property and Poverty: An Agenda for the Mid-80s*, London: Centre for Policy Studies.

Mount, F. (1986), *The Practice of Liberty*, London: Conservative Political Centre.

O'Gorman, F. (1986), *British Conservatism*, Harlow: Longman.

Phillips, J. (1988), *Policing the Family*, London: Junius.

Plant, R. (1988), *Citizenship Rights and Socialism*, London: Fabian Society, Tract 531.

Radice, G. (1989), *Labour's Path to Power: The New Revisionism*, London: Macmillan.

Raison, T. (1964), *Why Conservative?*, Harmondsworth: Penguin.

Rawls, J. (1973), *A Theory of Justice*, Oxford: Oxford University Press.

Redwood, J. (1988), *Popular Capitalism*, London: Routledge.

Seldon, A. (1975), 'Who Will Rid Us of This Tyrannical Paternalism', in R. Boyson (Ed.), *1985: An Escape From Orwell's 1984*, London: Churchill Press.

Shuller, T. (1985), *Democracy at Work*, Oxford: Oxford University Press.

Tawney, R.M. (1953), 'We Mean Freedom', in his *The Attack and Other Papers*, London: George Allen and Unwin.

Taylor, C. (1985), 'What's Wrong With Negative Liberty', in his *Philosophy and the Human Sciences: Philosophical Papers 2*, Cambridge, Cambridge University Press.

Thatcher, M. (1989), *The Revival of Britain: Speeches on Home and European Affairs 1975–89* (Ed. A.B. Cooke), London: Aurum.

Titmuss, R.M. (1970), *The Gift Relationship*, London: Allen and Unwin.

Utley, T.E. (1970), 'Permissive Society or Free Society', *Solon: A Right Wing Journal*, 1.

Utley, T.E. (1989), 'Thatcher's New Crusade', in C. Moore and S. Heffer (Eds.), *A Tory Seer: The Selected Journalism of T.E. Utley*, London: Hamish Hamilton.

Walzer, M. (1987), 'The Prophet as Social Critic', in his *Interpretation and Social Criticism*, Cambridge, Mass: Harvard University Press.

Whitehead, P. (1984), 'Education and the Disadvantaged', in B. Pimlott (Ed.), *Fabian Essays in Socialist Thought*, London: Heinemann.

Wright, A.W. (1979), *G.D.H Cole and Socialist Democracy*, Oxford: Clarendon Press.

Citizenship and rights

Political debate is currently dominated by the language of rights. Today, all the main political parties, most pressure groups, and individuals of almost every ideological persuasion, make their demands and define our identity as citizens in terms of rights. Thus, dissidents in Eastern Europe referred to their rights to legitimise their opposition and justify calls for democratic reform. Similarly, groups campaigning against discrimination, such as women or ethnic minorities, regularly turn to rights to articulate and institutionalise their demands. Rights are also increasingly used in international relations by those, such as the poor in the Third World, seeking to emphasise the obligations of countries other than their own towards them. Over the whole range of political issues, therefore, rights have become the preferred method for pressing one's case and judging a state's, a government's, or a social and economic system's legitimacy.

Perhaps because our political thinking and practice has become so suffused with talk of rights, we rarely question its attractiveness or coherence. The appeal of rights, like the rights themselves, is frequently regarded as being self-evident. In this chapter, I want to challenge that assumption by pointing out some theoretical difficulties with the concept of rights which I believe weaken its practical effectiveness. I shall start by examining the two main ways of characterising the links between rights and citizenship found in the most recent literature on the subject. In the first section, I shall discuss some of the abstract philosophical arguments for what I call a 'rights-based conception of citizenship'. In the second section, I turn to the more sociological form of analysis that underpins a 'communitarian conception of citizenship and rights'. I shall claim this second conception articulates many of the unexamined and, in my opinion, dubious social assumptions of the first view. Finally, in the third section I shall outline an alternative 'republican conception of citizenship', which places duties before rights.

In laying out my argument in this fashion, I also wish to achieve a secondary purpose, that of illustrating a particular approach to political theory. I hope to show that, whilst clear and logical thinking is indispensable, abstract theorising of the kind discussed in section one is insufficient in itself to mount a convincing argument. Rather, it needs to be supplemented with the sorts of sociological and distinctively political or institutional considerations raised in sections two and three respectively.

Rights-based citizenship

Rights-based conceptions of citizenship draw on doctrines of human rights. An initial distinction needs to be made at this point between human rights and institutional rights. Human rights claim to be fundamental and universal. As such, they must be capable of being extended equally to all persons regardless of social status, country of origin, colour, creed or sexual inclination. They ought to be upheld by all legitimate states, whatever their particular cultural, ideological or religious traditions and practical commitments. In certain important respects, therefore, human rights make us citizens of the world – an aspect that those campaigning on behalf of relief for the hungry or oppressed have often sought to exploit in order to generate international co-operation to tackle these issues. However, the universality of rights does not negate our membership of different states or cultures, nor does it mean that all states must adopt precisely the same laws and institutional structures. Human rights only aim to define the essential moral conditions that ought to be guaranteed citizens in any social and political order. They are necessary but not sufficient elements of morality or politics, which purport to be compatible with a wide variety of different sets of moral beliefs and political and economic systems. As a result, human rights are usually framed in sufficiently abstract and general terms to be met in a number of highly diverse ways.

Institutional rights consist of the rights recognised and incorporated into the laws and regulations of particular countries or other associations. Clearly, for any human right to be operative, it will need to be institutionalised and formulated in detail. Thus, the right to a fair trial will in practice require further specification in numerous institutional rights detailing what sort of evidence the police can or cannot bring against you, the composition and procedures of the court, access to legal support, the framing of the laws used against you, and so on. Similarly, a right to welfare will need spelling out in terms of a system of social security benefits, health care, housing provision etc. These institutional rights give members of a particular society an entitlement to a whole range of benefits subject to meeting certain well-defined criteria. However, a country's institutional rights may be deemed to conflict with or fail to provide for certain human rights. In these instances, human rights activists believe that the laws, and in some cases even the entire political system, have to be reformed, possibly radically.

This distinction between human and institutional rights lies behind attempts to get international agreement on various charters of rights, such as the United Nations Universal Declaration of Human Rights of 1948 or the European Convention for the Protection of Human Rights of 1953. None of the signatory nations to these charters have precisely the same legal, social, economic or political arrangements, and there are often huge cultural differences not only between countries but within them too. Yet all claim in their different ways to meet certain standards safeguarding basic civil rights, such as the right to a fair trial; political rights, such as a right to vote; and usually certain social rights as well, such as rights to a given level of education, health care and housing. However, when either the policies or the institutional rights enshrined within the law or conventions of a particular signatory state are deemed to have conflicted with human rights, then, according to the proponents of human rights, it is the offending law or policy that ought to change, even if that law reflects the democratic will of the population at the time. For example, Britain has been taken to the European Court of Human Rights on numerous occasions over matters such as its interrogation methods and policy of internment in Northern Ireland; corporal punishment in schools; employment legislation which endorses or gives inadequate protection against discrimination against women etc. In each of these cases, individuals who had no rights according to the institutional laws of Britain, and hence no case in British courts, were able to force the British government to introduce new legislation institutionalising new practices in line with the European Convention.

The thinking behind the human rights project should now be clear. Human rights aim to offer a meta-political moral framework for politics and social interaction, which is capable of providing criteria by which we can judge a given system or set of arrangements as just or not. The declared purpose of human rights is to ensure the just treatment of individuals and, on some theories, groups as well, either by protecting them from the incursions of others, as with rights against torture or unfair imprisonment, or, at least on certain interpretations, by enabling them in some vital respect, as with rights to food or shelter.

Human rights have an obvious political appeal for activists of all kinds. By getting their claims accepted as rights, they can seek to alter established conventions, policies and legal and institutional frameworks by questioning their moral validity. They can insist that the legally accepted authorities – governments and the courts of the land – do not have the final say. There are universal principles by which their decisions may be evaluated and called to account. A demand that human rights be respected can have a liberating effect, therefore. For those that invoke rights may challenge not just the practices but the very values of the established order. In this guise, rights can serve to promote radical changes, as in the cases cited in the opening paragraph. However, they may equally operate to block reforms or preserve the status quo if the proposed innovations are held to infringe individual rights. Some of the ambivalence that both the left and right have expressed about rights arises from the fact that, whilst Conservatives have generally deplored the first aspect of rights discourse and welcomed the second, socialists have usually liked the first and condemned the second. The British Labour Party, for example, see the Social Chapter of the Maastricht Treaty as offering a means for securing worker's rights. The Tories, in contrast, have seen it as involving undue interference with the property rights of employers and the individual's freedom of contract.

These sorts of disputes reveal a paradox generated by the very appeal of rights. For to be at all useful, human rights must speak not only to those seeking change but also to those capable of instituting it. To achieve this goal, human rights must be able to lay claim to a degree of universality and objectivity that places them above political debate. As a result, they must meet two fairly stringent conditions. First, to achieve widespread support, human rights must be capable of appealing to a plurality of different people and types of institution motivated by often diverse principles and goals. In particular, they must be able to sustain in a plausible manner their claim to be fundamental and universal conditions of a just social order, that are capable of applying equally to all individuals. To meet this condition, a distinction needs to be drawn between the 'right' and the 'good', between the framework of basic rights and the conceptions of the good people may pursue within that framework. Human rights cannot themselves be based on any particular ethos or conception of the good, therefore. Secondly, whilst being sufficiently general and abstract to meet the first condition, rights must also be precise enough for us to be able to apply them to concrete circumstances, and the criteria defining what counts as a right must be stringent enough to prevent each and every goal or preference we have becoming the subject of a human right. Those who doubt the usefulness of rights language have usually been particularly critical of the tendency for the class of human rights to expand seemingly indefinitely to include each and every person's favoured cause.

Most philosophers now believe that the two traditional foundations for human rights, a divinely ordered natural law and an appeal to human nature, are inadequate because they fail to meet these two conditions. Given that the world contains not only wide differences of religious belief but also a large proportion of atheists as well, God is too contentious a starting point for a theory of rights aiming at near universal acceptability and applicability. The secularism of modern science has rendered human nature a similarly problematic basis for rights. Those theorists who begin from here, argue that our rights should protect and possibly promote the conditions necessary for human beings to flourish. We establish these rights by identifying the distinctive characteristics of the human species and the circumstances necessary for them to develop. However, numerous difficulties arise with this procedure (Williams, 1972). In the first place, one immediately comes up against the 'is' 'ought' problem. That something happens to be a fact about human beings tells us nothing in itself about its moral significance. After all, there are many human traits that mark us out from other animals, such as cruelty and killing for reasons other than food, which most people would find morally repugnant. Moreover, even those traits that appear to be rather more attractive, such as rationality or creativity, may be put to morally ambiguous or positively immoral uses, such as devising sophisticated and subtle forms of torture. Indeed, the empirical evidence tends to suggest quite a variety of often conflicting forms of human flourishing even within the range that most people would find acceptable. Thus, the selection of the distinguishing marks inevitably presupposes certain moral judgements about the nature of the good life, so that it is our views about morality rather than any empirical facts about human beings *per se* that actually do the work in our selection of human rights. As a result, the appeal to human nature will not get us very far. It will generate as many conceptions of rights as there are moral views and hence fail to pass our two conditions.

Most contemporary philosophers faced with this dilemma have opted for a 'transcendental' argument for human rights.[1] In other words, they have tried to associate rights with the preconditions necessary for us all to make moral judgements and choose to flourish in any recognisable form at all. This basis for rights is generally held to issue in an equal right to liberty (see Hart, 1950 for a classic statement of this argument). On this view, claims to particular rights will be settled on the basis of whether they can be construed as a universal right to liberty that can be held equally by all. If there are many consistent such sets of compossible rights,[2] then the maximum set guaranteeing the greatest degree of individual liberty compatible with a like freedom for everyone else is to be preferred. John Rawls' 'first principle of justice' offers a neat summary of this formulation, according to which 'each person is to have an equal right to the most extensive total system of liberties compatible with a similar system of liberty for all' (Rawls, 1971, p. 302).[3]

Even if the form of moral agency assumed by this argument is clearly the Western liberal one of the autonomous chooser, and hence not so uncontentious as its proponents often assert, the reasoning behind it appears perfectly cogent: namely, to provide the optimal framework for a plurality of individuals living together in society to carry out their various projects in a peaceful and just fashion. Since freedom seems necessary to undertake any project at all, by making liberty the basis of rights they claim to have satisfied the two conditions for a coherent theory of rights set out above. Unfortunately, matters are not so simple. To be plausible, this thesis requires near universal agreement on a common conception of liberty. Most of the recent debates about rights arise because, rhetoric apart, no such consensus exists.

Although there are a number of intermediary positions, the debate over rights to liberty is essentially between those who take a 'negative' view of liberty and those who hold a 'positive' view. For the former, mainly New Right libertarians (e.g. Nozick, 1974; Barry, 1990), freedom consists of an absence of intentional interference by others. The most important rights are, therefore, the traditional civil and political rights guaranteeing a right to life, security of property, freedom of speech and belief, and rights to engage in economic activity free from the intervention of the State or others. For the latter, who range from social liberals to democratic socialists (e.g. Gewirth, 1982; Plant, 1990), freedom also includes the capacity to undertake certain actions, and hence must include a number of social or welfare rights to basic human needs, such as to food, health care, shelter and education.

If a conception of rights based on liberty is to work, this debate has to be settled. For these are not just two different views of liberty rights but two incompatible views. As New Right theorists eagerly point out, if I have an unrestricted right to property and to trade in the market, I cannot have unrestricted rights to welfare (and, of course, vice versa). To avoid this dilemma, these thinkers have insisted that only a negative conception of liberty can make sense of the rights project. They argue that basing rights on positive liberty inevitably leads to conflicts between rights and so brings into play unresolvable moral questions about the quality as opposed to the quantity of our liberty, and so renders the concept of liberty rights inherently unstable. In the rest of this section I shall very briefly examine their case against positive liberty rights and show that it is equally telling against their own arguments for negative liberty rights. I will conclude that these criticisms seriously weaken the whole rights-based conception of citizenship.

Negative libertarians standardly argue that rights based on 'negative freedom' merely require restraint on the part of others (e.g. Cranston, 1973). As a result, they are capable of being universally applied to all and generate perfect duties on everyone that do not infringe any other negative liberty rights. For example, in sitting quietly at my word processor, as I was when writing this sentence, I can respect each and every person's rights not to be attacked etc. and everybody else can show an equal respect for my right just as easily. Positive liberty rights, in contrast, require action on my part which is often costly, frequently conflicts with another of my rights, and is in some instances impossible to extend equally and universally to all.

These three criticisms of positive rights are related. Because they are costly, they lead to conflicts and so cannot be universal equal rights. If I tried personally to meet the welfare rights of my fellow human beings, for example, I would quickly exhaust my financial and physical resources, thereby restricting the exercise of my own liberty rights to do other things, and make only the smallest of contributions to the relief of suffering. Many of these difficulties remain even if I attempt to get around some of the problems, as most advocates of positive rights propose, by holding that respecting other people's welfare rights merely entails an obligation to support agencies, such as social workers, a national health service etc., that can provide a more universal system of benefits than any single individual could. For the negative libertarian, there would still be a conflict between the taxation needed to run these services and my right to do what I will with my own rightfully acquired property. Robert Nozick goes so far as to argue that such taxation is the moral equivalent of granting property rights in another person and 'is on a par with forced labour' (Nozick, 1974, p. 169).

Even if we do not accept this extreme view of property rights, proponents of welfare rights admit that the scarcity of resources means that competing claims will result in conflicts between rights that will have to be sorted out somehow (Waldron, 1989). If two people require a particularly expensive form of treatment, for example, and there only exists resources for one of them, then inevitably one person's right to health care will have to be weighed against the entitlement of another person. Equally, governments are likely to be faced with competing claims between different sorts of rights, between education and housing for instance, which may prove even trickier to resolve. In each of these sorts of cases, it will be hard for anyone to say which policy maximises freedom. What metric could we use to say whether housing, health care or education produces more freedom, or to decide whether one person's liberty would be increased more than another's?

Resolving conflicts between rights in this way places the whole concept in jeopardy. To engage in these sorts of interpersonal comparisons in order to maximise the utility of the whole goes against what is traditionally regarded as one of the chief virtues of rights: namely, that rights attach themselves to individuals and prevent or 'trump' (Dworkin, 1977) any attempt to sacrifice a person or minority for the good of a majority or collectivity (e.g. Rawls,

1971, pp. 3–4, for an explicit statement to this effect). To countenance calculations of interpersonal utility, therefore, constitutes a slippery slope that undercuts the very logic of rights theories. Moreover, negative libertarians believe it reveals what they regard as the central incoherence at the heart of positive liberty rights: the confusion of freedom with ability. For once liberty gets linked to my capacity to do something, then the only way clashes between different liberty rights could be avoided is by everyone becoming omnipotent (Hayek, 1960, p. 19).

Proponents of positive liberty rights usually grant a watered down version of these criticisms, but respond by pointing out that negative liberty rights give rise to the self-same problems (e.g. Plant, 1991, Ch. 7, 1992). After all, my negative rights to security of my person and possessions, a fair trial etc. require a police force, prisons, courts of law and so on if they are to be upheld, all of which are just as costly to keep up and lead to similar utilitarian comparisons between rights and persons. Indeed, the cost of total security is probably as far beyond our resources as meeting everyone's welfare needs, and could only be achieved at a similarly unacceptable moral price. For as most attempts to increase security lead to clashes and trade-offs with other rights, such as the right to privacy or free speech, a totally secure society would not only break the exchequer but have to be an extremely coercive police state as well.

Developing this argument, advocates of positive liberty counter the charge of having absurdly identified freedom with omnipotence by arguing that any view of freedom will be bounded by qualitative moral judgements, at least some of which will entail notions of ability.[4] Negative libertarians have attempted to avoid this dilemma by adopting physicalist accounts of liberty that define coercion in the narrowest terms as a direct, intentional, absolute, and practical hindrance to our performing a given action, such as imprisoning someone. However, outside the realm of metaphor, the view of the individual sheltering behind a barricade of rights within an 'inviolable moral space' proves very hard to sustain (the metaphor is Nozick's (1974, pp. 10, 56, 57)). To be remotely plausible, this conception has to rely on a number of debatable empirical assertions, such as the view that people's choices are not constrained by prevailing social prejudices or fears, for example, or that the effects of market transactions can neither be intended nor foreseen. But even if we grant these usually unargued assumptions, evaluative difficulties will still crop up about defining when the individual's physical space has or has not been infringed. Thus, is the loud music emanating from the flat below mine a hindrance to my freedom or not? If so, to what degree, and at what point does it cease to be so? It seems hard to answer these questions without getting embroiled in knotty questions concerning the various degrees to which different physical acts impose on people. Such questions involve making some sort of appeal to basic human interests and our capacity for protecting them etc. These considerations in turn will lead to the problem of how to make balanced judgements between conflicting liberty rights. After all, stopping my noisy neighbours surely will entail some interference with their property rights?

If no objective view of freedom exists, then the project to make universal equal rights to liberty foundational runs into grave problems. Faced with differing and often conflicting views of freedom, it may not be possible even to agree when collisions between liberties occur, let alone to rationally resolve such disputes. Moreover, we have seen that this dilemma arises even within attempts to deduce rights from a single conception of liberty. These theoretical weaknesses give rise to even more debilitating practical difficulties. Once the 'right' can no longer be separated from the 'good', then in a pluralist society one will be faced with an ever expanding number of rival and disproportionate assertions of rights between which no mediation is possible. Think, for example, of the way the debate over abortion and related issues, such as population policies in the Third World, degenerates once it is conducted in terms of rights. Between the 'right-to-lifers' and the defenders of the mother's right to control her own body, little or no compromise has been possible without what has usually been felt to be an unacceptable compromising of one or other side's principles.

The only way to circumvent these obstacles to a coherent theory of human rights is to smuggle certain communitarian assumptions into the foundationalist position. Whereas foundationalists seek to separate the right from the good and come up with a set of human rights valid for all societies, communitarians situate rights within the context of a certain kind of community that promotes a particular conception of the individual and his or her relations with others. From this communitarian perspective, rights emerge in their true character as secondary rather than primary principles. Instead of being prior to the good, rights operate to co-ordinate a given way of life motivated by a certain common conception of the good.[5] The tacit reliance on communitarian reasoning was apparent in the way classical rights theorists typically appealed to a pre-political 'natural' society in order to ground their argument, Locke's *Second Treatise of Government* being the paradigmatic example of this approach.[6] Contemporary rights theorists do just the same, but less openly. For example, advocates of negative liberty rights frequently champion the market on the grounds that it offers the most plausible realisation of their conception of rights as rights to non-interference. But really the line of argument is the reverse of this: namely from the market to a conception of rights rather than the other way around. Closer reflection reveals that it is quite implausible to characterise the market as the spontaneous outcome of exchanges between rights bearing individuals. Far from this system being constituted by individual rights, these rights depend upon certain social institutions and values which give them purpose and facilitate their exercise. In spite of the apparent liberal reliance on the invisible hand to derive public benefits from the selfish pursuits of egoistic individuals, the successful operation of this mechanism assumes that all recognise the collective good of the market itself. As the originators of this theory, notably Adam Smith, well knew, the market consists of a complex network of conventions concerning such notions as fair dealing, promise keeping, and the avoidance of restrictive practices such as the formation of price cartels or monopolies which would destroy its competitiveness. The market only benefits the public, as opposed to certain private individuals, so long as these regulatory structures remain in place. For someone to insist on their rights to the point of destroying these social arrangements, thereby preventing others from enjoying the same rights in the future, would be nonsensical.

At the extremes, radically individualist theorists of rights, such as Nozick, recognise this paradox – for example, when they admit that the owner of the only water hole in a desert infringes the rights of others by charging extravagantly for them to use it (Hayek, 1960, pp. 135–7; Nozick, 1974, pp. 178–82). This concession amounts to an acceptance that rights cannot exist in a social and moral vacuum. They can only be enjoyed in a certain situation, defined by the presence of certain collective goods and shared understandings. Thus, the benefits arising from the various rights protecting economic freedom presuppose the market and its values. To subvert them is ultimately to destroy those rights. The upshot of this recognition of the market as a public good is to compromise the stringency of the negative libertarian version of the human rights thesis. The vital conditions necessary for the form of life allowed by the market may require in certain circumstances that some rights be violated in order to protect the whole system of rights. It is only the tacit assumption that rights serve some other good that makes the quasi-utilitarian trade-offs that always occur between conflicting rights both acceptable and possible. Needless to say, a similar argument could be made about theories of positive rights, as I shall demonstrate in the next section.

The upshot of our analysis so far has been to call into doubt the coherence of the thesis that human rights can act as foundational principles for any acceptable social and political order. For rights have been shown to presuppose, rather than to pre-exist, a given way of life. Constructions of rights implicitly rely on a certain conception of society which seeks to provide a range of options enabling various patterns of human development and social inter-action. As such, different conceptions of human community and flourishing will generate different conceptions of rights. It is to the coherence of these various communitarian justifications of rights that we must now turn.

Communitarian conceptions of rights and citizenship

If foundationalists maintain that rights inhere in individuals and exist both logically and morally prior to any society or state, com-munitarians associate our rights with membership of a particular kind of society or state.[7] However, we have seen that the foundationalist position ultimately collapses into the communitarian one, since any coherent theory of rights necessarily proposes an ideal form of mem-bership and hence a certain type of community. A number of rights theorists have deliberately grasped this nettle. They argue that the foundationalist enterprise can be given a communitarian basis in the nature of modern industrial societies. They contend that the evolution of contemporary capitalism has promoted the very form of agency presupposed by foundationalist theories of human rights: namely, the view of the individual as an autonomous chooser of ends, capable of freely contracting into different social relationships.

As we saw at the end of the last section, New Right proponents of negative liberty rights believe this mode of action is best satisfied within a somewhat idealised model of the capitalist market. In contrast, proponents of positive rights have argued that, although capitalism provided the initial impetus for the development of notions of rights, the subsequent elaboration of this doctrine by a variety of groups struggling to gain a degree of control over their lives has radically transformed both the capitalist system and the character of rights themselves (e.g. Marshall, 1950; Giddens, 1985; Held, 1989). Consequently, rights can no longer be assessed solely in terms of their ideological significance for class relations within capitalist society. Rather, new claims of rights have created new forms of citizenship and community. In what follows, I shall offer a different interpretation of this process. I shall argue that the changes within modern societies that both these sets of theorists have correctly associated with the growth of rights, have served to undermine the communitarian assumptions on which any coherent conception of human rights must rely.

In order to focus my argument, I shall centre it around an analysis of probably the most influential sociological explanation of the development of human rights, T.H. Marshall's famous essay 'Citizenship and Social Class' (Marshall, 1950). Marshall linked modern rights-based citizenship to the growth of capitalist relations based on the division of labour within the context of the modern nation-state. The creation of a national economic infrastructure and the resulting need for a mobile workforce, possessing a generic training and able to communicate in a standard idiom, produced a transformation of the relationship between the individual, society and the state. State and society became gradually separated, with the state's role shifting from one of direct control to the regulation, albeit of an increasingly extensive nature, of the social relations of free and equal rights-bearing individuals. Nationalism played an important part in this new economic and administrative structure. It provided the common cultural identity required by a form of citizenship that was defined by adherence to a shared set of legal, socio-economic and political norms and institutions. Within this set-up, rights co-ordinated our relations both with each other and with the state and other agencies. However, like the proponents of positive liberty rights, Marshall believed that rights not only served to stabilise the industrial capitalist order, but to reform it. He saw the establishment of welfare rights as a prime instance of this reformist potential, regarding them as one of the principal means whereby the working class acquired full membership as equal citizens of the modern state.

Marshall provided a brilliant synthesis of the historical evolution of the modern conception of citizenship and rights in Britain. He divided this process into three phases. The 'first phase took place, roughly speaking, in the eighteenth century and saw the consolidation of civil rights, such as 'liberty of the person, freedom of speech, thought and faith, the right to own property and to conclude valid contracts, and the right to justice.' The second phase, occurring generally during the nineteenth century, witnessed the consolidation of political rights 'to participate in the exercise of political power, as a member of a body invested with political authority or as an elector of the members of such a body'. Finally, the third phase, which was largely a twentieth century phenomenon, involved the creation of social rights extending 'from the right to a modicum of economic welfare and security to the right to share to the full in the social heritage and to live the life of a civilised being according to the standards prevailing in society' (Marshall, 1950, pp. 10–11).

Marshall did not regard these three categories of rights as distinct or exclusive but as complementary. Our exercise of our political rights, for example, entails not only the civil rights guaranteeing our freedom to speak without fear of harassment or arbitrary arrest, but also (in his view) a sufficient level of education and welfare to be able to make informed and independent decisions. The three phases of their establishment formed part of a dialectical process whereby rights had been changed from the privileges of a few within the hierarchical social order of the feudal system, into the universal entitlements of all members of modern egalitarian societies (Marshall, 1950, pp. 11–14). The three only appeared to be in conflict during the intermediate stages of their transformation, as when the establishment of the civil right to freedom of contract clashed with the semi-feudal social rights based on ascribed status protecting the privileges of certain classes and categories of worker to pursue particular trades or professions. However, when all three came to be reconstituted as aspects of our equal status as citizens of the community, he believed they would once again be harmonised. Summing up his argument, he observed how:

Citizenship is a status bestowed on all who are full members of a community. All who possess the status are equal with respect to the rights and duties with which the status is endowed. There is no universal principle that determines what those rights and duties shall be, but societies in which citizenship is a developing institution create an image of ideal citizenship against which achievement can be measured and towards which aspiration can be directed. The urge forward along the path thus plotted is an urge towards a fuller measure of equality, an enrichment of the stuff of which status is made and an increase in the number of those on whom the status is bestowed... Citizenship requires a... direct sense of community membership based on loyalty to a civilisation which is a common possession. It is a loyalty of free men endowed with rights and protected by a common law. Its growth is stimulated both by the struggle to win those rights and by their enjoyment when won. (Marshall, 1950, pp. 28–9, 40–1)

Marshall's linking of modern citizenship rights to the shift from status to contract as the organising principle of modern societies, essentially offers a historicist and communitarian explanation of the foundationalist view that we possess our human rights as persons entitled to equal rights to freedom to pursue our own lives in our own way. Indeed, given the pivotal role of social rights in his argument, foundationalist advocates of welfare rights have happily welcomed his interpretation of rights as providing an empirical grounding of their own case for positive rights (Plant, 1988; King and Waldron, 1988). They thereby acknowledge the communitarian background informing their own justification of rights.

However, Marshall's communitarian thesis has a number of advantages over the foundationalist position. First, although the general justificatory principle informing his discussion is the same, namely our entitlement to equal concern and respect, Marshall's more relativist perspective can accommodate different understandings of this principle far more consistently than the foundationalist position can. Second, because Marshall's argument makes better historical and sociological sense of the meaning of rights, in many ways it makes better philosophical sense too. Rather than viewing rights as universal dictates of pure reason, an approach we saw to be largely vacuous, Marshall's account unites the theory and practice of rights and plays the two off against each other. His starting point was not an *a priori* principle, but a widely shared premiss implicit within the customs and practices of modern states. He then showed how a direct appeal to this ideal provided a benchmark against which existing institutions could be challenged and reformed. In this way, for example, campaigners for women's rights have been able to argue that there is no plausible way equal rights can be defended for half the human race whilst denying them to the other half. On this account, a philosophical defence of rights follows from an inherent critique of our present arrangements rather than a transcendent critique of the kind adopted by most contemporary philosophers. Finally, Marshall's explicit acknowledgement that rights operate as functional components of a shared social life makes the resolving of conflicts between rights far easier. For on this theory, the individual has not just rights but social duties to sustain the community that makes the exercise of those rights possible (Marshall, 1950, pp. 59, 70).

Unfortunately, the social assumptions on which Marshall's case ultimately rests have come under a great deal of criticism from a number of recent commentators (e.g. Giddens, 1981; Mann, 1987). They have maintained that Marshall's argument relies on a dubious teleology to sustain it; pays insufficient attention to the role of historical contingencies, such as war and political struggle, in determining the shape of citizenship and rights within different countries; and is generally over-optimistic about the inherently beneficent and irreversible character of rights. Others, though, have defended him from these accusations (e.g. Held, 1989; Turner, 1986, 1990). They note that there is nothing in Marshall's analysis to suggest that he saw the particular development of rights in Britain as either inevitable or smooth. On the contrary, he was well aware that the establishment of certain rights has often generated conflict and hindered as well as promoted the struggle for others. For example, he stressed the way the granting of the negative liberty rights associated with the market had produced huge inequalities of social, economic and political power, and he saw the struggle of working class movements for political and social rights as attempts to rectify these inequities. Moreover, if in the light of the New Right attack on welfare rights he appears to have been rather optimistic in his hope that the expansion of social rights would continue to modify the capitalist system so as to abolish class distinctions and economic inequalities altogether, both the New Right assault and the resistance it has met testify to the very real gains that have been made in the direction Marshall desired (Turner, 1986). Finally, those who have noted the limitations of Marshall's concentration on Britain have generally supplemented rather than overturned his analysis.

For there is nothing in his argument to suggest that he was unaware of or would have been surprised at the divergent forms citizenship took due to the various ruling class strategies allowed by particular patterns of industrial development within different countries (Esping-Anderson, 1990).

If many of the traditional objections to Marshall fail to convince, however, there are others which are more telling and which threaten the whole communitarian basis for rights. Marshall believed that the modern industrial community would ultimately stabilise. The class conflicts that continued to characterise it were a transitionary phenomenon associated with the move from the feudal to the modern rights-based social morality (Marshall, 1950, pp. 47, 77). Underlying this belief was a dubious social ontology or nature of being derived from the 'new liberal' thinkers, such as T. H. Green and L. T. Hobhouse, who had provided much of the ideological support for this transformation of the state at the turn of the century (Freeden, 1978; Vincent and Plant, 1984; Plant 1992).[8] This thesis made social membership intrinsic to individual flourishing to the extent that each person's self-realisation becomes assimilated into the progress of society as a whole. This ontology is best described as offering a secular equivalent of the natural law doctrines that underpinned classical liberal theories of rights, and was acknowledged as such by its new liberal originators (e.g. Green, 1986, paras. 5–7; Durkheim, 1953, p. 52). However, some such thesis seems essential for a communitarian (and hence any) conception of rights (see Freeden, 1990, 1991 for an explicit defence of rights along these lines). For it provides the only convincing way either of defending a particular set of compossible rights or of reconciling conflicts of rights through appeals to social utility or the common good, tasks which, as we saw in section 1, no coherent theory of rights can avoid.

Of doubtful plausibility in the 1890s, in the 1990s this position appears highly implausible. Not only has the onslaught of policies inspired by the New Right destroyed the post-war social democratic conciliation of negative and positive rights, at least in Britain and the United States, but new sources of tension and conflict have developed that have undermined the social homogeneity communitarian theories assume. Marshall and his immediate followers centred their discussion of citizenship on class and capitalist relations of production. However, we have noted already that in recent years the debate has been broadened to involve the struggle for recognition of a far more diverse number of groups. These groups have ranged from movements struggling for the rights of women and ethnic minorities, to campaigns for rights for children, the poor of the Third World and even ecologists asserting the rights of animals and the planet generally.

This proliferation of rights claims derives in large part from the fragmentation of traditional conceptions of membership and citizenship associated with the break up of the nation-state. The related processes of greater functional differentiation and the globalisation of economic, social and political activity has subjected the state to two corresponding countervailing pressures: the one calling for greater heterogeneity at the local and regional level, the other stressing greater interconnectedness at an international level. As a result, the nation-state appears too large for some purposes, too small for others (Bell, 1987, p. 14). The consequence of this dual pressure has been the disintegration of the relatively homogenous national cultural identity that previously defined citizenship of a particular state, and its challenging by the various groups listed above.

As I observed earlier, some theorists of positive rights have interpreted these new social movements as simply shifting and widening the definition of social and political membership to encompass previously excluded and oppressed groups (Turner, 1986, pp. 85, 92; Held, 1989, pp. 199–203). They look to an expanded set of rights to match a broader and cosmopolitan conception of citizenship. Rights come in this way to define our identity as citizens of a global community (Held, 1991, 1992). In spite of its popularity, this belief appears unfounded. Without in any way denying the many positive social developments that lie behind these new right claims, the hope that they can be incorporated in some drastically reformed and fuller conception of citizen's rights is theoretically and practically misconceived.

There are two main problems that undermine this optimistic thesis. First, the bases on which these different assertions of rights are made are by no means compatible with each other. Typically they invoke not just different interpretations of common values, such as liberty, but often different and conflicting values as well. From the point of view of anyone not sharing the same moral principles as the rights claimants, their appeal to rights will appear completely arbitrary. Second, precisely because many of these pronouncements of new rights represent assertions of difference and a rejection of currently accepted norms, they make no claim to universality or equality.

Many are avowedly demands for special treatment. Certain radical feminists, for example, in demanding reproductive rights for women have been concerned to avoid justifying this claim on the grounds that it is necessary in order to equalise their position with men in terms of job opportunities etc. For they have seen in this argument not an expansion of citizenship to include women, but the incorporation of women into a model of the citizen defined by traditional male roles (e.g. Young, 1989). The problem with the cosmopolitan rights-based conception of citizenship, therefore, is that it cannot avoid appealing to an idealised form of universal agency that many of these new movements reject.

Other theorists, of both negative and positive rights, have tried to argue that the pluralism and complexity of modern societies can be contained within a more minimal conception of human rights. Indeed, they contend that in a disenchanted world, in which the old solidarities of nation, class, culture or religion have become increasingly frag- mented and people's motivations and aspirations have become increasingly subjective and individualistic, the only common bond likely to prove at all appealing is our basic human rights. Rights within this conception operate not just as enablements but also as barriers that help us to separate out the different spheres of our lives – the religious and moral from the political, for example, and both of these from the economic. In this guise, rights supposedly operate as regulators of a world in which the integration of all aspects of our lives into a final universal synthesis is no longer possible or acceptable. On this view, it is the very fragmentation of the modern world that has promoted the form of agency assumed by foundationalist theories of human rights. Namely, that of a global citizen who freely contracts in and out of a wide range of different sorts of relationships, that are often spatially far removed.

This argument may appear anti-communitarian, and generally critics have contrasted rights-based and communitarian theories on these grounds (e.g. Sandel, 1984). However, we have shown in the last section that rights-based theories have to trade on certain communitarian assumptions, so that it is more accurate to characterise such minimal rights theories as merely minimally communitarian in character.[9] As we saw, even the most minimalist negative libertarian conception of human rights appears to assume agreement on the good of the market and the form of agency underlying it, and viewed market relations as largely harmonious and self-sustaining. Similarly, the more positive libertarian thesis of John Rawls, who has made the communitarian basis of his theory increasingly explicit in his recent writings, relies on analogous assumptions when he characterises his principles of justice as providing a framework for a 'social union of social unions', in which 'everyone's conception of the good as given by his rational plan is a subplan of the larger comprehensive plan that regulates the community' (Rawls, 1971, p. 563).

Unhappily for this school of thought, the world fails to evidence the moral regularity which even these minimalist theories of human rights need to be made coherent. Indeed, the self-same features of modern societies that human rights theorists point to in order to stress the attractiveness of their arguments have, in reality, undermined their theories' plausibility. For the increased social differentiation and the accompanying ethical and cognitive pluralism associated with the globalising tendencies of contemporary economies, not only has generated a plethora of conflicting claims but has undercut any common basis for their reconciliation. The tensions generated by the increasingly individualistic appeal to human rights is vividly illustrated, for example, by the way in which an insistence on negative liberty rights has steadily eroded any collective responsibility for the positive liberty rights of welfare. Moreover, as I remarked at the close of section one, there is every reason to expect that the unchecked exercise of negative liberty rights by some will steadily undermine the possibilities for others to avail themselves of them. Far from stabilising at an equilibrium point of perfect competition, as anarcho-capitalist champions of the market claim, a free market consisting solely of individuals exercising negative-liberty rights would soon give rise to monopolistic and corporate practices that would destroy the value of the market itself.

Once rival claims to human rights become pressed outside a shared form of life, they assume the character of opposed ontologies between which no compromise is acceptable. Take the Salman Rushdie affair, for example. Although a liberal or a Muslim fundamentalist may be capable of balancing the right to free speech against the right not to be offended within their respective traditions of thought, there is no sensible way in which a liberal view of the right to freedom of speech can be reconciled with a Muslim fundamentalist's notion of a right not to be offended. Both operate with incommensurable interpretations of the purposes these different rights serve. Appeals to human rights in such circumstances has only resulted in a hardening of their respective positions.

The argument of this section has been that modern societies fail to provide a secular communitarian substitute for the natural societies of classical natural rights theorists. Rather than converging on the sort of common moral framework needed for either an extended or minimal conception of human rights, modern societies appear increasingly differentiated and pluralistic. The contention that human rights can offer a framework for the pluralism of modern societies is confuted by the fact that theories of rights presuppose a high degree of social and ethical homogeneity for their coherence. Within a pluralistic society, particular assertions of rights can only be successful at the cost of squashing or driving out all rival assertions by others. If this dilemma is to be avoided, then we need an account of the political mechanisms whereby the struggle for rights may be institutionalised without degenerating into a raging war between polarised camps. In the next section I shall argue that such an enterprise rests on a very different conception of citizenship to those examined so far, one which places duties before rights.

Republican citizenship: From duties to rights

Rights-based theories of citizenship see human rights as defining and delimiting the sphere of the political. The existence of certain basic rights, such as freedom of speech and the right to vote in regularly held elections, not only ensures equal access by all citizens to the political process. These fundamental rights are also said to prevent governments from illegitimately interfering with or failing to promote certain vital liberties of individual citizens. Such thinking lies behind schemes for a written constitution and a Bill of Rights (see Chapter 6 by MacCormick in this volume, and Held, 1987, Ch. 9). From the perspective of a republican view of citizenship, however, this approach inverts the true relationship between politics and rights. Republicans regard rights as the products of the political process, rather than its presuppositions. They believe the moral framework of politics to be defined by a duty to participate in collective decision-making and to take the views of one's fellow citizens seriously, rather than a right to participation that one may or may not exercise. I shall argue that this offers the most plausible conception of rights and citizenship within modern pluralist societies.

Two important clarifications need to be made about the republican conceptions of rights and citizenship respectively. First, the rights that emerge from political deliberations are institutional rather than human rights. In other words, they are rights that derive from the particular laws and accords arrived at between citizens participating within the political process, rather than supposedly transcendent normative verities. Institutional rights of this kind have a number of advantages over doctrines of human rights. Unlike the latter, they do not invoke an idealised form of human agency and community of a putatively universal kind. Instead of representing inherent ontological attributes, they reflect socially determined purposes which are capable of reformulation to meet changing circumstances and attitudes. Legislation can be used to mediate between competing claims, granting rights which reflect the divergent requirements of different areas of social life, as in the case of reproductive rights for women, rather than conforming to a uniform standard. Furthermore, when rights are institutionalised then the counterpart duties can be allocated with precision so as to settle conflicts. These characteristics of institutional rights make them far more suited to the heterogeneity of modern societies than human rights.

Second, the term republican is used advisedly and in contrast to the civic humanist conception of citizenship, with which it is often confused. As Quentin Skinner has pointed out (Skinner, 1986), classical republicanism differs from civic humanism in seeing politics as a means rather than an end in itself. A form of Aristotelianism, the civic humanist tradition regards human beings as essentially political animals for whom political participation forms a necessary aspect of the good life. Civic humanism is a variety of communitarianism, therefore, which sees citizenship in terms of involvement in a common enterprise orientated towards a shared conception of the good. This view has been rightly ridiculed by rights theorists as advocating an unrealistic return to the solidary communities of the past. Moreover, it trades on a similar sort of ethical naturalist thesis to that employed by those who seek to derive a doctrine of natural rights from a view of human nature, a position we have already criticised for its circularity. Neither the ethics nor the practices of ancient Greece can be plausibily revived in the modern world.

Classical republicanism, in contrast, originates with Machiavelli and treats civic involvement as merely the condition for retaining our personal liberty. According to this line of reasoning, since the rights and liberties available to us depend upon the priorities, norms and laws of the society in which we live, we shall only be free to the extent that we share in determining the character of that society. In addition, if these arrangements are to respect fairly the values and demands of all members of society, rather than just those of particularly well-placed and powerful persons and groups, then we have an obligation not only to participate personally in collective decision-making but to ensure others do so too.

At the heart of the republican conception of citizenship lies a set of prudentially motivated political duties. These duties provide the preconditions for political discussion and decision-making between a plurality of roughly equal agents and agencies. They reflect a situation in which no agreed transcendent principles of reason and truth exist, so that the only ground for a claim that a particular policy or decision is just or the object of a right is that it has been consented to by a public that allows the free expression of all relevant points of view.[10] The sorts of duties to emerge from this kind of reasoning would be those that entail only adopting those forms of conduct that are compatible with free communication between all members of the polity. Thus, deceit would be ruled out since it undermines the basis of discussion and could not be adopted as a universal obligation without self-contradiction: there is no point in lying when everyone else is. Similarly, to be systematically indifferent to human vulnerability is to ignore the degree to which our acts affect others and our independence is mutually dependent and socially engendered. Such considerations operate in most welfare legislation which aims to secure the conditions of agency for all, for example.

It has been objected that the notion of free consent which lies at the heart of this argument inevitably involves making the very sorts of idealisation about human agency I criticise in theories of rights.[11] The universal duties which I claim define citizenship are said to be too abstract to enable one to know whether particular agents are coerced or not. Since the actual consent of agents may be the product of coercion or indoctrination, the deliberative process itself cannot provide a foundation for the specification of our rights. This thesis must inevitably fall back on some notion of hypothetical consent between ideal rational agents, therefore, if it is to provide a legitimate foundation for principles of justice. This approach gives rise in turn to a theory of those rights necessary to take part in the process of

moral and political deliberation (see Gewirth, 1982 for an example
of this sort of argument).

Against these critics, I believe that it is not only possible but
necessary to steer a path between the idealised citizens of rights-
based theories and the relativist view of the communitarians. If the
problem with relativised accounts of citizenship is that they risk
legitimising the forces constraining individuals' choices within particular circumstances, the difficulty with idealised accounts is that
they often completely ignore such issues altogether. As feminists
have observed of liberal social contract theories, for example, such
approaches all too frequently assume that agents enter the world
white, middle class, adult and male (Pateman, 1980a, 1980b). To
avoid the Scylla of idealisation and the Charybdis of relativism, we
must rely neither on the hypothetical consent of idealised agents
nor the actual consent of possibly oppressed agents to ground moral
principles. Rather, to quote Onora O'Neill, whose thesis I am here
developing, the appeal should be to the *'possible consent* of *actual
agents'* (O'Neill, 1989). In other words, the specific interpretations
of these duties must reflect the view of those actually involved.
However, to avoid the problems of false consciousness or coercion
inherent to this thesis, consent must be capable of refusal or re-
negotiation. This emphasis on the opportunity for refusal follows
from the general approach of defining duties through the rejection
of those principles that could not be coherently universalised amongst
a plurality of potentially interacting agents and agencies. On this
view, it is the possibility of dissent rather than actual or hypothetical
consent that guarantees the legitimacy of policies and that should
guide the framing of those democratic institutions that, in a pluralistic
world, provide the only adequate basis for constructing the norms
regulating social life.

O'Neill has shown how making duties fundamental in this way
avoids many of the difficulties we encountered with rights-based
arguments (O'Neill, 1986, 1989). First, whereas the coherence of
constructions of basic human rights requires that we identify the
whole set of consistent, compossible rights, duties can be identified
successively via the rejection of those principles of action that are
incompatible with a heterogenous public sphere within which all
participate on roughly equal terms. Second, universal duties can
be formulated in ways that are both general and abstract without
entailing the idealisation of a particular form of human agency, a

requirement that mars the aspiration to universality of any conception of human rights. This non-idealising feature of duties makes them far better candidates for the fundamental principles of a pluralistic society than rights. Third, a moral theory consisting exclusively of rights is immensely impoverished. For it allows only for the perfect duties entailed by respecting the reciprocal rights of others. Acts of supererogation, virtue and the disinterested pursuit of excellence often provide far weightier reasons for action than those generated by a respect for rights alone, but tend to become debased within rights-based discourse. Note the way the demands of rights-based justice have relegated charity to the level of an optional extra, for instance. Fourth, rights by themselves give no indication as to how they might be exercised. Far from always requiring decent behaviour, within their sphere they give a title to do wrong if the right-holder so wishes (Waldron, 1981). Indeed, the logic of rights can lead us to ignore the social environment that makes their exercise possible and valuable. Making duties primary, in contrast, forces us to consider the collective arrangements entailed by a system of rights and their effects on the lives of others. Finally, the emphasis on duties provides a far more effective framework for action than rights because they speak directly to what ought to be done. There is a tendency for rights to be put into effect or asserted with little regard for what might be entailed for other people to meet them. This rhetoric speaks more to the powerless seeking a slogan around which to organise, than to those who are being called upon to act, for whom the assertion of a right is liable to appear too indeterminate. What really defines a right is the complex of obligations within which it is situated. When we seek to work out what is involved in a right to life, for example, we are asking essentially what kinds of things we ought or ought not to be doing if certain risks are to be avoided and needs met. To make a discussion of rights primary, therefore, is to approach such problems of applied ethics from the wrong end.

These advantages of making duties rather than rights fundamental are well illustrated by the issue of welfare (O'Neill, 1989, Ch. 12). As we noted in section one, libertarians are able to object to the idea of a human right to welfare on the grounds that there can be no universal correlative obligations on the part of an individual to help all those in need. The most any single person can offer is selective help. This argument reflects many of the distortions of the rights-based view. A universal refusal to give aid draws its plausibility from an implicit appeal to a model of idealised independent agents. These paragons of self-sufficiency apparently suffer none of the usual human frailties and requirements, such as the propensity to fall sick and the need for food, that lead ordinary men and women to call on the help and support of others at various times in their lives – particularly in childhood and old age. According to the duty-based view, in contrast, amongst ordinarily needy and vulnerable human beings a principle of universal indifference could never be adopted. If we are only to adopt principles all can act upon, then we must necessarily reject principles that undermine or threaten the capacity for agency of others. True, the duty so established remains an imperfect obligation, but it does not follow that we have no duty to do anything. Rather, the argument creates a requirement to institutionalise and allocate recipients of welfare to agents and agencies capable of supplying these needs. Institutional rights to welfare will thereby be created which can be tailored to the character and conditions of particular societies. These rights, however, clearly depend on the prior establishment of both a fundamental general duty and more special obligations to help others.

Duty-based thinking gives greater rather than less consideration to the preconditions for action than rights, since it emphasises the need to pay attention to those real circumstances of actual persons that may inhibit their option of refusal. This approach also has profound consequences for how we think about politics. A duty-based politics yields a very different style of citizenship to a politics derived from rights. Rights-based forms of citizenship are ultimately passive and anti-political. The universalising and homogenising character of rights displaces politics from smaller forms of association and relocates it at a more comprehensive level – in the past the nation-state, in more recent formulations some kind of global organisation (e.g. Held, 1992). At the same time, however, power gets shifted from democratic institutions, such as the legislature, to bodies, such as the judiciary and bureaucracy, that claim to be untainted by popular pressures, and hence better able to decide issues of principle in an objective manner and uphold the individual's basic rights against the tyranny of the majority. Although rights are often presented as protecting the individual against the state, in reality they strengthen it and reinforce the concentration and centralisation of power. For every demand for rights necessarily entails a greater regulation and institutionalisation of social life so as to conform to a uniform pattern, and a concomitant withdrawal of more and more issues from the realm of democratic decision-making. As a result, individuals find themselves enmeshed in a growing array of obligations not of their own making. However, their self-image as free choosing rights-bearers cannot sustain this degree of engagement in the affairs of others. Using a process of logical argument, continual insistence on the priority of right ultimately alienates individuals from public responsibility. Political discussion gives way to irreconcilable conflicts between rival rights claims. A framework of duties, in contrast, provides the basis for a participatory form of citizenship in which we collectively decide on our legal rights through the exercise of our civic obligations.

This republican conception of citizenship may seem as elegiac as the civic humanist's. Within complex and large-scale social systems, individuals simply lack the time, knowledge or ability to participate directly in the political process. Even if new technology could help them to do so, decision-making with the consent of everyone seems hardly plausible amongst such a massive number of people, and involving such a wide range of opinions and interests. The advantage of a rights-based political system, its proponents claim, is that the entrenchment of rights within a constitution frees individuals from politics and enables them to get on with their lives in peace and security. Similarly, international conventions of rights can regularise the relations between states and introduce a measure of justice and order into an otherwise anarchic world (Cassese, 1990; Vincent, 1986). However, as we have seen, such stability can be acquired only at the price of a high degree of imposed conformity. Since moves in this direction go against the trend towards greater plurality and differentiation within modern societies, appeals to rights are far more likely to prove as destabilising as they are ineffectual (Bull, 1977, Ch. 4).

To meet the challenge of the complexity and pluralism of modern societies, we need to move away from the model of the sovereign, centralised state and conceive of politics as operating within a complex plurality of interrelated political units. This objective fits with the duty-based, participatory model of citizenship far better than it does with the rights-based view. It requires the distribution of decision-making power throughout society and the designation of distinct areas of competence so as to limit the scope of central authority. Such a system increases the areas of public life where a more active participation by citizens is possible. Putting pressure at the lower levels of the political system also serves to improve the accountability and responsiveness of our representatives to the views and aspirations of people at large.

Rights theorists frequently voice the fear that increasing democracy in this way raises the spectre of a tyrannical majority squashing the views of non-conforming individuals or minority groups. This objection is misplaced. In practice, formal statements of rights establish very little. After all, even under Stalin the USSR boasted a written constitution guaranteeing the rights of its citizens. Individual freedom is not protected by written statements, however worthy, but by the existence of agencies which enable persons to act in certain ways and offer them a means of defence against being hindered by others. This protection is best provided by having a variety of different areas of power, that respects the autonomy of different spheres and levels of social life, and restricts the possibilities for any one group or agency to dominate all others. Such a system replaces the substantive, 'moralistic', constitutional constraints on majority rule and government action of rights, with 'realistic', procedural, democratic checks and controls.

The republican form of citizenship also helps overcome the alienation we associated with rights-based politics. Participation not only promotes the instrumental exercise of freedom by citizens, but also educates them into a perception of the dependence of their social relations and individual autonomy upon collective rules and arrangements. Thus free riding and other self-defeating forms of self-interest are discouraged. Moreover, by providing a forum for public discussion, it enables preferences to be transformed and not just aggregated, allowing opposed interests to find agreement on common values which can offer new forms of individual expression for all.

Finally, a framework of duties offers a better starting point for international co-operation and the mediation between the different spheres of our lives than rights. As we noted above, duties provide more effective action-guiding principles than rights. Above all, they encourage the creation of the political mechanisms through which it is possible to establish the policies and priorities which institutionalise rights and so give them a meaningful existence. The various charters of rights have only had an impact on international politics to the extent that they have been authenticated by a political process capable of mobilising the interests of a significant number of states behind them. As a result, human rights have been appealed to in a highly selective and frequently hypocritical manner. However, this situation will not be made better by putting into effect ever more sophisticated and detailed conventions of human rights. Because of the unstable foundations of rights, discussed in section one, such proclamations will only increase the number and contestability of rights claims, increasing in the process the ability of states to recognise only those rights, and only in those circumstances, that suit them. As in the domestic arena, rights-based theories approach the problem of justice in international relations from the wrong end. Here too, the legitimation of value cannot be distinguished from the distribution of power. The rethinking of the international political system in ways that foster co-operative decision-making and supply the means for interest aggregation between states is a precondition for, rather than a product of, a coherent policy of world rights.

Conclusion

This chapter has made the following three points. First, I showed that a coherent theory of fundamental human rights assumes a fairly homogenous human community oriented around a common human good, a thesis traditionally provided by a doctrine of natural law. Second, I contended that modern societies are too fragmented to provide a secular communitarian foundation for a doctrine of human rights. Indeed, the complexity and pluralism of modern societies leads to unresolvable and infinitely expanding claims of rights. Third, I argued that resolving these disputes between contesting rights claims is a distinctively political matter, calling for a duty-based conception of participatory citizenship. This approach involves a shift from assertions of human rights to the formulation of institutional rights built around particular policy initiatives.

Notes

1   In this respect they adopt a line of argument originating with Immanuel Kant.

2   The notion of compossibility derives from the metaphysics of Leibniz and was introduced into moral and political philosophy by Bertrand Russell, a distinguished Leibniz scholar. Here the term denotes non-conflictability

and harmony. With regard to theories of rights, the idea is that rights should dovetail in such a way that the upholding of one right need not involve contravening another (Gray, 1989, p. 147).

3   Held offers a similar view, whereby:

persons should enjoy equal rights (and, accordingly, equal obligations) in the framework which limits the opportunities available to them; that is, they should be free and equal in the determination of the conditions of their own lives, so long as they do not deploy this framework to negate the rights of others. (Held, 1991, p. 228)

4   Lack of space dictates that my treatment of this issue can only be very brief. My account draws on the following, who provide the detailed arguments I can only hint at: O'Neill, 1979; Miller, 1984; Plant, 1991, Ch. 6; and, for a libertarian's acknowledgement of the same difficulties, Gray, 1989, Ch. 9.

5   I have developed this argument in more detail in Bellamy, 1992a, pp. 89–98.

6   The communitarian nature of Locke's account of rights is one of the implications of the analysis of Tully, 1980. For an important study of the links between classical rights doctrines and their modern counterparts, see Shapiro, 1986. Shapiro's realist account of liberal theories of rights inspired much of the following argument of this and the next section.

7   Communitarian arguments are as ideologically and epistemologically diverse as foundationalist views of rights. There are conservative (Burke, 1969; Oakeshott, 1975), socialist (Marx, 1844; Miller, 1989), rationalist (Finnis, 1980) and relativist (Walzer, 1983) versions of communitarianism. Since the rationalist versions tend to rely on the sort of controversial view of human nature that I have already criticised as a basis of rights, I shall not consider them here. My concern will be with the widely held tacit communitarian assumptions about modern societies that I believe ground most contemporary rights-based theories of citizenship.

8   See too Bellamy, 1992b, Ch. 1 for a much more critical examination of this movement, that places it in a comparative perspective with similar changes in other European countries. The parallel with Durkheim, 1894, examined in Ch. 3, is particularly strong.

9   The view that the contrast between communitarian and rights-based theories has been over-stated has become increasingly common. See Bellamy, 1989; Kymlicka, 1988 and Taylor, 1989 for details. Gray, 1989, Ch. 11 and Parry, 1992, pp. 168–73 offer an interesting portrayal of Michael Oakeshott's conception of a 'civil association' as offering a communitarian account of the liberal theory of basic human rights.

10   The inspiration for this argument is Habermas's 'communicative ethics' and shares his theory's Kantian ancestry (e.g. Habermas, 1983). However, whereas Habermas develops a theory based on a public composed of hypothetical agents, my thesis requires that discussion take place between actual agents.

11   By David Held and Leo MacCarthy in their helpful and detailed
comments on an earlier version of this chapter.

Bibliography

Barry, N. (1990), 'Markets, Citizenship and the Welfare State: Some Critical Reflections', in Plant and Barry (1990), pp. 34–77.

Bell, D. (1987), 'The World and the United States in 2013', *Daedalus*, 116: 1–32.

Bellamy, R. (1989), 'Defining Liberalism: Neutralist, Ethical or Political', in R. Bellamy (Ed.), *Liberalism and Recent Legal and Social Philosophy*, Stuttgart: Steiner, pp. 23–43.

Bellamy, R. (1992a), 'Liberal Rights, Socialist Goals and the Duties of Citizenship', in Milligan and Miller (1992), pp. 88–107.

Bellamy, R. (1992b), *Liberalism and Modern Society: An Historical Argument*, Cambridge: Polity.

Bull, H. (1977), *The Anarchical Society: A Study of Order in World Politics*, London: Macmillan.

Burke, E. (1969), *Reflections on the Revolution in France*, Harmondsworth: Penguin.

Cassese, A. (1990), *Human Rights in a Changing World*, Cambridge: Polity.

Cranston, M. (1973), *What Are Human Rights?*, London: Bodley Head.

Durkheim, E. (1953), *Sociology and Philosophy*, tr. D. F. Pocock, London: Routledge & Kegan Paul.

Durkheim, E. (1984), *Division of Labour in Society*, tr. W. D. Halls, London: Macmillan.

Dworkin, R. (1977), *Taking Rights Seriously*, London: Duckworth.

Esping-Anderson, G. (1990), *The Three Worlds of Welfare Capitalism*, Cambridge: Polity.

Finnis, J. (1980), *Natural Law and Natural Rights*, Oxford: Oxford University Press.

Freeden, M. (1978), *The New Liberalism: An Ideology of Social Reform*, Oxford: Oxford University Press.

Freeden, M. (1990), 'Human Rights and Welfare: A Communitarian View', *Ethics*, 100: 489–502.

Freeden, M. (1991), *Rights*, Milton Keynes: Open University Press.

Gewirth, A. (1982), *Human Rights: Essays in Justification and Applications*, Chicago: University of Chicago Press.

Giddens, A. (1981), *A Contemporary Critique of Historical Materialism, Vol. I, Power, Property and the State*, London: Macmillan, pp. 226–9.

Giddens, A. (1985), *The Nation State and Violence: A Contemporary Critique of Historical Materialism, Vol. II*, Cambridge: Polity.

Gray, J. (1989), *Liberalisms: Essays in Political Philosophy*, London: Routledge.

Green, T. H. (1986), *Lectures on the Principles of Political Obligation and Other Writings*, P. Harris and J. Morrow (Eds.), Cambridge: Cambridge University Press.

Habermas, J. (1983), *Reason and the Rationalisation of Society*, Boston: Beacon.

Hart, H. L. A. (1950), 'Are There Any Natural Rights?', *The Philosophical Review*, LXIV: 175–91.

Hayek, F. A. (1960), *The Constitution of Liberty*, London: Routledge.

Held, D. (1987), *Models of Democracy*, Cambridge: Polity.

Held, D. (1989), *Political Theory and the Modern State*, Cambridge: Polity, Ch. 7.

Held, D. (1991), 'Democracy, the Nation-State and the Global System', in D. Held (Ed.), *Political Theory Today*, Cambridge: Polity.

Held, D. (1992), 'Democracy: From City-states to a Cosmopolitan Order?', in D. Held (Ed.), *Prospects for Democracy, Political Studies*, Special Issue, XL: 10–39.

King, D. S. and Waldron, J. (1988), 'Citizenship, Social Citizenship and the Defence of Welfare Provision', *British Journal of Political Science*, 18: 415–43.

Kymlicka, W. (1988), 'Liberalism and Communitarianism', *Canadian Journal of Philosophy*, 18: 181–203.

Locke, J. (1960), *Two Treatises of Government*, P. Laslett (Ed.), Cambridge: Cambridge University Press.

Mann, M. (1987), 'Ruling Strategies and Citizenship', *Sociology*, 21: 339–54.

Marshall, T. H. (1950), *Citizenship and Social Class and Other Essays*, Cambridge: Cambridge University Press.

Marx, K. (1844), 'On the Jewish Question', in D. McLellan (Ed.), *Karl Marx: Early Texts*, Oxford: Blackwell, 1972.

Miller, D. (1984), 'Constraints on Freedom', *Ethics*, 92: 66–86.

Miller, D. (1989), *Market, State and Community: Theoretical Foundations of Market Socialism*, Oxford: Oxford University Press.

Milligan, D. and Watts Miller, W. (Eds.) (1992), *Liberalism, Citizenship and Autonomy*, Aldershot: Avebury.

Nozick, R. (1974), *Anarchy, State and Utopia*, Oxford: Blackwell.

Oakeshott, M. (1975), *On Human Conduct*, Oxford: Oxford University Press.

O'Neill, O. (1979), 'The Most Extensive Liberty', *Proceedings of the Aristotelian Society*, 80: 45–59.

O'Neill, O. (1986), *Faces of Hunger: An Essay on Poverty, Justice and Development*, London: Allen & Unwin.

O'Neill, O. (1989), *Constructions of Reason: Explorations of Kant's Practical Philosophy*, Cambridge: Cambridge University Press.

Parry, G. (1992), 'Conclusion: Paths to Citizenship', in U. Vogel and M. Moran (Eds.), *The Frontiers of Citizenship*, Basingstoke: Macmillan, pp. 166–201.

Pateman, C. (1980a), ' "The Disorder of Women": Women, Love and the Sense of Justice', *Ethics*, 91: 20–34.

Pateman, C. (1980b), 'Women and Consent', *Political Theory*, 8: 149–68.

Plant, R. (1988), *Citizenship, Rights and Socialism*, London: Fabian Society, Tract 531.

Plant, R. (1990), 'Citizenship and Rights', in Plant and Barry (1990), pp. 1–32.

Plant, R. (1991), *Modern Political Thought*, Oxford: Blackwell, Chs. 6, 7.

Plant, R. (1992), 'Citizenship and Rights', in Milligan and Miller (1992), pp. 108–33.

Plant, R. and Barry, N. (1990), *Citizenship and Rights in Thatcher's Britain: Two Views*, London: Institute of Economic Affairs.

Rawls, J. (1971), *A Theory of Justice*, Oxford: Clarendon Press.

Sandel, M. (Ed.) (1984), *Liberalism and its Critics*, Oxford: Blackwell, 'Introduction'.

Shapiro, I. (1986), *The Evolution of Rights in Liberal Theory*, Cambridge: Cambridge University Press.

Skinner, Q. (1986), 'The Paradoxes of Political Liberty', in S. McMurrin (Ed.), *The Tanner Lectures on Human Values*, VII, Cambridge: Cambridge University Press.

Taylor, C. (1989), 'Cross Purposes: The Liberal-Communitarian Debate', in N. Rosenblum (Ed.), *Liberalism and the Moral Life*, Cambridge, Mass.: Harvard University Press, 159–82.

Tully, J. (1980), *A Discourse on Property: John Locke and his Adversaries*, Cambridge: Cambridge University Press.

Turner, B.S. (1986), *Citizenship and Capitalism: The Debate over Reformism*, London: Allen & Unwin.

Turner, B.S. (1990), 'Outline of a Theory of Citizenship', *Sociology*, 24: 189–217.

Vincent, A. and Plant, R. (1984), *Philosophy, Politics and Citizenship: The Life and Thought of the British Idealists*, Oxford: Blackwell.

Vincent, R.J. (1986), *Human Rights and International Relations*, Cambridge: Cambridge University Press.

Waldron, J. (1981), 'A Right to do Wrong', *Ethics*, 92: 21–39.

Waldron, J. (1989), 'Rights in Conflict', *Ethics*, 99: 503–19.

Walzer, M. (1983), *Spheres of Justice: A Defence of Equality and Pluralism*, Oxford: Martin Robertson.

Williams, B. (1972), *Morality: An Introduction to Ethics*, Cambridge: Cambridge University Press.

Young, I. M. (1989), 'Polity and Group Difference: A Critique of the Ideal of Universal Citizenship', *Ethics*, 99: 250–74.

Social justice and equality

Introduction: Love is all you need?

The questions to be asked in this chapter concern, very broadly, social justice and equality. Should the state distribute welfare and resources to achieve some notion of social justice? Is the implication of this distribution some form of welfare state? What are the political consequences of that? Or, is the market the most efficient way of achieving fair distribution? Is the implication of that an uncaring, unloving society? Are market and welfare two hostile principles which will always be in opposition to each other? What sort of ethic do the notions of welfare and market imply? How can we evaluate these rival ethics?

We have heard a lot about the 'crisis of the welfare state' and I do not intend to discuss this in detail here (see Chapter 5 for a discussion of this point). Rather, I will note that the crisis did bring about the collapse of an old ideological consensus between the Labour Party and 'One Nation' Conservatives which broadly accepted a degree of state intervention in the economy. This intervention was not only for reasons of economic efficiency but also for redistribution so as to achieve some sort of equality or social justice. Neither form of intervention was felt to affect property rights too much. The collapse of this consensus has brought arguments for and against the market to the fore again. On the one hand, the market is presented as the saviour of society. The re-marketisation of society is supposed to bring both efficiency and morality back to peoples' lives. It gives them freedom. On the other hand, the market is represented as destroying any sense of social solidarity. The market's opponents claim that its concentration on the individual and his/her desires gets rid of any possible caring society. Crudely, the anti-market side can contrast a selfish market society with a caring non-market one. The pro-market side replies in the same vein by saying that 'the road to hell is paved with good intentions'; that all the talk about caring masks a massive and usually progressive disregard of individual rights, coupled with a progressive diminution of economic efficiency.

The parable of the labourers in the vineyard is a classic examination of some of these themes. Here, God's love comes up against the labourers' demands to be treated justly. The themes of welfare, deserts, equality, justice, contractual rights all come up in varying mixes. However, this should be understood in its biblical setting. We can use it here to explain different visions of society and different moral principles of social organisation. This is the relevant text from 'The Gospel according to St Matthew':

For the kingdom of heaven is like unto a man *that is* an householder, which went out early in the morning to hire labourers into his vineyard. And when he had agreed with the labourers for a penny a day, he sent them into his vineyard. And he went out about the third hour, and saw others standing idle in the market place. And said unto them, 'Go ye also into the vineyard, and whatsoever is right I will give you.' And they went their way. Again he went out about the sixth and ninth hour and did likewise. And about the eleventh hour he went out, and found others standing idle, and sayeth unto them, 'Why stand ye here all day idle?' They say unto him, 'Because no man hath hired us.' He sayeth unto them, 'Go ye also into the vineyard; and whatsoever is right, *that* shall ye receive.' So when even was come, the lord of the vineyard sayeth unto his steward, 'Call the labourers, and give them *their* hire, beginning from the last unto the first.' And when they came that *were hired* about the eleventh hour, they received every man a penny. And when they had received *it*, they murmured against the goodman of the house, saying, 'These last have wrought *but* one hour, and thou hast made them equal unto us, which have borne the burden and heat of the day.' But he answered one of them, and said, 'Friend, I do thee no wrong: didst not thou agree with me for a penny?' Take *that* thine *is*, and go thy way: I will give unto this last, even as unto thee. Is it not lawful for me to do what I will with mine own? Is thine eye evil, because I am good?' ('The Gospel according to St Matthew', Ch. 20, vv. 1–15)

The case for markets: Hayek and the 'Great Society'

One way of looking at the parable is to say that love is its own reason; that the love of God knows no bounds and He gives to all what they need. We can, however, turn this into a contractarian argument against the more 'caring society', by pointing out that God is a special case, being all-knowing as well as all-good. Since God knows all, he knows what is best for everyone; being all-good, he can be trusted to will it for everyone being all-powerful, he can achieve it for everyone. However, we cannot be God and so cannot know the best thing to do. F. A. Hayek has taken this as the nub of an argument for the market and against welfare and state intervention. God might know what every individual human being is doing and what is best for him or her in the context of what everyone else is doing, but this is beyond the capacity of human beings. Caring only works if you know what you are doing. From the point of view of society as a whole, humans cannot know what everyone wants. They can only know what they want and what they need to do.

How does Hayek argue for this thesis? We start off with the idea of order. For Hayek there are two models of social organisation. First, there is the 'spontaneous order'. We can never know everything about social life. In non-command societies, order grows up spontaneously and is self-generating. It requires general rules that have to be obeyed, which can emerge through, and are best left to, natural selection. Secondly, there is a 'constructed order'. This kind of order assumes that there must be some purpose and end to the order as a whole and that intervention can help it better to achieve its function.

For Hayek, societies and social institutions arise by evolution. The criteria of success is the survival of one social form in competition with another. Societies are the product of unwitting actions on the part of countless individuals. No one intends to produce any specific distribution of goods or services; it is merely the product of their countless actions. Hayek calls this spontaneous order a *cosmos*. Human society as *cosmos* is the product of human action, but not of human design. This sort of order functions through abstract rules.

In a social order the particular circumstances to which each individual will react will be those known to him. But the individual response to particular circumstances will result in an overall order only if the individuals obey such rules as will produce an order. Even a very limited similarity in their behaviour may be sufficient if the rules which they obey are such as to produce an order. Such an order will always be considered an adaptation to the multitude of circumstances which are known to all members of that society together but which are not known as a whole to any one person. (Hayek, 1973, p. 45)

We have to distinguish this spontaneous order from a deliberately constructed order or *taxis*. A *taxis* functions through rules which are specific for the particular function or effect that they want to achieve. They are regulations that are not general in the way that the rules of the *cosmos* are. Rather they are instrumental devices for gaining particular ends. They have a specific purpose in mind and, indeed, they have been made with that purpose in view. The *cosmos*, in contrast, cannot be said to have a particular purpose since it has not been constructed deliberately. It is the outcome of countless intentional actings but not of an overall plan. A *cosmos* merely enables people to harmonise their various competing desires and to pursue them in some sort of co-ordinated and orderly way. It does not pursue any particular goal. Therefore, the *cosmos* is far more hospitable to complexity than a *taxis*. It does not have to deal directly with each individual and his or her particular needs and desires and try and match them with the needs and desires of everyone else. Instead, it is concerned with the procedure of just co-ordination. It deals with the general and abstract and thus ignores, to an extent, the particular.

Liberal legal order and the market economy can be seen as examples of a *cosmos*, and here also Hayek's notion of the 'Great Society' makes its appearance. One of the defining characteristics of such a society is the equal respect and treatment of all human beings under the liberal form of law; this to consist of general and abstract rules. This overarching system of universal rules, implying a philosophy of right and duty and equal treatment, is the only rational way that people can live in a community. It is a move from the morality of the tribe and the solidarity of the small group to the great society of equals before the law. We do not have the same depth of feeling in such a society that one finds in traditional communities but that is the price one has to pay for civilisation. It is no wonder that such a society is very fragile. For Hayek, this is the essential characteristic of Western civilisation, and it is this which makes that fragile entity, the 'Great Society', superior to all others.

This conflict between what men still feel to be natural emotions and the discipline of rules required for the preservation of the open society is indeed one of the chief causes of what has been called 'the fragility of liberty': all attempts to model the Great Society on the image of the familiar small group, or to turn it into a community by directing the individuals towards common visible purposes, must produce a totalitarian society. (Hayek, 1976, p. 147)

This 'Great Society' of Hayek can be seen as the *Gesellschaft* type society that I discuss later on in the paper (see p. 90). One can say that it has strong connections to notions of legality. Legality here can be described as a view:

according to which matters of legal regulation or controversy ought to, so far as possible, be conducted in accordance with predetermined rules of considerable generality and clarity in which legal relations comprise rights duties powers and immunities reasonably clearly defined by reference to such rules and in which acts of government however desirable teleologically must be subordinated to respect for such rules and rights. (MacCormick, 1989, pp. 1–2)

Fuller (1969) can be seen as giving a more concrete version of this liberal conception of the rule of law. He sets out eight necessary features of 'the discipline of rules' and thus what a system of abstract, universal and formal rules might mean. These eight features are not to be applied mechanically – legality is an art and we must balance them against each other so that we achieve the best mix. They must, however, all be present in some degree. Legality implies:

1) Rules which are universal in scope. Though they might apply to a single person, they will be applied each time the conditions for their application arise.
2) They must be widely available in the sense that people must have access to the laws. This implies that they be intelligible *per se* or that lawyers (through legal aid if necessary) help people understand and use them.
3) Laws should not in general be retroactive; though in the context of prospective rules it might sometimes be necessary to have retroactivity as a curative measure.
4) They must be clear and the too frequent use of vague concepts like 'reasonable' and 'fair' be avoided. Otherwise the law is vague, unpredictable and susceptible to great discretionary power.
5) Laws should not be contradictory.
6) Laws must not demand the impossible.
7) Laws should have some constancy over time but should not stay so static as to ossify.

8) There must be some congruence between official action and
   declared rules.

A market economy is another component of the Great Society.
Here again we see the opposition between *cosmos* and *taxis*:

Much of the opposition to a system of freedom under general laws arises
from their inability to conceive of an effective co-ordination of human
activities without deliberate organization by a commanding intelligence.
One of the achievements of economic theory has been to explain how such
a mutual adjustment of the spontaneous activity of individuals is brought
about by the market, provided that there is a known delimitation of the
sphere of control of each individual. (Hayek, 1960, p.159)

How does that happen? Adam Smith was one of the first to provide
an explanation. He showed how individual actions are co-ordinated
through markets not because this is what markets were designed for
but because markets happen to have this property. They do so
because in an open market there is a tendency for activities to be
co-ordinated. Those who produce a commodity that is desired at the
lowest price are rewarded. The market is the most efficient system
of communicating the information, in the form of prices etc., that
people need to achieve that goal. In the pursuit of their own interest,
they are led to favour the general interest. Hayek called this system
a *catallaxy*. This is a system which has no particular end but can be
said to have as many ends as there are people involved, 'serving the
multiplicity of separate and incommensurable aims of its members'
(Hayek, 1976, p.159). Hayek asks us to think of it as a wealth-
producing game which depends upon both skill and luck. This game
allows different ends to become compatible with each other. What
is important to note here is that prices are the means of giving
information: they show what ought to be bought, made or sold.
They are not a reward or punishment for good or poor judgement.
They give the information that is necessary for the system to work
and resources to be distributed. The chances that everyone can have
their expectations fulfilled are thus maximised. It is also important
to note that there is no deliberate distribution; momentary outcomes
are the result of all the individual transactions made under the rules.
If this is the case, then no one momentary holding can be said to
be just or unjust since no one chooses that any given individual
should have any particular holding.

The metaphor that best describes this process of distributing resources is that of the 'invisible hand'. 'Invisible' should be read here as 'not existing' rather than some superhuman hidden force. There is no God behind the system co-ordinating everything with some pre-ordained plan of which He alone has the knowledge. Rather, what we have is a system where the intentional actions of many particular people can be co-ordinated and made coherent. This can be effected without these people having to desire the particular outcomes that the system as a whole brings about.

There is both an epistemological point and a moral point involved here. Epistemologically, the point is that we cannot know everything. We cannot know all the facts and particulars that exist in the world. We would need to know all these in order to make an absolutely correct decision in the context of the society as a whole and our particular plan for it. Science will not advance in such a way that it will become the equivalent of God. It will be unable to become as God because it has to deal with the world at a general level. This will not lessen the multiplicity of particular facts in the world and will not help us to know them. For Hayek, it will always be the case that a single human will not be able to know all the 'particular facts which are known to some men but not as a whole to any particular person' (1973, p. 16). This makes Hayek attack what he calls constructivist rationalism; that is, the idea, stemming from the Enlightenment, that one can design social orders from scratch. Order for Hayek is not like this. Social orders do not have designers in the sense of being the product of deliberate human design. Any attempt to design order would anyway end in failure since we cannot know everything and it is arrogance that makes us think we can do so. We can make grand designs which aim at a particular end but what actually transpires will never correspond to the designed aims. We cannot design societies from scratch; we can only go along with the flow of a spontaneous order. This is not, however, to say that reason has no part to play. We can, first of all, learn to interact with the institutions in which we find ourselves and not stand against them, seeking to construct them anew. Secondly, we can get round our ignorance of the particulars that might exist by dealing with abstractions and generalities. In practical terms, we have to confine ourselves to making sure that the market runs properly; that everyone plays the game fairly; and that the rules that define the market are followed.

Morally, the argument stems from the epistemological point

discussed above. We cannot direct the market order because we cannot know all the particular facts that exist. Trying to do so would in fact distort our ability to do anything at all. Our activity would distort the role of the market as a system for providing information for action, and would hold back the hidden hand of the market. Moreover, the attempt to inject some sort of design into the system in the form of planning has consequences for liberty. Hayek explains these in the *Road to Serfdom* (1944). As planners tried to push the society in certain ways, society would gradually become more directive and managerial. There would be no order where there was no purpose as a whole. Instead of individuals following their own desires aided by information from the market, they would be forced in the planners' directions. This would lead to a lack of liberty; to a lack of negative freedom.

It is important to note that this is not a situation where evil-intentioned planners would force decisions on unsuspecting citizens. The argument is that even those with good intentions would be at fault. Though they would be trying to act for the good of society, they could not know what this good might be. Neither could they know all the consequences of their interventions. All that they would succeed in doing would be distorting the very information mechanisms people use when deciding how best to act. People would not be able to do what they thought was best for them but would have to follow the orders of those who claimed (misguidedly) that they knew better. This would inevitably lead to a totalitarian state. The road to hell is, for Hayek, truly paved with good intentions. Intervention implies a system of legal ordering which the American legal theorist L. Fuller (1969) calls managerialism. In this schema, law is a system of regulation that directs us towards particular ends, paying scant regard to rules or legality. Fuller contrasts this 'rule by managers run amok' with legality. In the latter we place ourselves under 'the governance of rules'. We can see then that our epistemological arrogance, in thinking we know what is right, has severe moral consequences.

How do we get round that arrogance? Hayek argues that though we cannot clearly tell what is right, we can more easily tell what is wrong. We ought, therefore, to try to refrain from doing wrong. If we follow the rules that we have laid down beforehand, this will at least ensure that we do no wrong. Here we can see the argument for legality; by following the rules we minimise our chances of doing wrong and this is all we have in our cognitive power to do. If we positively try to do good, then since we do not have that cognitive capacity, we will inevitably make mistakes and commit greater acts of immorality.

The case against markets: Pashukanis and capitalist society

So far, we have seen a view of society based on a market model. Not only is it claimed that this would be the most efficient way of organising society but also that it is the only moral way to operate. Only in this way, it is argued, can we ensure that people can pursue their own individual interests freely. That the labourers in the vineyard freely contracted to work for a penny is, on this view, the key point of the parable. Whoever gets what he or she bargained for has no complaint, especially not about others getting what they bargained for. To re-shape market outcomes for some state-favoured purpose, even 'social justice', in fact upsets these bargains. The purposive state is intrinsically illegitimate. For Hayek the 'Rule of Law' provides a framework for freedom and is inextricably linked with market society; it is ideally suited for the market society and does not fit well into a policy of welfare state intervention.

I now turn to consider the view of the Soviet Marxist scholar E. B. Pashukanis. Pashukanis, though agreeing with this description of capitalist society, draws different cognitive and normative conclusions. Pashukanis agrees with Hayek that law and economy are intimately connected. But it is in Pashukanis' way of formulating that connection that we get an idea of his objections to capitalist society. For Pashukanis, the connection is not best described in causal terms, such as that the forces of production cause the superstructure, that epiphenomenal edifice consisting of law, morality, religion, art etc. For him, the connection is best expressed by concepts such as 'constitute', 'reflect', 'mirror'. What does this mean? Marx said:

It is plain that commodities cannot go to market and make exchange on their own account. We must therefore have recourse to their guardians who are also their owners. Commodities are things and therefore without the power of resistance against men. If they are wanting in docility he can use force. In other words he can take possession of them. In order that these objects can enter into relationship with each other as commodities, their guardians must place themselves into relation with each other as persons whose wills reside in these objects and must behave in such a way that each does not appropriate the commodity of the other, and part with his own except by means of an act done by mutual consent. They must therefore recognise in each other the rights of personal proprietors. This juridical relation, which expresses itself in contract, whether such a contract be part of a developed legal system or not, is a relation between two wills, and is but a reflex of the real economic relation between the two. (Marx, 1970)

Pashukanis interprets this analysis of market exchange as follows. Capitalist society is where generalised commodity production obtains. Here goods are, in a generalised way, produced for their exchange rather than their use value. In other words, goods are not produced for their intrinsic worth but in order to exchange for other goods that people might want. Bread, for example, is not produced because it is 'the staff of life' (its use value) but because people want to buy it (its exchange value). What they want it for is irrelevant, as is the commodity's social value. I might just as well produce pet rocks if people want to buy them.[1] This being the case, mechanisms are needed which enable commodities to be transferred and to be owned by those doing the transferring. Exchange cannot operate unless someone owns a commodity and can transfer his or her rights in it. It is clear that I could not sell you the Tower of London unless I owned it. Similarly, I could not do so if society as a whole owned it. If all property is held in common, as in a monastic community, I cannot transfer goods in the same way as in a capitalist society – though I may have things for my own personal use. The relation between commodities exchanged in this way is only expressed through the wills of those claiming ownership. This relation of wills is expressed through law, through the juridical relation. It is not the pet rock and the money that are related, but the pet rock that I own and want to transfer and the money that you own and want to transfer. The personal pronouns are the most important descriptors, thus goods become as persons. But this does not, as one might think, make people most important. For you and I become abstract legal persons. The fact that it is the rights we claim in commodities that are most significant means that we are looked on, not as concrete persons, but as bearers of right. This abstract bearer of right, the legal person, only has existence in the commodity that it lays claim to. The irony is that though the commodity becomes as a person, that person is an abstract legal subject which only has concrete existence in the commodity. Marx calls this the 'fetishisation of commodities'. This fetishisation makes commodities, rather than the people who made them, appear to be the movers in social life. We live our life through them. It is not what I put into them that becomes important but rather what they exchange for on the market. We lose control over our own actions. We do not think we can interfere in the process of distribution for exchange follows a logic of its own. We cannot go against the 'invisible hand'. This postulates an individualism where individual interest is all that matters and where 'society' does not exist except as the sum of individual human actions. Things always have to belong to someone; there can be no conception that they belong to society as a whole and be used to benefit that society and the individuals in it as they need.

Pashukanis sees the juridical relation as the one which makes commodity-producing society possible. For it enables us to have the institutional facts of commodity and exchange. The whole society is constituted as capitalist through its central institution, the market. The market is, in turn, constituted through the juridical relation. Law, then, is a central feature in the form of organisation of a society. We saw, when we looked at Hayek, that this view is also mirrored on the right. The rule of law and the political liberties of the West are seen as being inextricably linked with market society. Hayek sees market society as one where distribution is based on a formal principle of equality and a negative conception of liberty and applies universal laws equally to all. Who gets what is determined by the operations of the market. That is fair because the market works on the principle that when people freely buy and sell, they exchange goods that have equivalent value. Thus everyone gets what they want. This freedom from coercion, from being told what to do, is guaranteed by universal rules, equally applied.

But for Pashukanis this is precisely what is wrong with capitalist society. Capitalism appears acceptable because of the equivalence of the market. Since everything is equal and free in the market — I freely exchange my goods for those of equivalent value — there seems to be no exploitation. But this is mere formal equality and ignores the realities of the situation. The reality is the exploitative nature of the capitalist production process. There is differential ownership of the means of production and the surplus value produced by the proletarian is appropriated by the capitalist. Capitalist society may offer freedom and equality but money is unevenly distributed and freedom is the offer 'you can't refuse'. For Hayek, both rich and poor are equally free to stay at The Ritz even though only the former can avail themselves of this opportunity.

Pashukanis wants to replace this formal equality with a system of distribution based around a substantive principle of equality and a positive conception of liberty that treats people as individuals according to their respective needs. Freedom is not just freedom 'from', but the freedom positively to fulfil oneself.[2] This means we cannot just apply a measure to people and treat them equally in respect of it. The rule that everyone is free to go to The Ritz is no use. We have to treat each person individually and see whether they need to go to The Ritz and what they will gain from it. The implication of this is that society is a co-operative venture, where people confront each other in all their facets and not as buyers and sellers or bearers of rights and owners. The freedom of each becomes the condition of the freedom for all and distribution occurs naturally: from each according to his abilities, to each according to his needs.

Law and market society

For both Hayek and Pashukanis law has a centrally important role because it constitutes a particular sort of society. Both sides argue that one cannot have a socialist law, in the sense of legality and the rule of law. Since that form is so bound up in the society, to do so would mean accepting a capitalist society.

What does that mean more concretely? Fuller (1969) shows us this in his *The Morality of Law*. Where the ideal of legality exists, official action is enmeshed in, and restrained by, the web of rules. No power is immune from criticism or completely free to follow its own bent, however well intentioned. It prevents us being dominated by the arbitrary will of officials and others who claim to know what is best for us. It acts as a curb on their power. An opposed view, which sees law as merely a technique, emanating from the will of someone authorised to make it, Fuller calls managerialism. Such a theory does not see the ordering of society as somewhere where the 'rational ordering of rules' obtains. Rather, society is likened to something akin to an economic enterprise. This is run by executives and managers who direct the enterprise and those working in it by reference to its objects. Thus all regulation would be cast so as to achieve efficiently the objects of the enterprise. Rules would be contingent and not the stable fixed entities they are under legality. They would change in response to changing conditions of which the managers would be the sole judges.

We can explain this by looking again at the parable. We may think of the master adopting a welfare role to his labourers – giving them what they need. But the trouble with the criterion of need or 'welfare' is that it cannot be fixed in advance. It cannot be incorporated under the equality of universal rules. It is irredeemably particular, depending upon the circumstance of the particular case. When you judge by need you are looking to the consequences of your action for the welfare of the particular person. That will differ from person to person and from time to time. 'Equal pay for equal work' is irrelevant because what counts is what you need and that will differ in each individual case.

Let us take a more concrete example. Examiners do not take into account the welfare needs of students when marking their degrees. We might say that the maxim, 'equal pay for equal work' obtains. For the same quality of work students get the same marks. We do not consider it relevant that one student might have greater need of the degree than another – he is poor and this is his only means of supporting his family. If we did, it would be unfair for many reasons. One of those would be that equality could not prevail since each student would have to be judged differently.

Let us look at the case where the moral choices are not so obvious. If social security benefits are to be given on the criterion of need, this gives great discretionary power to those who hand them out. Because each person's welfare will be different, one cannot make a general rule which defines in what cases a particular benefit is to be given. This will depend on the individual judgement of need. One cannot 'care' for an abstract proposition but only for a concrete person. Rules will be more akin to rules of thumb. They will be broken when necessary for the good of the individual or institution. This negates legality and can be, as we have seen, the beginning of the slide into a dictatorial regime. And anyway, it seems unfair to look to need at the expense of equality. This is what the labourers in the vineyard recognised. In this light, we can view them as expressing a sort of capitalist morality. What they are saying is that some sense of reciprocity, here defined as equality, measuring equality of pay against equality of work, must obtain. The exchanges they make for their labour must be equal as against all the other labourers. The rule is not equality of the persons as concrete individuals but as

D

personified in their labour — the commodity they have to exchange. It is only when the commodities exchanged are equal, that the labourers are treated equally. Thus 'equal pay for equal work' — what they deserve is to be paid according to the amounts of work done and to be treated equally. They think this to be the only fair way. Otherwise one gets the despotism of someone who believes they know what is good for you. That path leads to slavery.

The foregoing shows how Fuller argued that market societies remove managerial arbitrariness. But the 'capitalist morality' of the labourers leads us into a second point: namely the form of equality which is imposed by the rule of law and how it is related to other forms of ordering. This can be seen in the work of Kamenka and Tay (1975). Using Tönnies (1955) and Pashukanis, they pick out three ideal types of legal—social order. Capitalist society is characterised by *Gesellschaft* law (what one might call societal law). This arises out of, and constitutes, atomic individualism. The community is not seen as an organic whole; rather it is the sum of individual bearers of rights, all standing equal before the law and all pursuing their own interests. Contract is the paradigm form of such a law. There is a distinction between the public and the private, between the moral and the legal. This type of law is best expressed in individualistic, *laissez-faire* societies, each individual's interest being just one competing and sometimes overriding interest among many. One can see how equality becomes a key feature of this sort of society. Everyone is equal under the law and everyone is equal in the market. Everyone can do what they want under the abstract and universal rules which apply equally to everyone. 'Equality under the Law' is the slogan of these societies, and it is a powerful one. This feature is what makes it an improvement on and an advance from feudal society which can be characterised as a *Gemeinschaft* society (one might call law here communitarian law). Here justice is substantive and expressive of the organic community. There is no distinction between public and private, between political, moral and legal issues. All are one in the community but differentiated by status. Capitalist society, with its emphasis on freedom and equality, cuts a swath through the old feudal society where everything depends on status. The individual is set free of the old status hierarchies which no longer bar his advancement.

Finally we have what Kamenka and Tay call the bureaucratic administrative order. This seeks to regulate an activity and not to adjudicate in collisions between individuals; its fundamental concern is with consequences rather than with fault or *mens rea*, with public need or public interest, or the interest of the public activity itself, rather than private rights or individual duties. (1975, p. 139)

It is clear how this is a form that would be characteristic of welfare states and those where some overarching purpose (such as the construction of socialism) is given to the organisation of national life. When Pashukanis says law will wither away under communism, he means that *Gesellschaft* type law will go to be replaced by something like the bureaucratic administrative mode.

The morals of markets

We seem to have arrived at our answer. After all, what could be more proper than equality under universal rules? What could be a better way of organising a society than this legal–market model? This alone seems to save us from the worse excesses of dictatorial regimes: from their immorality and inefficiency. We have only to look to the failures of the East European 'socialist' regimes to see that.

But it is not quite as simple as that. For even in that case we saw that what Hayek thought good and useful, Pashukanis thought bad and useless. We have examined the case for Hayek's views. Let us now turn to examine the moral case for Pashukanis. In *Past and Present*, Thomas Carlyle says:

True, it must be owned, we for the present with our Mammon-Gospel, have come to strange conclusions. We call it a Society; and go about professing the totalest separation, isolation. Our life is not a mutual helpfulness; but rather, cloaked under due laws-of-war, named 'fair competition' and so forth, it is a mutual hostility. We have profoundly forgotten everywhere that *Cash-payment* is not the sole relation of human beings; we think nothing doubting, that *it* absolves and liquidates all engagements of man. 'My starving workers?' answers the rich mill-owner: 'Did I not hire them fairly in the market? Did I not pay them, to the last sixpence the sum covenanted for? What have I to do with them more?' – Verily Mammon worship is a melancholy creed. When Cain for his own behoof had killed Abel, and was questioned, 'where is thy brother?' He too made answer, 'Am I my brother's keeper?' Did I not pay my brother *his* wages, the thing he had merited from me? (quoted in Acton, 1971)

The claim here is that markets encourage greed instead of selflessness. Indifference to one's neighbour rather than concern. Selfishness and avarice is promoted to the level of a virtue.

Carlyle makes three claims about the way the market economy structures human relations. Firstly, there is the claim that I do not do things for others. I always do things for myself and say, without any justification, that this is the best for others. There is thus no community and no co-operation − everyone pursues their own self-interest. Moreover they have to. If they do not, the market mechanism will be upset and things will get worse: 'you can't buck the market'. It appears that a morally acceptable society can come out of something that, by most moral criteria, is considered a vice. Avarice and greed are not transformed into virtues because everyone practises them.

Acton (1971) attempts to answer this point. He claims that the market does not imply that one uses the economic necessity of the other to help oneself. It is merely the way the economic system works. One does not have to see market activity as 'using others to help oneself'. It could just as easily be conceptualised as 'doing something for someone else in order to satisfy myself'. Here we have something much more like the 'cool self love' of Bishop Butler. The bottom line however, is satisfying *yourself*. In a sense everything depends on motivation. There obviously is a sense in which this sort of market ethos is morally acceptable. If it were not, we could not make sense of the Christian imagery of 'losing your life in order to gain it'. How far, however, someone can act selflessly *for the sake* of someone, while knowing it will be for their gain, is a fine question. And this is especially so in a system where the organisation of social life is based specifically and generally upon self-interest. A self-interested society makes for a self-interested individual. The rise of the 'yuppie' in the '80s is instructive.

Secondly, Carlyle claims that a market society is a competitive one, where 'the law of the jungle' replaces co-operation. This is a strong theme in the moral criticism of capitalism. Competitiveness generally is attacked as unworthy. For a while, this extended to discouraging competitive games as instilling the wrong sort of values. Do they? One must, as Acton says, distinguish competition from rivalry. In rivalry people want to defeat each other as well as gain the prize. In competition this is not the case. Defeat of others is not wanted for its own sake. They are indifferent to the other competitors except as a means to the end of winning. 'The law of the jungle' with its connotations of Hobbes and anomie is a misnomer when talking about competition. There are rules in competition. It is not the case that 'anything goes' but rather that everything must be done according to the rules. Again, we are dealing with a question of motivation here. It is a fine point as to whether a society based on competition will not slide over into what Acton calls rivalry. In the real world there is a fine distinction between wanting to win; wanting to win *and* wanting the other person not to win; and finally just wanting the other person not to win. Some of the activities of our more famous enterpreneurs fall into the last category.

This brings me to Carlyle's third point, which is about what a market structure does to human relations in general. Accepting Acton's point about competition creates a problem of its own. For in competition one is indifferent to the other person – what is important is following the rules of the game. The other's success or failure is not a matter of your concern. Your only relation to your fellow competitors is as someone else following the rules. You only care that they follow them. It is, as Acton says approvingly, a rather impersonal relationship. But this is precisely what some see as morally questionable. For we are completely indifferent to one another. Except in so far as we have obligations and duties to each other under the rules, we do not have to care. This is the attitude exemplified by Carlyle's mill-owner.

We can see the equality and indifference that the market needs and promotes operating in the *Gesellschaft* order. It cuts a swath through the old feudal society, attacking status and substituting the equality of all under the law. But how does this equality work? How can we consider people to be the same when they are so obviously profoundly different? What happens is that we strip away from them all the things in respect of which they are different. Finally we come to something in respect of which we can say they are the same and can be treated equally. But this is not something concrete. Rather it is the abstract concept of the legal person. It is as legal persons, the abstract bearers of rights and duties under the law, that we treat concrete people equally. Thus the real human person becomes an abstraction – a point at which is located a bundle of rights and duties. Other concrete facts about them are irrelevant for the law. What this amounts to is that the law ignores as irrelevant the circumstances and material conditions of the particular concrete individual.

We are equally able to go to The Ritz in theory but only those with money actually can. We are all equally able to sleep under the bridges of the Seine. Treating unequals equally merely compounds inequality.

What is more, treating people as abstract makes them abstract (the way in which the commodity and the person merged in Pashukanis). They become things and not real living persons, who feel and care. You do not help a person but give them their rights. It becomes more worthy to visit your dying mother in hospital because you have an obligation so to do rather than because you love her (cf. Anscombe, 1958). See also what happens to the parable of the Good Samaritan in the law. In that parable, being a neighbour is a matter of what you do, a matter of the prior relation you have with the other person. When the law looks to the parable and asks in what cases we should make people answerable for any damage they cause to others by careless actions, it is the other way around. It seeks to define and place, under a prior web of rules, the neighbour relationship.[3]

The person's attitude to self would also be affected. Self also disappears into this abstract point. The concrete person would not do anything, only his abstract self would. He would not experience except in so far as the buyer and seller in the market, and thus the commodity, would. What is meant by this can be seen in the way art becomes corporate entertainment, sport is experienced on the TV and so on.

Conclusions

We seem to have come back to our starting point. It appears that the moral minuses of the anti-marketeers are the moral pluses of the pro-marketeers. Where do we go from here? If we go to the labourers in the vineyard we seem to be on the side of everyone at once. We see that the disappointed labourers have a point and we also approve of the love shown by the master. Is this an example of our wanting to have our cake and eat it? Only if we consider that the two principles we have been discussing are contradictory and that one must drive out the other. And in fact, many have considered the principles as a sort of zero sum game. In the former societies of Eastern Europe, non-market principles were applied everywhere, including economy and law. In the West, there was, and indeed still is, an attempt to marketise all fields of social life, including the 'caring' institutions. For the Marxists, the commodity form (the market principle) tended to spread and infect all forms of social life. For the liberals, command economy principles tended to spread and drive out the other forms.

This zero sum view of it might be true as a matter of sociological and historical fact. Powerful institutions in society do spread their values and their ways of going about things. But this need not necessarily be the case. Society is not a site of logically contradictory or counter principles where the one drives out and hides the other. To the contrary, social life and its institutions are based upon a mixture of principles which are in tension, one with the other. Particular social institutions will resolve this tension in different ways. They will balance the principles in particular ways in differing concrete circumstances. But this will not be a compromise in the sense that more of one will mean less of the other. When we come to looking at political institutions we will not necessarily justify them by the grand and abstract principles of 'freedom' or 'welfare' or 'equality'.

Let us take a look at equality. My argument has been that market equality implies the application of a single measure equally without concerning itself as to the concrete particularities to which it is applied. In so doing it reduces these particulars to the lowest common respect in which they can all be equal. Thus we saw how 'equality under the law' is achieved by making every concrete person that abstract bearer of right, the legal subject. In this way the legal person is stripped of any history. But this formal view of equality is incomplete. Take the example of reverse discrimination. According to this conception of equality, women, or ethnic minorities, should not get special treatment in respect of jobs or resources. For that would be unfair on others since it would treat them unequally. Equality, viewed in an abstract way, would here be compromised. However, other forms of egalitarianism, such as equality of life chances, might demand that we treat women more favourably than men in certain circumstances. We might need to be abstractly unequal in order to be concretely unequal. This will also depend on the institutions with which we are dealing and other moral imperatives. In the trial, the form of 'equality under the law' I mentioned might be no bad thing. All these have to be balanced in the concrete case (cf. Dworkin, 1985; Raz, 1986).

The same is also the case for freedom. Thus the market definition of absence of coercion will not be the one always applied. Freedom from poverty, freedom to organise, etc. will also be in play. These particular freedoms will be pursued at particular times and places and will be weighed against each other. Likewise with welfare, this will mean different things in differing circumstances and differing concepts will be balanced against each other. The problems of choice that arise in political life will not be susceptible to reduction to one principle or another. When we look at institutions in our society then the question is not the abstract one of whether market or welfare principles are best. We cannot rule out market or welfare principles *per se*. The solution to problems of professional power will depend on the particular circumstances involved and the ethical choices demanded therein. Solving them by marketisation or 'customer power' will not be appropriate in all cases. Compare students, patients, passengers and prisoners. Should all the areas involved, education, health, transport and the prison system, have customers instead? Do market principles for the distribution of goods necessarily detract from the principle of care? In health and education, for example, market principles in certain areas of choice might make those institutions better. But that is not to say that the institutions as a whole should be marketised.[4]

The collapse of the command economies of Eastern Europe shows the failure of societies constructed overwhelmingly on non-market principles. My argument implies that this does not mean that we should attempt to construct societies solely on the market principle. It does not mean the triumph of one principle over the other. Rather, it forces us to look closely at what is appropriate in particular concrete institutions of society. We must not initially dismiss this as impossible. That would imply as much arrogance as thinking that we always know what is right. We should be mindful that getting our concrete institutions well balanced in this way will not be easy. We must always think of our solutions as provisional and susceptible to challenge. If this appears difficult, then it is. After all, society is a complicated place – uncomplicated answers will not change that.

Notes

1 According to Hayek, as we saw, this shows the virtues of the market as a means of distribution of the social product. It is not dependent upon what planners decide but what people want.

2   See Ch. 1 for a fuller discussion of the negative/positive liberty distinction.

3   In *Donoghue* v *Stevenson*, 1932, AC 599, Ld Diplock said:

The rule that you are to love your neighbour becomes in law: You must not injure your neighbour, and the lawyer's question: Who is my neighbour? receives a restricted reply. You must take reasonable care to avoid acts or omissions which you can reasonably foresee would be likely to injure your neighbour. Who then, in law, is my neighbour? The answer seems to me to be persons who are so closely and directly affected by my act that I ought reasonably to have them in contemplation as being so affected when I am directing my mind to the acts or omissions which are called in question. This appears to me to be the doctrine in *Heaven* v *Pender* as laid down by Lord Esher.

4   Cf. Le Grand and Estrin (1989) for an interesting discussion of some of the ways market and other principles could be balanced. They discuss the use of vouchers in health and education. They argue that this could produce a form of 'market socialism'.

References

Acton, H. B. (1971), *The Morals of Markets*, London: Longman.

Anscombe, G. E. M. (1958), 'A Modern Moral Philosophy', *Philosophy*, 33.

Dworkin, R. (1985), *A Matter of Principle?*, Cambridge, Mass.: Harvard University Press.

Fuller, L. (1969), *The Morality of Law*, New Haven: Yale University Press.

Hayek, F. A. (1944), *The Road to Serfdom*, London: Routledge and Kegan Paul.

Hayek, F. A. (1960), *The Constitution of Liberty*, London: Routledge and Kegan Paul.

Hayek, F. A. (1973), *Rules and Order*, London: Routledge and Kegan Paul.

Hayek, F. A. (1976), *The Mirage of Social Justice*, London: Routledge and Kegan Paul.

Kamenka, E. and Tay, A. (1975), 'Beyond Bourgois Individualism: the Contemporary Crisis in Law and Legal Ideology', in *Feudalism, Capitalism and Beyond*, Canberra: ANU Press.

Le Grand, J. and Estrin, S. (1989), *Market Socialism*, Oxford: The Clarendon Press.

Marx, K. (1970), *Capital*, London: Lawrence and Wishart.

MacCormick, D. N. (1989), 'Legalism', *Ratio Juris*, 1–2.

Pashukanis, E. B. (1951), 'The General Theory of Law and Marxism', in *Soviet Legal Philosophy*, Babb, H. and Hazard, J. N. (Eds.), Cambridge, Mass.: Harvard University Press.

Pashukanis, E. B. (1980), *Selected Writings in Law and Marxism*, Ed. P. Beirne and R. Sharlet, London: Academic Press.

Raz, J. (1986), *The Morality of Freedom*, Oxford: The Clarendon Press.

Tönnies, F. (1955), *Community and Association*, tr. C. P. Loomis, London: Routledge and Kegan Paul.

Welfare and citizenship

The last decades have seen a dramatic transformation of the social and political agendas of modern societies. A period of political stability and social conformity in Western societies in the 1950s had by the late 1960s given way to division and social conflict. A New Left was in the ascendant accompanied by new forms of political militancy which seemed to indicate a fundamental instability of Western capitalism. For their part, the bureaucratic regimes of communist Eastern Europe seemed stable and enduring despite their lack of popular legitimacy. By the end of the 1980s, however, the situation was reversed. Communist regimes in Eastern Europe had collapsed, while government in Western capitalism was increasingly dominated by New Right political ideologies. These social and political events were mirrored by developments within social and political theory. During the sixties, Marxism emerged as an intellectual force and a challenge to liberal theory; by the end of the eighties it was being laid to rest and neo-liberal theory now holds the centre of debate.

We need not be detained too long by the question of whether or not the regimes in Eastern Europe represented a true test of communism, or were some perversion of it. Problems for Marxist theory would remain however that argument is resolved. If, as Cohen (1978) argues, the central mechanism of the Marxist theory of history is the contradiction between the forces and the relations of production, then the absence of polarised classes in capitalism means, at a minimum, that the characterisation of capitalism by such a contradiction is called into question. At the same time, it would seem to be 'actually existing socialism' that confronts 'fetters' that its social relations place upon the development of productive forces and the 'market' that is the solution to this impasse.

Yet, even if 'we' are the solution to 'their' problems, that does not mean that we have no problems or that we have the means of solving them. Indeed, despite the seemingly fundamental changes of the last two decades, there has been one constant – criticism of the welfare state. Social and political theorists in the 1950s had proclaimed an 'end of ideology' (Bell, 1960; Parsons and Smelser, 1956), where an important part of their claim was an end to fundamental conflict between the individual and the collective provision of wants, between 'capitalism' and 'socialism'. It seemed to them that this division had been transcended and that that transcendence was institutionalised in the welfare state. Since the 1960s this view has been subject to continued criticism, first by the New Left, then by the New Right.

The crisis of welfare and citizenship in our own societies is not diminished by the triumphalism in some quarters occasioned by the demise of communist regimes. In the West, it would seem that the New Right inherited the 'prize' which the New Left had argued would flow from the 'contradictions of welfare in a capitalist society' (Gough, 1979; Offe, 1984). But the 'victory' of the New Right might be short-lived. Problems of explanation on the left are matched by problems on the right. If Marxists, or others in the New Left, who previously explained the growth of the welfare state by its functionalism for capitalism, face the problem of explaining *how* it came to be called into question, and *why* they would now defend it, those neo-liberals who would question it as contradictory for capitalist relations have an equivalent problem of how to explain its growth.

Paradoxically, however, we shall see that, although New Left and New Right arguments make different judgements about how they would replace current welfare arrangements, they often describe those arrangements in a similar way. New Left arguments have been adopted by New Right critics and vice versa. New Left criticisms of the welfare state helped to create the current dominance of the New Right political agenda. Having criticised the failures of state welfare the New Left found those alleged failures enthusiastically promulgated by New Right writers. Even sympathisers of the political project underlying the welfare state now seem to be on the defensive, calling into question its so-called 'statist' predilections (Pierson, 1991; Plant, 1990). In this essay, then, I shall argue that what appears to be a 'normative' conflict of opinion over preferred outcomes disguises more fundamental agreement. However, I shall suggest that these common perceptions of the nature and consequences of welfare arrangements are mistaken. My claim is that some of our current social and political dilemmas will be answered by a different socio-logical approach to issues of welfare and citizenship.

Convergent criticisms

Two broad traditions in the discussion of issues of welfare and citizenship in political philosophy can be identified (Bellamy, Ch. 3, this volume; Kymlicka, 1990; Plant, 1991). The first is *liberal-individualism* with its emphasis upon the framework of laws which govern the *means* by which individuals pursue what are held to be essentially *private ends*. This entails a concern with a system of economic freedom involving (supposedly) uncoerced market exchanges. The second is the *communitarian* approach which emphasises a *community of ends*, or common good, to be realised in the structures of citizenship. On this perspective, the subordination of economic transactions to the wider purposes of the community is regarded as appropriate.

Although current political debates seem to be dominated by New Right liberals and 'left' communitarians, these traditions do not reduce to a simple right—left opposition. There are 'conservative' and 'pluralist', as well as 'socialist', forms of communitarianism and 'social democratic' as well as right wing forms of liberalism. In fact, historically, with its hostility to conventionalism, liberalism is associated with the radical criticism of status hierarchies and privileges. This association would seem to open the opportunity for some kind of synthesis between liberal—individualism and an egalitarian communitarianism of a pluralist or a socialist kind, whose proponents might see in the liberal—individualist tradition some of the substance of the equality that they suppose the community might embrace. Moreover, if the task of communitarian political philosophy is to explicate the moral 'tradition' that the community embodies, then liberal philosophers as part of our community would seem to require explication as contributors to the 'tradition'.

It would seem, then, that the two traditions of political theory overlap in their claims. Yet what is undoubtedly also the case is that this 'centre' does not hold. For some, even this limited description of a common project is a contradiction of terms. The 'self-regarding' substance of individualism is at odds with the 'other-regarding' character of communitarian sentiments. Thus, Plant (1991) regards the two traditions of political thought to be in some fundamental respects incommensurable. Not only is this a common view in discussions of political philosophy, but practical discussions of welfare are similarly polarised. Many liberal theorists – in particular, those neo-liberal theorists associated with the New Right – remain strongly opposed to any idea of agreement upon ends and any form of redistribution to meet needs (King, 1987). For their part, many communitarians would characterise any individualistic community as anomic and, therefore, not a community at all. But this produces a paradoxical consequence. The communitarian criticism of liberalism would seem to accept the liberal characterisation of modern society as comprising self-regarding individuals externally connected. In consequence, it frequently appears that communitarian writers are utopian in their hopes, unable to ground them practically as immanent within current arrangements. Within communitarian approaches, Marxism took on something of an exemplary status as a demonstration of the limits of liberal–individualism, at least with regard to its sociological limits.[1]

Yet, developments in the substance of welfare arrangements in Western societies have not been consistent with liberal conceptions of an appropriate system. Most liberal writers, and New Right liberals, in particular, are severely critical of the modern welfare state. From a communitarian perspective might we not explain the growth of welfare institutions that deviate from neo-liberal principles as a substantive demonstration of the insufficiency of those principles and as the embodiment of the claims of human community? Certainly, there is some support for this interpretation in arguments, such as that of T. H. Marshall, which explain the growth of the welfare state in terms of the elaboration of *social rights* of citizenship (Barbalet, 1988; King and Waldron, 1988; Marshall, 1963).

Marshall writes of citizenship as a status bestowed upon full members of a community where those included within the status are recognised as equals as to their rights and duties. He distinguishes three categories of rights of citizenship – civil, political and social rights – each the object of struggle over definition and inclusion. Broadly speaking, civil rights refer to an individual's rights before the law, while political rights concern an individual's rights to participate in democratic processes. These rights comprise the substance of liberal citizenship. However, according to Marshall, while citizenship entails an equality of status, the ability of any individual to exercise these rights is substantially affected by the inequalities of the class system. Marshall argues that these inequalities become the focus of social rights. In policies which take their legitimacy from social rights, the substantive problems of market capitalism are to be met through the ameliorative role of the state.[2]

However, the relation between the different rights cannot be reduced to a simple statement of the mutual consistency of civil and political rights versus the contradictory claims of social rights, as neo-liberal writers have wished to suggest. Marshall argues that the claims of an equality of citizenship and the inequalities of class were more or less compatible in developments through to the end of the nineteenth century, but in the twentieth century they have been at 'war'. That 'war' owes much to the strengthening and extension of political rights which created the means by which social rights could be claimed. In consequence, for Marshall,

> the political rights of citizenship, unlike the civil rights, were full of potential danger to the capitalist system, although those who were cautiously extending them down the social scale did not realise how great the danger was. (Marshall, 1963, p. 97)

Marshall's insight is reflected in that extensive body of political science research that seeks to identify an 'overload' upon democratic political systems (Crozier et al., 1975; King, 1975; Rose and Peters, 1977). Moreover, it indicates the extent to which any attempt to deny the meaningfulness of the idea of 'social rights' of citizenship must have implications for other forms of citizenship. Attempts to reverse the development of 'social rights', for example, would confront issues of 'civil' and 'political' rights, too.

This *interpenetration* of the different forms of rights is made more acute by Marshall's identification of a supplementary level of citizenship, that of the 'secondary system of industrial citizenship', which has implications for each of the three types of rights. Thus, rights of collective bargaining for trades unions are an extension of civil rights for workers, but,

> these civil rights became, for the workers, an instrument for raising their social and economic status, that is to say, for establishing the claim that they, as citizens, were entitled to certain social rights. (Marshall, 1963, p. 97)

More importantly, as we shall see, the system of 'industrial citizenship' crucially affects the way the welfare state is organised. In particular, it is one of the major forces underlying the linkage between welfare benefits and employed status which has profound implications for gender inequalities.

Whatever the weaknesses of Marshall's argument – critics have most frequently taken issue with the implication of a teleological unfolding of the rights of citizenship – it is hard to resist the conclusion that it was written at the wrong time. In the immediate postwar period in Britain much of it seemed, perhaps, self-evident. In the 1960s and 1970s it seemed too complacent, too much a part of arguments for an 'end of ideology'. To more radically minded, New Left writers at that time, if there was a 'war' between class inequality and citizenship, class had won. Since the institutions of the welfare state were adapted to the requirements of capitalism, so the argument went, the criticism of capitalism had to be extended to a criticism of its integral welfare arrangements. As Pierson summarises the position, the welfare state came to be regarded as 'a particular form of the developed capitalist state. It functions to secure the long-term circumstances for the continued accumulation of capital' (Pierson, 1991, p. 53).

For right-wing critics, whose voice was beginning to be heard more insistently in the 1970s, these arrangements represented an institutionalising of trades union interests and the development of a form of corporatist State which denied liberal precepts. Thus, we begin to see a polarisation of political commitments which is combined with a common rejection of the modern welfare state. For the most part, the institutions of the modern welfare state are not what critics of capitalism, including many communitarians, mean by an acceptable alternative and they frequently appear to be as critical of them as any neo-liberal writer.

The role of Marxism as a supposedly exemplary demonstration of the limits of liberal–individualism gives rise to explanations of the welfare state as 'class struggle from above' (Miliband, 1989) or as part of technocratic 'administered capitalism' (Habermas, 1976). From the perspective of neo-Marxist, or New Left, approaches, the welfare state is part of corporatist arrangements for the discipline of organised labour to secure the management of the economy in the interests of large-scale capital. Thus, Ginsburg writes that,

from the capitalist point of view state welfare has contributed to the
continual struggle to accumulate capital by materially assisting in bringing
labour and capital together profitably and containing the inevitable resistance
and revolutionary potential of the working class. (Ginsburg, 1979, p. 2)

Defence of the prevailing order by the state is, for Miliband, 'a
major contributing factor in the expansion of State power and
"statism" '. (Miliband, 1989, p. 13)

Following Marx's critique of reform (albeit one made in radically
different circumstances), it is argued that 'true' welfare objectives
could not be met within the constraints of capitalism. According to
Miliband this criticism can be extended even to social democratic
governments which 'have also tended to limit the scope of reform,
and have given to the "welfare state" a highly bureaucratic and often
rebarbative character' (Miliband, 1989, p. 73). Indeed, even where
it is accepted that the motive force of welfare developments comes
from below, it is argued that where the working class chooses a
'reformist', rather than a 'revolutionary', route it necessarily produces
the consequences identified by Miliband or Ginsburg. Thus, Gough
argues that, in these circumstances,

labour indirectly aids the long-term accumulation of capital and strengthens
capitalist social relations by struggling for its own interests within the state.
One could apply this approach to much welfare policy this century. (Gough,
1979, p. 55)

The consequence of applying such an analysis to welfare policy
is severe: all 'victories' turn to ashes. Przeworski (1985) interprets
reform versus revolution in terms of a choice that workers face
between improving their conditions under capitalism, or better
conditions under socialism. However, to get to socialism they must
traverse 'transition valley' and their current conditions under
capitalism are better than the conditions they must endure during
that trek. Reforms are possible, but not a reformist strategy to
transform capitalism. Thus, he accepts that 'poverty and oppression
are with us and will not be alleviated by the possibility of a better
future', and writes further that, 'the struggle for improving capitalism
is as essential as ever before. But we should not confuse this struggle
with the quest for socialism' (Przeworski, 1985, p. 248). If reforms
are not organised by the principles of socialism, this begs the question
of what, precisely, are the principles which do organise them? The
further pathos of his position is that the success of any such struggle

within capitalism is the production of the conditions under which 'transition valley' is deeper and wider; the success of reformism produces the conditions in which it is 'rational' to choose capitalism. The claims of the welfare state to modify inequalities have also been challenged. It is not only Marxist writers who have argued this, but non-Marxists such as Goldthorpe and Parkin in their criticism of 'end of ideology' theorists (Parkin, 1971; Goldthorpe, 1974). Indeed, Barbalet, in his recent discussion of citizenship, offers a nice summary of this 'sociological' position. He writes:

systems of class inequality involve not only disadvantage but also privilege and the power to preserve it, [therefore] it is unlikely that any changes brought to the class system through the development of citizenship, in which the powerful and privileged are included, would be fundamental. (Barbalet, 1988, p. 5)

Barbalet, for example, allows that the development of social rights has had some impact upon inequality. However, other processes are at work. He writes:

there can be no doubt that the development of citizenship during the twentieth century has altered the pattern of social inequality. Yet it would be unnecessarily narrow to suggest that citizenship was the only factor in this process. Improvements in the conditions of ordinary people can in many instances be attributed to directly economic causes. (Barbalet, 1988, p. 45)

Much effort, then, has been put into demonstrating the resilience of capitalism whose abolition, or modification in certain aspects, these theorists devoutly desire. Ironically, their arguments contribute directly to the neo-liberal critique of welfare. This is explicit in the work of Norman Barry. For example, he writes:

some socialists, and all consistent Marxists, have to regard the typical welfare institutions as in a very real sense harmful because they are structured on a pre-existing capitalist order. Their thriving would be inimical to the future aim of abolishing the capitalist order ... Indeed, in theoretical Marxism, since the state is defined in essentialist terms as a coercive force to protect class interests, any welfare role that social theorists might attribute to it must be illusory. Almost all overt socialists saw welfare as a form of social control, as indeed it was. (Barry, 1990, p. 41)

Plant, in a debate with Barry, accepts this 'convergence' without demur, writing of 'the sense of dependency which both the right and the left now accept has been a feature of bureaucratically provided public services' (Plant, 1990, p. 29).

For his part, Barry seems unwilling to examine the implication that he shares with Marxism a similar 'essentialism' – in his case, the optima of competitive markets and private exchanges – with the corollary that it is *the 'essentialism' of either approach* which gives rise to the attribution to state welfare of a coercive form. In either case, the economy is understood in terms of market relationships formally independent of political processes. The state is identified with the regulation of production and other institutional requirements of a system of private exchanges. It does not much matter whether, as in Marxism, it is class relationships that are held to explain the underlying structure of market relationships, or whether, as in liberal theory, these are held to be the aggregated outcome of individual tastes and preferences. Each position presents an image of the state *intervening* in an economy whose basic processes are held to be antecedent to the activities of the state.

On the liberal view, economic power is dispersed in the operation of competitive markets, while the state is associated with the organisation and centralisation of political power which, in the development of modern states, comes to be legitimised by civil and political citizenship rights. For Barry, as for other neo-liberal writers, the growth of welfare represents the state exceeding the proper grounds of its legitimacy, involving an intrusion of non-market concerns into market processes. The principles of 'economy' and 'polity' with regard to the distribution of social resources are, then, antithetical. Since politics is about collective decisions which are binding upon individuals, the extension of state activities expands the collective at the cost of voluntary, individually determined outcomes. Thus, in discussing the distinction between markets as the expression of 'self-interest' and the welfare state oriented to 'need', Barry comments that 'the correct dichotomy should be between freedom and coercion', (Barry, 1990, p. 70). Consider, then, the weakness of Plant's defence of social rights of citizenship after he has accepted most of the arguments by which they are rendered problematic. He writes:

if we are interested in empowering all people in society this has to be done certainly by the market, but it cannot be done wholly by it. We still require state-provided or state-guaranteed services. But we on the Left should not try to reinvent yesterday and go back to forms of welfare institutions which, with the best intentions, actually put very little power in the hands of those they were designed to help. (Plant, 1990, p. 32).

The problem from any perspective is the acceptance of such a distinction between 'politics' and 'economics'. The consequence of accepting it is that the claims of social citizenship to the *re*-distribution of the social product must face a contrary claim to justice which resides in the principle by which the initial distribution of resources is held to be produced. For Barry, and other neo-liberals, the initial set of outcomes is market-determined, reflecting the operation of an 'invisible hand' balancing the expressed wants of individuals. In consequence, any redistribution by the 'visible' hand of politics in the name of 'higher' values must be a denial of at least some of the 'values' expressed in the primary determination. As Barry puts it, 'voting is an obvious surrogate for the market, but majoritarian procedures, even if they work perfectly, do involve the imposition of decisions on unwilling people' (Barry, 1990, p. 51). Neo-liberals, like Barry, would be quite happy to endorse Barbalet's view, cited earlier, of 'economic causes' of the improvement of the conditions of ordinary people, since it would suggest that markets and needs are not antithetical. Moreover, the association of markets with 'efficiency' means that any redistribution appears as a 'distortion' of market outcomes. It is a source of 'inefficiency' without a secure normative foundation.

In these circumstances, the negative evaluation of the redistributive efforts of welfare states contributes to the neo-liberal critique. Neo-liberals are concerned that the public distortion of private arrangements is at a price which includes a cost to those currently in receipt of benefits. In this connection, Barry utilises 'leftist' criticism of welfare state attempts to effect an egalitarian redistribution of incomes. For Barry, there is indeed redistribution, but it is to the middle class as a consequence of their electoral dominance. Political rights of citizenship have produced a pressure to use 'politics' against 'markets'. But whereas classic liberals were concerned by the threat posed by the working class under a mass suffrage, the problem now appears to be what Barry, following LeGrand (1982), calls the 'sharp elbows' of the middle class. 'Targeting' would, then, appear to be a more effective means of both meeting needs and securing any minimal, necessary redistribution, since the impact of high-spending welfare states appears small and out of proportion to the size of welfare expenditure. This thesis would seem to be what underlies Barry's rather whimsical suggestion that, 'the only possible way that [middle class sharp elbows] could be countered would be an electoral alliance between rich and poor – a most unlikely occurrence' (Barry, 1990, p. 107). We might rather conclude that what is unlikely is that the proposed 'centrifugal' redistribution away from the 'middle class' would spin very much to the poor. Barry provides no account of how his proposed electoral alliance would work, given the conditions which have otherwise served the middle class. Indeed, the consequence of such attempts – if we may so regard the policies of the Conservative government in Britain over the last decade – has been cuts to the welfare programmes affecting the poor and maintenance of those programmes affecting the middle class (LeGrand, 1990). If there has been no spin off to the poor, the spin off to the rich is very evident.[3]

Marxists, such as Miliband, and neo-liberals, such as Barry, propose a theory of capitalism whose basic categories (and the processes believed to be intrinsic to those categories) are at odds with current social arrangements. For each, developments within the societies in which they believe their theories have relevance have not confirmed the processes of their theories. However, there is an asymmetry in their relation to this situation. For Marxists, current circumstances deviate not merely from their core understanding of capitalism, but from those by which their preferred outcome would be achieved. For neo-liberal writers, a similar lack of fit appears as an immediate 'policy opportunity'. Their theory of capitalism provides a series of policy prescriptions by which 'deviant' social arrangements can be returned to 'rationality'. This rectification is not an outcome that Marxists would wish. However, since Marxists have a theory which cannot adequately account for 'non-market' forms, that theory cannot be a coherent defence of them. In the end, all Miliband offers us is a rhetorical gesture. The past and present do not conform to his theory, but the future may. 'Class struggle for the creation of democratic, egalitarian, co-operative, and classless societies', he writes, 'far from coming to an end, has barely begun' (Miliband, 1989, p. 234).

Our conclusion concerning the contribution of Marxism to the understanding of modern society must be severe. A communitarian political philosophy that would speak to our present circumstances requires a more fundamental reconstruction of ideas about modern society. A communitarian theory which can only offer us the future is unlikely to have much future. On the other hand, a neo-liberal theory designed to return us to a future we might previously have taken, but did not, is equally implausible.

Types of welfare state

Although the dominant sociological consensus has been that the redistributive achievements of the welfare state have not been impressive, recently there have been some cracks in that consensus. It is now argued that the extent of redistribution has been understated, that it does vary with levels of welfare spending (which, although not unproblematically, might be regarded as an index to the level and extent of social rights). (Ringen, 1987; Uusitalo, 1984)

In developing this argument, it is necessary to distinguish between types of welfare state – between, 'marginal' and 'institutional' systems (Korpi, 1983; Titmuss, 1974). The former can be understood in terms of the temporary provision of a 'safety net' against 'market failure', while the latter offers more continuous need provision outside market processes. We can understand the distinction in terms of Marshall's recognition that social policy addressed to perceived needs does not necessarily take the form of a right of citizenship. Thus, the 'marginal' type seeks to adapt welfare to the requirements of the market and is characterised by means-tested assistance, modest (if at all) universal transfers and modest social insurance plans. The consequence is a dualism between state-welfare recipients, who experience a relative equality of poverty and a majority of the population who meet their needs through some form of market-related provision, such as private insurances and occupational welfare programmes. In contrast, the 'institutional' system is one where need provision is assimilated to citizenship rights and is characterised by generous and universal welfare benefits. In such a system, there would be no dualism because all social groups would be incorporated. Inequalities of income remain, but, as Marshall argues, in recognising a 'universal right to real income which is not proportionate to the market value of the claimant' (Marshall, 1963, p. 100), rather than 'dualism' there is the equality of status necessary to a right of citizenship.[4]

For neo-liberal critics of the welfare state, however, this universal status within an extended form of social citizenship is merely the generalisation of *dependence*. Barry (1990), for example, accepts that 'markets' cannot be the whole answer to needs, but suggests that they could be complemented by other voluntary associations – mutual aid and charity – without any contradiction of liberal principles. However, there is a crucial asymmetry in Barry's treatment of charity as a possible alternative to state welfare. His concern is entirely that of the voluntary, rather than coercive, character of charity from the point of view of the donor. He gives no consideration to the consequences upon the identity of those in receipt of charity. We might regard their subordination to the moral order of donors a most oppressive imposition.

This emphasis upon charity, however, has its parallel among left-wing critics of the welfare state. Thus, Walzer (1988) criticises the 'nationalisation' of welfare, arguing instead for a 'socialisation' of welfare, involving self-help and voluntary groups (see also Wolfe, 1989). For Walzer, the consequence of the 'nationalisation' of welfare has not been an empowerment of the population, but an increase in material welfare that has gone hand in hand with an extension of dependency. He writes, 'now we measure the advance of the welfare state – but we can hardly measure its success – by the growing number of dependents each working citizen must support, and to many citizens these days the number seems insupportable' (Walzer, 1988, p. 6). For Walzer, as for Barry, the decline of charitable activities associated with the rise of the welfare state is an indication of the decline of voluntary service as an ideal.

This political debate over the 'contradictions of universalism' betrays its roots in the public discussions of a specific, *marginal* welfare state, the USA. Murray's (1984) book, which argued that the welfare state created poverty and dependency, in particular by fostering the expansion and reproduction of an 'underclass', has been particularly influential. It does not seem to strike Murray that the fact that he is showing that the least developed welfare state has the most extensive welfare problems suggests the opposite of what he is claiming. Indeed, the adaptation of his argument to Britain (Murray, 1990) – that Britain seems to be following where the USA leads – suggests that the problems of an 'underclass' are produced by policies designed to 'de-institutionalise' welfare arrangements. This is the position argued by Myrdal (1962), who was one of the first to use the concept of an 'underclass' in his critique of American welfare policies. Myrdal argued that the specific welfare policies, which Murray subsequently judged and which were beginning to get underway when Myrdal wrote, would have the effect of, 'trap[ping] an "underclass" of unemployed and, gradually, unemployable persons and families of the bottom of a society in which, for the majority of people above that level, the increasingly democratic structure of the educational system creates more and more liberty – real liberty – and equality of opportunity, at least over the course of two generations' (Myrdal, 1962, p. 40). This is one of the first arguments to identify the issue of 'dualism' in welfare arrangements and, for Myrdal, the problem was the failure to effect a fully 'institutional' welfare system, in particular one that addressed issues of full employment.[5]

With this in mind, we can reinterpret the claims about 'nationalised' welfare arrangements. Much of Barry's (and Walzer's) perceived deficiencies of the welfare state are those associated with 'marginal' welfare states and are, therefore, properly viewed as a *consequence* of attempting to accommodate the requirements of 'markets'. Thus, it is 'targeted' welfare programmes which are associated with an inadequacy of need provision, wider inequalities of income, and the very 'perverse' effects of welfare such as 'poverty traps', 'dependency' and 'work disincentives' that neo-liberals seek to excise (and which some left-wing critics accept uncritically as the consequence of state-welfare programmes). Indeed, the sort of popular sentiments that are accepted as confirming the view that public welfare provision creates dependency, rather than empowers, are directly associated with means-tested welfare benefits. For example, there would seem to be little popular sentiment that adequate, publicly provided old-age pensions would create dependency. In contrast, there is considerable popular resentment about the inadequacy of pensions which for many gives rise to a necessary resort to means-tested supplementary benefits. Such negative sentiments are a consequence of the *failure to institutionalise* social rights, rather than a consequence of their institutionalisation.[6]

Given that one consequence of 'marginal' systems is the defection of the more advantaged groups to private forms of provision, it might be argued that middle-class capture of welfare through 'fiscal advantages' is greater than that which occurs through their direct consumption of publicly provided goods (Esping-Andersen, 1990; Sinfield, 1977).[7] Thus, middle-class advantages are likely to be more extensive, if disguised, in 'marginal' as opposed to 'institutional' welfare systems. Furthermore, the 'middle-class' capture of welfare in 'institutional' systems is associated with better outcomes for the 'poor'. Here we might adapt the liberal principle that seeks to justify the inequalities of 'market' systems on the grounds that those who seem to be disadvantaged are nonetheless better off than they would be without them, to argue that 'middle-class capture', however distasteful it might seem to some sensibilities, is the condition of more general advantage.

It is a sad comment that it has taken so long for social and political theorists to come to terms with the paradoxical and seemingly inegalitarian consequences of institutionalised, social rights of welfare. After all, Marshall pointed out that, 'a total scheme is less class-abating in a purely economic sense than a limited one, and social insurance is less so than a means-test service. Flat-rate benefits do not reduce the gaps between different incomes. Their equalising effect depends on the fact that they make a bigger percentage addition to small incomes than to large' (Marshall, 1963, p. 106).[8] If we press the argument a little further, we find that part of the problem lies with the way in which the question about the 'distributive' role of the welfare state is framed.

As we have seen, most writers approach social rights as a political, or social, category in terms of which social resources are *re*-distributed *after* their initial production and distribution on some other basis. Yet, institutional welfare states – in particular, the social-democratic welfare state of Sweden – are associated with a narrower range of initial incomes (Rein and Rainwater, 1986; Hedstrom and Ringen, 1987). For most writers, the primary allocation of resources is 'economic' and determined by market processes. It seems perverse to regard the more egalitarian 'primary' distribution of social democratic welfare states to be a consequence of 'economic' factors. Rather, it would appear that the 'standards' expressed in the social rights of secondary distributions also appear in the primary distributions.

We have some clue to the processes in Marshall's 'secondary system of industrial citizenship' – involving, for example, trades union rights of collective bargaining. One of the features of the social-democratic welfare regime – for example, that of Sweden – is a commitment to full employment and a 'wages solidarity' incomes policy which operates across categories of workers. In these circumstances, it seems especially inappropriate to regard the primary allocation of incomes as 'market-determined'.[9] However, a similar argument also applies to 'marginal' welfare states. Such welfare states are not characterised by the absence of a 'secondary system of industrial citizenship', but by a particular and limited form. Thus, in the United States, specific sectors of employment afford access to company-based health insurance, pension arrangements and the like. These particular arrangements are not 'generalised' as they are in 'institutional' systems and access to them is frequently an issue of gender, race and ethnicity, but, nonetheless, they structure the distribution of incomes. Thus, writers have noted a 'dualism' of the labour market into 'primary' and 'secondary' sectors (Doeringer and Piore, 1971). We can regard this 'dualism' in industrial citizenship as continuous with the dualism in social status already discussed as characteristic of the welfare systems of 'marginal' welfare states.

There are differences between societies in the nature and form of social rights, yet, whatever their extent, they transcend any standard division of 'economics' and 'politics'. It is inappropriate to approach these differences by means of a theory which is held to contain an 'essential' statement of basic processes, despite the substantial deviation of concrete arrangements from that statement. Contrary to what Barry, and other neo-liberals, might suggest, the 'conventions' of the community are embodied not merely in 'politics', but also in 'economics'. This must call into question any claim that earnings are determined by competitive processes and the marginal productivity of labour and, therefore, the claimed 'justice' of the primary distribution of earnings.[10]

Gender and welfare

It will not have escaped attention that I have discussed issues of welfare and citizenship without discussing gender. This has been deliberate. It has been made easy by the fact that none of the writers discussed so far deals with issues of gender. However, the sociology and politics of gender has, to a large extent, replaced the sociology and politics of class as the focus of critical discussions of welfare and citizenship. It has seemed appropriate to 'exhaust' the discussion of class before approaching the question of gender. If, as I have suggested, the approach to class issues has involved a problematic 'debunking' of the welfare project, we should be on our guard against a similar treatment of gender issues.

Feminist criticisms within liberal social and political theory have focused upon the way in which that theory has operated with an implicit, or not properly examined, distinction between a private realm of familial relations and a public realm of autonomous individuals pursuing their private ends while reflecting upon what collective considerations might rationally bind them. If issues of class intruded into these debates to force a recognition of the particularity and socially situated character of the self assumed in liberal arguments, the gendered character of that self was neglected as a consequence of the absence of a direct and self-conscious reflection upon the private/public distinction itself (Coole, 1988; Okin, 1989; Pateman, 1989). The individual of liberal theory appears gender-neutral only because liberal theory lacks the means to address the gendered character of the social arrangements that that conception of the individual seems to authorise. Thus, according to feminist writers, an adequate social and political theory requires the address not merely of civil society and state, but of the family as well, and the interrelations among the three.

What is striking is that when the family is addressed nearly all theorists are communitarian. There is, for example, a curious inversion in the public–private dichotomy favoured by liberal theorists. The 'public' realm is a realm of 'private' individuals, but the 'private' realm of the family has the character which is denied as possible in the 'public' realm. Not only are most social theorists communitarians concerning the family, they are frequently 'socialist' communitarians. For example, Hume (1961) reflects upon the possibility of a society organised on altruistic sentiments and discounts it. Fanatics may attempt a community of goods but its inconveniences and selfishness bring a return of separate property. Nonetheless, the community of goods in the family is not a fanatical idea. In the family we have a 'society' composed of 'enlarged minds' which are 'replete with friendship and generosity'. We should not be surprised at such an argument. This particular conception of familial relations is necessary in order to justify their 'privacy'. Enforceable rules of justice governing familial relations are unnecessary because the family is justice realised unreflectively. In contrast, feminists argue, the family is a *political* society with the same issues of power, coercion and co-operation as are found in the state (Okin, 1989; Pateman, 1989). Moreover, the 'communitarianism' of theories of the family brings to feminism an understandable caution about communitarian theory itself owing to what Kymlicka calls the community's tolerance of 'what was often a racist and sexist "common good"' (Kymlicka, 1990, p. 226).

On the face of it, the situation of gender inequality in modern welfare states is quite straightforward. Women experience a systematic disadvantage in citizenship and the distribution of social resources when compared with men (Jenson et al., 1988; Lister, 1990). Not only are all welfare states gendered in the substance of their social policies, so too are employment structures gendered. In this way, the argument in the previous section is reinforced by a consideration of gender inequalities – for example, Treiman and Roos (1983) have shown that the patterns of inequalities in earnings can be explained by no available theory of market processes, whether human capital, Marxist, or whatever (see also Stewart et al., 1985). Most importantly, these features are equally evident, or at least have been equally claimed, for 'marginal' or 'institutional' welfare states. Whatever the claim for the 'universality' of the 'institutional' welfare state, that claim is immediately contradicted by the reality of gender inequalities. On gender issues, it seems, all welfare states are 'dualist'.

For many feminists, this is an indication of a *patriarchal* social structure and a *patriarchal* welfare state (Barrett, 1980; Pateman, 1989). However, there is a paradox in the presentation of the substance of patriarchal practices. For Gilligan (1982), for example, the distinction between public and private spheres and the socialisation of men and women in terms of differential participation in these spheres has meant that men and women speak in 'different voices'. The male voice is of self-determination, reason and universal morality, while the female voice stresses interdependence, care and moral particularism. It is perhaps easy to see this distinction applied to the state in terms of the development of civil and political rights of citizenship, yet the development of social rights of citizenship would seem to involve 'female' principles of care. Indeed, Hernes (1988) coins the rather apt phrase that with social rights of citizenship, reproduction moves from the private sphere and 'goes public'. On the face of it, does it not seem more appropriate to regard social rights of citizenship in terms of a 'feminisation' of the state, rather than of an accentuation of its patriarchal character? [11]

Some writers, looking for the connection between 'capitalism' and 'patriarchy', argue that 'patriarchy' serves the reproduction of capitalism in a fashion that is strongly reminiscent of arguments about how the welfare state served capitalism (Hartmann, 1981). If there has been a 'war' in the twentieth century between equality of citizenship and class inequality, the conclusion we would draw is somewhat different. It would appear that the consequence of some of the class 'victories' in that war has been the creation of the current form of gender inequalities in citizenship. Yet it is unlikely that these inequalities could be adequately addressed except through the institutions of social citizenship. Thus, it would seem to be that where gender inequalities have been effectively addressed it has been through activities of the state (Ruggie, 1984; Nelson, 1984; Hernes, 1988). Indeed, Walzer's 'communitarian' view that welfare could be 'socialised' would seem to be particularly problematic from the point of view of gender issues, since informal and 'voluntary' caring places particular burdens upon women (Lister, 1990). It seems that in the approach to issues of gender inequalities we face some of the paradoxical consequences that we faced in approaching class inequalities.

If we pursue the implications of the relation between class inequalities and gender inequalities a little further, we can see that the arrangements that are currently argued by feminists to be oppressive to women also represent (however problematically) a realisation of women's interests. We should remember that the demand for social rights of citizenship was a response to the perceived consequences of the development of a market system, especially a market for labour. The development of a fully commodified, individualistic wages system would mean that those without independent means of subsistence would be driven to sell their labour power and those unable to do so would be dependent upon others. Competition among workers would drive the level of wages down to the reproduction costs of individual labour power. In a market system of wages the claims of dependants could form no part of the determination of wages. Thus, a major social crisis of capitalism in the nineteenth century concerned child poverty. Put simply, the welfare of children was, in large part, met by some version of a 'family wage' system of higher wages for married men. This challenge to a market-determined wages system is continuous with the rise and development of welfare states (Brenner and Ramas, 1984; Humphries, 1977). The details of 'family wage' systems vary, but characteristic are age-related payment systems, protections for seniority, child allowances within wage payments and unemployment benefits for fathers, etc. Exclusionary practices maintain sectors of (relatively) high paying jobs for 'appropriate' categories of workers. For her part, Radcliffe-Richards has suggested that, 'if women had been fully involved in the running of society from the start they would have *found* a way of arranging work and children to fit each other' (Radcliffe-Richards, 1980, p. 114). However, this misses the point of the particular social circumstances in which strategies have to be developed (Brenner and Ramas, 1984; Humphries, 1977).[12] The absence of supposedly 'patriarchal' practices and relatively equal access to jobs for men and women was not associated with women's welfare, but low incomes and poverty for men *and* women (and their children).

Obviously, the 'family wage' system also has negative consequences for women. One currently pressing issue is the feminisation of poverty and child poverty upon marital breakdown (Nelson, 1984). With the dependence of children upon male earnings comes a dependence of wives upon husband's earnings, especially during the period of childbirth and the early years of children. This is a 'dependency culture' within 'welfare' arrangements that neo-liberals do not discuss. Where women work, they have what Hernes (1988), for example, calls 'untidy life patterns' compared to the 'tidy' patterns of men and this is reflected in different earnings-levels and income trajectories. The patterns of female employment that are observed, such as part-time employment, can only be understood in their relation to male employment and to family formation (Siltanen, 1986). These inequalities between men and women are then embodied in the structures of social citizenship through earnings-related benefits or employment-related entitlements (just as they are embodied systematically in the various 'private' forms of provision, such as insurances or occupational pensions).

The current issues of an equality of citizenship between men and women cannot be separated from issues of the relation between family, employment, non-employment and the state. It could not be restricted to the sphere of social citizenship rights as these are usually understood. Equally as important is the restructuring of the form of 'industrial citizenship' ('employment citizenship', would, perhaps, be the better term). What is challenged is not simply current relationships between family and employment, but the *current meanings of employment*. Yet we have got here by challenging meanings in the past and, however unacceptable current arrangements are, no useful critical purpose is served by giving them over to processes which are held to operate wholly against the interests of women. The modification of class inequalities which has produced the current structures of industrial and social citizenship that feminists rightly criticise has also served women's interests. What we require is an approach in which we can understand how the process of change produces different conceptions of interests without projecting current conceptions of interests back into the past as somehow their 'true' underlying meaning.

Conclusion

The traditional issues of political philosophy and social theory are pressing concerns for us, but I do not think that we can remain satisfied by the standard answers. This essay has examined the common assumptions in seemingly very different approaches and found them to be wanting. The challenge is to produce an approach to citizenship and welfare which embraces more of current arrangements than is presently fashionable. The issues of gender are central to this undertaking. It is likely, when the history of our present period comes to be reviewed, that the 'fragility' of welfare arrangements and the 'crisis of welfare' that so dominates current arguments, will be revealed as an artefact of a particular transitional period in our societies. The transition I have in mind is that from a welfare state grounded in male employment experience to one grounded in an equality of experience between men and women.

Notes

1   It is evident that many communitarian theorists have, implicitly or explicitly, relied upon some version of Marxist class theory in their characterisation of modern societies. MacIntyre, for example, comments that while Marxism is 'exhausted' as a political tradition it is 'still one of the richest sources of ideas about modern society' (MacIntyre, 1981, p. 262). For avowedly Marxist communitarians, the problem of their political tradition is specific; the 'proletariat' in whose name they would act do not seem to agree with the proposed solution, even where their circumstances can be described as insufficient to guarantee a proper obligation to liberal arrangements.

2   Marshall was aware that 'ameliorative' social policies were not always a consequence of the status of citizenship. In his discussion of the nineteenth century Factory Acts, for example, he recognised that the legislation refrained from affording protection to all workers on the grounds of a claimed respect for citizenship. Thus, protection was afforded to women and children precisely because they were not accorded the status of citizen (Marshall, 1963, p. 84).

3   Bracewell-Milnes, in a recent IEA Inquiry into universal child benefit, for example, recommends its replacement by tax allowances with the comment that, 'at the philosophical level the treatment of the higher rate [of tax] illustrates the difference between a tax allowance and a government hand-out. The latter is a collectivist concept, and its expression is inevitably egalitarian. A tax allowance, by contrast, like the personal allowance or married couple's allowance of income tax, is based on the opposite principle of benefiting the richer taxpayer more than poorer if the richer is taxed at a higher rate' (Bracewell-Milnes, 1991, p. 6).

4   Recent arguments for the welfare state distinguish two types of 'institutional' welfare state, the 'social-democratic' and the 'corporatist-statist' (Esping-Andersen, 1990). The former has the characteristics of the institutionalised welfare state discussed above and is argued to be a product of a strong labour movement. It is particularly associated with Scandinavia. The latter type involves general welfare programmes that embody status differentials. They are strongly influenced by Catholic social movements which emphasise the maintenance of traditional family values. Examples of this type are Germany, Austria, France and Italy. These differences are important historically, but post-war developments would seem to involve a convergence between them (Holmwood, 1991).

5   Myrdal's solution to the problem of an 'emerging underclass' was characteristically robust, arguing for 'movements of protest on the part of the underprivileged' (Myrdal, 1962, p. 45).

6   Hoggart, for example, writing not long after Marshall, gives a characterisation of popular attitudes of 'them' and 'us' strongly formed by the experience of 'means-tested' benefits. He writes, ' "them" includes the policeman and those civil servants or local authority employees whom the working classes meet – teachers, the school attendance man, "the Corporation", the local bench. Once the Means Test Official, the man from "the Guardians" and the Employment Exchange officer were notable figures here' (Hoggart, 1957, p. 72).

7   We should be careful to distinguish between those public goods which the middle class 'captures', and which can be incorporated under the category of citizenship rights, and those that represent other aspects of state activities. For example, subsidies to British Rail commuters may benefit the middle class, but they hardly represent a 'right of citizenship'.

8   Compare Marshall's statement with the 'radical' analysis by Goodin and LeGrand. They write, 'whether or not you think the beneficial involvement of the non-poor in the welfare state is undesirable depends on what you suppose the goals of welfare to be. If the goal is an egalitarian one, then the beneficial involvement is likely to be undesirable ... If the goal in view is reducing poverty or guaranteeing everyone minimum standards, then the objection to beneficial involvement is not nearly so strong. The most that can be said is, in these terms, that it is wasteful. But if weeding out non-poor beneficiaries is even more costly, then we should in these terms

be prepared to accept that level of wastage in pursuit of our poverty-reduced goals' (Goodin and LeGrand, 1987, p. 218).

9   Barry notes the development of earnings-related benefits, writing that, 'when these transfers are earnings-related they preserve into retirement the inequalities of the prevailing income structure' (Barry, 1990, p. 117). The implication is that this is a further indication of the operation of middle-class sharp elbows and an undermining of the redistributive potential of 'institutional' welfare states. However, his argument fails to take into account the context of narrowing differentials in the prevailing income structure. Moreover, the 'privatisation' of welfare provision is associated with widening income differentials at the same time as it, too, would preserve income structures into retirement.

10   It is, for example, precisely in terms of such a theory of competitive markets that Barry identifies the superiority of neo-liberal principles of citizenship. He writes, 'perfectly competitive markets are in fact quite egalitarian: each factor of production is paid its marginal product, there is no "wasteful" profit, and the whole system is geared towards the satisfaction of the uncoerced wants of rational individuals' (Barry, 1990, p. 95).

11   The right-wing, populist epithet for the welfare state, the 'nanny state', would seem to indicate that social rights embody the 'ethics of care'. We have also seen (note 1, above) that Marshall recognised that protective employment legislation was initially introduced for women on the basis of an inequality of citizenship between men and women. By that token, the generalisation of such legislation for both sexes could not be argued to reflect patriarchal principles.

12   Put bluntly, in the circumstances of early industrialisation, state activities were designed to reinforce work-discipline and were unsympathetic to the welfare claims of working-class families.

References

Barbalet, J. M. (1988), *Citizenship: Rights, Struggle and Class Inequality*, Milton Keynes: Open University Press.

Barrett, M. (1980), *Women's Oppression Today: Problems in Marxist Feminist Analysis*, London: New Left Books.

Barry, N. (1990), *Welfare*, Milton Keynes: Open University Press.

Bell, D. (1960), *The End of Ideology: On the Exhaustion of Political Ideas in the Fifties*, Glencoe: Free Press.

Bracewell-Milnes, B. (1991), 'Child tax allowances: the solution to the problem of child benefit', *Inquiry*, No. 22, February, London: Institute of Economic Affairs.

Brenner, J. and Ramas, M. (1984), 'Rethinking women's oppression', *New Left Review*, No. 144.

Cohen, G. A. (1978), *Karl Marx's Theory of History: A Defense*, Oxford: Oxford University Press.

Coole, D. (1988), *Women in Political Theory: From Ancient Misogyny to Contemporary Feminism*, Brighton: Wheatsheaf.

Crozier, M., et al. (1975), *The Crisis of Democracy*, New York: New York University Press.

Doeringer, P. and Piore, M. J. (1971), *Internal Labour Markets and Manpower Analysis*, Lexington: D. C. Heath.

Esping-Andersen, G. (1990), *The Three Worlds of Welfare Capitalism*, Cambridge: Polity Press.

Gilligan, C. (1982), *In a Different Voice*, Cambridge, Mass.: Harvard University Press.

Ginsburg, N. (1979), *Class, Capital and Social Policy*, London: Macmillan.

Goldthorpe, J. (1974), 'Social inequality and social integration in modern Britain', in D. Wedderburn (Ed.), *Poverty, Inequality and Class Structure*, Cambridge: Cambridge University Press.

Goodin, R. and LeGrand, J. (Eds.) (1987), *Not Only the Poor: The Middle Classes and the Welfare State*, London: Allen and Unwin.

Gough, I. (1979), *The Political Economy of Welfare*, London: Macmillan.

Habermas, J. (1976), *Legitimation Crisis*, London: Heinemann.

Hartmann, H. (1981), 'The unhappy marriage of Marxism and feminism: towards a more progressive union', in L. Sargent (Ed.), *The Unhappy Marriage of Marxism and Feminism: A Debate on Capitalism and Patriarchy*, London: Pluto Press.

Hedstrom, P. and Ringen, S. (1987), 'Age and income in contemporary society: a research note', *Journal of Social Policy*, 16 (2).

Hernes, H. M. (1988), *Welfare State and Woman Power*, Oxford: Oxford University Press.

Hoggart, R. (1957), *The Uses of Literacy*, London: Chatto and Windus.

Holmwood, J. M. (1991), 'W(h)ither welfare?', *Work, Employment and Society*, 5(2).

Hume, D. (1961), *Enquiries Concerning the Human Understanding and Concerning the Principles of Morals*, Oxford: Clarendon Press.

Humphries, J. (1977), 'Class struggle and the persistence of the working class family', *Cambridge Journal of Economics*, 1(3).

Jenson, J., Hagen, E., and Reddy, C. (Eds.) (1988), *Feminization of the Labour Force: Paradoxes and Promises*, Cambridge: Polity Press.

King, A. (1975), 'Overload: problems of governing in the 1970s', *Political Studies*, 23(2).

King, D. S. (1987), *The New Right: Politics, Markets and Citizenship*, London: Macmillan.

King, D. S. and Waldron, J. (1988), 'Citizenship, social citizenship and the defense of welfare provision', *British Journal of Political Science*, 18(3).

Korpi, W. (1983), *The Democratic Class Struggle*, London: Routledge and Kegan Paul.

Kymlicka, W. (1990), *Contemporary Political Philosophy*, Oxford: Clarendon Press.

LeGrand, J. (1982), *The Strategy of Equality: Redistribution and the Social Services*, London: Allen and Unwin.

LeGrand, J. (1990), 'The state of welfare', in J. Hills (Ed.), *The State of Welfare in Britain: The Welfare State in Britain Since 1974*, Oxford: Clarendon Press.

Lister, R. (1990), 'Women, economic dependency and citizenship', *Journal of Social Policy*, 19(4).

MacIntyre, A. (1981), *After Virtue: A Study in Moral Theory*, London: Duckworth.

Marshall, T.H. (1963), 'Citizenship and social class' in *Sociology at the Crossroads and Other Essays*, London: Heinemann.

Miliband, R. (1989), *Divided Societies*, Oxford: Clarendon Press.

Murray, C. (1984), *Losing Ground: American Social Policy 1950–1980*, New York: Basic Books.

Murray, C. (1990), *The Emerging British Underclass* (with contributions by F. Field, J.C. Brown, N. Deakin, A. Walker), London: Institute of Economic Affairs Health and Welfare Unit.

Myrdal, G. (1962), *Challenge to Affluence*, London: Victor Gollancz.

Nelson, B. (1984), 'Women's poverty and women's citizenship', *Signs*, 10(2).

Offe, C. (1984), *Contradictions of the Welfare State*, London: Hutchinson.

Okin, S.M. (1989), *Gender, Justice and the Family*, New York: Basic Books.

Parkin, F. (1971), *Class Inequality and Political Order*, London: Paladin.

Parsons, T. and Smelser, N. (1956), *Economy and Society: A Study in the Integration of Economic and Social Theory*, London: Routledge and Kegan Paul.

Pateman, C. (1989), *The Disorder of Women: Democracy, Feminism and Political Theory*, Cambridge: Polity Press.

Pierson, C.W. (1991), *Beyond the Welfare State*, Cambridge: Polity.

Plant, R. (1990), 'Citizenship and rights', in R. Plant and N. Barry, *Citizenship and Rights in Thatcher's Britain: Two Views*, London: Institute of Economic Affairs Health and Welfare Unit.

Plant, R. (1991), *Modern Political Thought*, Oxford: Basil Blackwell.

Przeworski, A. (1985), *Capitalism and Social Democracy*, Cambridge: Cambridge University Press.

Radcliffe-Richards, J. (1980), *The Sceptical Feminist: A Philosophical Enquiry*, London: Routledge and Kegan Paul.

Rein, M. and Rainwater, L. (1986), *Income Packaging in the Welfare State: A Comparative Study of Family Income*, Oxford: Oxford University Press.

Ringen, S. (1987), *The Possibility of Politics: A Study of the Political Economy of the Welfare State*, Oxford: Clarendon Press.

Rose, R. and Peters, B. G. (1977), *Can Government Go Bankrupt?*, New York: Basic Books.

Ruggie, M. (1984), *The State and Working Women: A Comparative Study of Britain and Sweden*, New Jersey: Princeton University Press.

Siltanen, J. (1986), 'Domestic responsibilities and the structuring of employment', in R. Crompton and J. M. Mann (Eds.), *Gender and Stratification*, Cambridge: Polity.

Sinfield, A. (1977), 'Analyses in the social division of welfare', *Journal of Social Policy*, 7(2).

Stewart, A., Prandy, K. and Blackburn, R. M. (1985), 'Gender and earnings: the failure of market explanations', in B. Roberts, R. Finnegan and D. Gallie (Eds.), *New Approaches to Economic Life*, Manchester: Manchester University Press.

Titmuss, R. (1974), *Social Policy*, London: Allen and Unwin.

Treiman, D. and Roos, A. (1983), 'Sex and earnings in industrial society: a nine-nation comparison', *American Journal of Sociology*, 89(3).

Uusitalo, H. (1984), 'Comparative research on the determinants of the welfare state: the state of the art', *European Journal of Political Research*, 12(3).

Walzer, M. (1988), 'Socializing the welfare state', in A. Gutmann (Ed.), *Democracy and the Welfare State*, Princeton: Princeton University Press.

Wolfe, A. (1989), *Whose Keeper? Social Science and Moral Obligation*, Berkeley and Los Angeles: University of California Press.

Constitutionalism and democracy

To discuss constitutionalism and democracy is to confront the inter-section of politics and law. A constitution is a legal framework for a state and the exercise of power in it. Politics is about the exercise of power, especially state-power. Democracy is a mode of exercise of state-power, for democracy is people-power (more or less literally, in the Greek original of the English term). How then should people-power stand in relation to constitutions and constitutionalism? Should constitutions restrict the democratic exercise of power, and should respect for these limits be insisted on in the name of constitutionalism? Or should the people always have moment-by-moment power over the constitution of their state? How, anyway, can the people be empowered in the circumstances of modern mass-society in the post-industrial state? Does constitutionalism help secure democracy, or simply subvert it by giving unelected judges powers to second-guess the people or their elected representatives in Parliament or Congress?

These questions are of concern throughout the (more or less) constitutionalist and (more or less) democratic world of advanced 'Western' societies. They put at issue the wisdom or necessity of having formally enacted, or 'written', constitutions, subject to special procedures for change, often requiring supermajority voting in one form or another. The USA, Australia, Canada, Switzerland, Denmark, Germany, to a degree France, and many others exhibit the potentialities of the written constitution, and, in varying degrees, the value of constitutionalism in such a context. The UK has for a long time been a unique bastion of the 'unwritten constitution' where the fundamental rights of the people and the powers of the rulers alike depend on an amalgam of laws and conventions which, although constitutional in character, are wholly co-ordinated with the ordinary law of the land, and as easily alterable by parliamentary enactment as any other parts of the general law. Yet even in the UK, voices arise more and more insistently urging a reconsideration of the prospects for constitutionalism and democracy under the traditional constitutional order, which seems to grow more and more anomalous with every year that passes and bears witness to yet another new start of a more formal constitutionalism in yet another new state, or old one reborn. Discontent expressed through Charter '88, through devolutionary or nationalist parties and groupings in Scotland and Wales, and other like sources of political pressure, bear witness to the growth of reforming constitutionalist sentiment in the UK. Even the monarchy comes under more critical scrutiny than for a hundred years. But the monarchy has defenders too. And equally, against pressures for a written constitution, distinguished counter-voices argue for parliamentarianism as both the soundest democracy and the safest constitutionalism.

The present chapter starts from a consideration of the concepts of politics and of law, with the aim of clarifying the concepts of state and constitution, and thus showing how the state can come to be subject to law. This analysis introduces the key idea of the state-under-law, or *Rechtsstaat*, and the related idea of the 'Rule of Law'. All this presupposes the distinctiveness and importance of constitutional law. Constitutionalism, the subject of the second section of this chapter, is the political virtue of respect for the constitution and the limits it sets to lawful power. Subsequent sections review in various ways how far constitutionalism is either antithetical or essential to democratic government.

Section I

Politics is about power. The study of politics is essentially about the power of decision-making in human communities on matters of communal importance. It is the study of how this power is allocated and exercised, and of how people compete for, and obtain, the power to make effective decisions on matters that concern the well-being of the community and its members. The state is of central concern to politics, being itself a locus for the exercise of power, a maker of decisions and the primary political community for most human beings in the contemporary world. The state is a political community of a special kind. It is a territorially organised political community, within which power is exercised over the territory with respect to the economic resources available in it, and to the use of force in interpersonal relations. Conceived as an acting subject, the state acts through individuals and organised groups of people who take and implement decisions in the name of the state and who, in their deciding, purport to be the state's officials or organs. It has effective means of defence against external interference, and effective means of coercion over persons within it, in order to ensure that its decisions are by and large implemented. It is a normal claim of states that they have a monopoly over legitimate use of force in or in respect of the state territory.

Law is about normative order. Wherever there is law, there is normative order; wherever normative order is institutionalised, there is law. Normative order is a kind of ideal order that lays down the difference between right and wrong conduct, stipulating which modes of conduct are required of people as their duties, providing that people have rights to proper conduct by others, and (so far as not constrained by duties) have rights to conduct themselves as they choose. It is possible for some duties to be duties of obedience to decisions made by other persons; where this is so, the decision-maker is said to have 'normative power', or 'authority', to make the relevant decisions affecting the duties of others (compare Raz, 1979). The institutionalisation of normative order arises through the erection of standing forms of authority (normative power) held by some individuals or groups. Crucial forms of authority are the authority to make general rules of conduct, and the authority to make binding decisions about alleged breaches of duty or infringements of right.

Institutionalised authority to make rules and to make adjudicative decisions is what essentially differentiates law from morality, whose authority, albeit ultimate, is not institutional, but grounded solely in practical reason and sentiment. On account of its institutional character, the normative order of the law is not a purely ideal order, but has also an actual and positive quality, whereas morality's importance lies in its being a purely ideal order, actualised (if at all) by the free decisions of humans unconstrained by institutional decisions, and showing respect for institutional decisions only so far as these morally merit moral respect.

This brief and summary conceptual explication shows why in practice law necessarily implicates politics and politics necessarily implicates law. On the one hand, law as institutional normative order cannot function as such without relying on some measure of political power, for in the long run the authority of legal decision-making depends, in the context of the state, on there being respect for legal decisions, or power to enforce them where respect is lacking. On the other hand the enduring organisation of political power in a state is almost inconceivable without some measure of legal–institutional authority. So legal institutions may be constitutive of political power, or, through the legitimacy they confer on political agents, a substantial contributor to political power. The need to engage people's sense of obligation, or of rightfulness and legitimacy, means that any standing decision-making power in a society tends to present itself as normative power: hence political power tends to legalise itself. Yet again, in consequence political power reciprocally shapes the normativity of the law. Legislation is the input of the political process into the law. Politics is necessary both to uphold the law's authority with the backing of temporal power, and to contribute to the processes of legal change.

The legal and the political can and should be held conceptually distinct. They are distinct despite manifest overlap. But overlap there always and inevitably is, by virtue of the interconnecting content of the two concepts. Politics has legal backing and (often) a legal framework; law has political inputs and (usually) the support of political power. In any stable society there must be some standing balance between the legal and the political, with reasonably high mutual respect and reciprocal regard for mutual boundaries.

What is not here assumed is that law is, as many think (e.g., Kelsen, 1960), essentially coercive, as well as institutionalised and normative (see MacCormick and Weinberger, 1986). While breach of any kind of law doubtless brings in its wake some form of sanction, if only that of the notorious illegality of the delinquent's conduct, the existence of institutionalised, organised and physically coercive sanctions belongs to one species of law, not to the genus as a whole, as the examples of canon law, the laws of sporting associations, or even something so imposing as international law or as massively institutionalised as the law of the European Community, all illustrate. The species of law to which the attribute of physical coerciveness belongs is state law, the law peculiar to the state as a political community of the kind described above. It is the state's pretension to a legitimate monopoly of coercive power within state territory that endows the state's law with coerciveness, not the character of law itself which brings coercion into the state.

Nevertheless, the existence of legal order in a state may be of the greatest importance in enabling it to function effectively as a coercive political order. Police forces, even secret ones, prisons and prison services, courts, even politically subservient ones, armies and militias, could not be organised to their coercive tasks in large-scale modern societies without a formidable body of reasonably formalised and reasonably coherent standing rules and regulations issued by some rule-making authority, and in practice somebody has to decide what counts as proper application of the rules and regulations, and to decide on disputes about whether they are being properly observed or flouted. Institutional normative order, that is, law, is then a necessary element within the state's coercive apparatus. So state law is coercive, and at the same time law of some kind is a necessary element in the state's coercive power.

The paradox, however, is that law is not only essential to the state's coercive self-organisation; it is also, according to received wisdom, an essential and indispensable instrument for limiting the power of the state and its agencies. Where there is law, and where the power of the state and its organs or agencies is deemed to be defined and conferred by law, then by the same token that power can (presumbly) be limited by law. Of any power exercised in the state's name, it will be possible to ask: was the decision in question really within the power granted? Did it avoid violating any limits or restraints imposed on the power granted? And judges can judge of such questions – provided they are impartial, and not themselves implicated in the challenges exercises of power. It will be possible for all concerned to act with a view to the law and the restrictions it imposes. A thoroughgoing respect for the law will in this case ensure that state power, albeit still coercive, is limited power. Where there is such thoroughgoing respect for law, the 'Rule of Law' is observed (though there is more to say regarding this concept below). Thus the Rule of Law is a guarantee that no state power is unrestricted power.

The German idea of the *Rechtsstaat* is one of the historically most important expressions of this idea. Originating in the nineteenth century, the theory developed of a differentiation between types of state, for example, those oriented towards policies of overall well-being according to the arbitrary discretion of their rulers, contrasted with those in which the pursuit of governmental ends was restricted in accordance with public law and respect for private rights. The latter, the state-under-law, is the *Rechtsstaat* (Bähr, 1864; Zippelius, 1985). This concept has in turn been exported to other linguistic and legal traditions as *Etat de Droit, Stato di Diritto*, and the like, but strangely lacks an English-language counterpart, perhaps because British constitutional usage avoids much reference to 'the state' as a concept at all, preferring to treat executive government as an emanation from 'the Crown', while legislation depends on a Parliament which was historically the rival of the Crown, not its partner, and the judiciary seek to distance themselves from both (Marshall, 1971; Chs. 5–7). The 'Rule of Law' is the politico-constitutional expression which perhaps comes nearest to capturing the type of value expressed by *Rechtsstaat*, but the continental terminology has the virtue of focusing on the quality of the concrete state which exists under the Rule of Law rather than on the purely abstract ideal state of affairs denoted by our term (MacCormick, 1984).

In any event, such a state (or such a state of affairs) is commonly and rightly assumed to be essential for securing the liberty and dignity of the individual. For there to be a state-under-law, there has to be law. That is, there have to be general rules of conduct, not particular instructions to individuals, and these general rules have to be published to the people they govern. They should be laid down by a legislature in advance of the cases they regulate, not made up by executive government in the process of governing. The government should be subject to the same rules as everyone else except when exercising powers clearly conferred by law, and subject to clear conditions and limits. People should be free from governmental interference in their lives except where clear powers are conferred and their exercise is reasonable and proportionate to the ends for which the power was conferred, and people should be free from state coercion except for clearly proven breaches of clearly preannounced laws providing for appropriate penalties or other forms of intervention. Those who exercise the different powers of the state should be distinct persons, and mutually independent in an institutional way, to ensure that each can to some extent check on the due performance of their functions by the others in the light of the authority actually conferred by law.

The legal structure envisaged in such a picture of the state clearly sees the political power exercised by state officials as dependent on legal grant. Hence it has to be envisaged that, in such a state, law sets a framework for the governing authorities, not just for those governed under law and subjected to the power of the state. The branch of law which concerns the establishment of governmental institutions for legislation, for execution and administration of law and the pursuit of public policy within law, and for adjudicating upon and enforcing allegations of punishable wrongdoing (crime) or remediable infringements of private or public right (civil law and administrative law), is of course constitutional law. Another important element in constitutional law in most modern countries, but not the UK, concerns the guaranteeing to individuals of fundamental human rights (civil and political rights, traditionally; nowadays social and economic rights to some extent as well). Since these are at their most important in setting limits to the legitimate power of any state official or agency, they properly belong in constitutional law as part of the limits on state power. (The UK, like most other members of the Council of Europe, is a full party to the European Convention for the Protection of Human Rights and Fundamental Freedoms, and hence affords its citizens judicial protection of their fundamental rights only through international, not domestic constitutional, tribunals.)

In most states, but not the UK, constitutional law, or its main part, is enshrined in a single documentary source (a 'written constitution'), and amendment of the provisions of the constitution is subject to special legislative processes making constitutional amendments more difficult to secure than the passage of ordinary laws. These arrangements have the effect of 'entrenching' any rights conferred on people in the constitution, and entrenching any elements of separation of power or other restrictions on power explicit or implicit in the constitution. Where such entrenchment is lacking, as in the UK, whose Parliament is held to be constitutionally sovereign, the protection of individuals may owe more to convention and to political tradition and the political process than to strict law. It becomes particularly important for politicians to give great weight to constitutional values, since the judges cannot second-guess them. But only a broadly based commitment to constitutionalism can then guarantee the *Rechtsstaat*.

Section II

The idea of a constitution is, as we have seen, that of a legal normative framework for the exercise of political power. A constitutional ordering, when duly observed, constitutes political power as legal authority, and can at the same time place restrictions and limits on the exercise of power. It has to be repeated, however, that constitutions are not merely normative frameworks for the exercise of political power, frameworks which determine who *may* exercise which powers, subject to what limits (limits which *ought* to or *must* be respected); they are also sources of *de facto* political power which can be exercised in defiance of those very limits. The two great American political scandals of Watergate and Irangate give vivid examples of this. The possession of constitutional authority was used as a source of political power which was then exercised in unconstitutional ways. (What must be added, of course, is that it was in each case through a triumph of American constitutionalism that the facts of the abuse of power were brought to public view within a relatively short time after their occurrence.)

A first working definition of 'constitutionalism' as a political creed or political virtue can be constructed on the basis of the argument so far. Constitutionalism is the creed according to which political power ought only to be exercised under constitutional provisions and subject to constitutional restrictions. For those who subscribe to such a creed, it is also a virtue − the virtue of exercising power and of conducting political debate in terms which fully respect and honour the constitution. It is probably uncontroversial that constitutionalism is a virtue in any case in which the constitution is accepted as a just and otherwise satisfactory framework for the polity and its politics. What is more controversial is whether constitutionalism remains a virtue even in the case of an unjust or imperfectly just constitution − for example, where voting rights are restricted on racial lines, or where certain political creeds or parties, or all but one creed or party, are proscribed under constitutional provisions. Is it in that case morally desirable or morally obligatory to restrict oneself to constitutionally permitted means for procuring amendment of the perceived (or, *a fortiori*, actual) injustice in the constitution?

Is constitutionalism an asymmetrical virtue? Do those who hold office or hold power under a constitution owe special duties of loyalty to it different from those (if any) which are incumbent on ordinary citizens? Is this relevant to the case of the partially unjust constitution? Or is it then specially incumbent on power holders to bend their powers and exceed their authority as, for example, Abraham Lincoln arguably did in procuring constitutional reforms and adjustments in the circumstances of civil war in the USA? The dangers of the argument that power holders may see dangers which only unconstitutional action can ward off have been made vivid by Watergate and Irangate. But the case of Lincoln does seem to pull the other way.

A possible response to this might be in terms of the direction, so to speak, of the illegality in question. It could be suggested that Lincoln's activities were bent towards removing injustice from the constitution, but not so Nixon's or Reagan's. The next step in the argument would then be to contend that the first working definition of constitutionalism as suggested above was too thin and formalistic. The point of the objection would be to deny that *any* organisation of power *whatsoever* should be acknowledged as a constitution, at any rate for the purposes of a theory of constitutionalism. This would be rather like a certain possible objection to Hans Kelsen's conception of the *Rechtsstaat*.

According to Kelsen, the state is the personification of the legal order, so necessarily every state is a *Rechtsstaat* (Kelsen, 1960, pp. 289–93, 314). But, it is objected, this leaves out of the account any qualitative stipulation as to the structure and content of the constitutional and legal order in view. Only given some material stipulations as to the form and content of the legal order can one accept the identification of state-as-legal-order with *Rechtsstaat* as political ideal (Zippelius, 1985, Section II, paras 3,30–4). Much the same may be said of constitutionalism: either as a creed or as a virtue (from the point of view of adherents to the creed), constitutionalism amounts to more than mere dedication to *any* constitutional arrangements of whatever sort. If the constitution were to say no more than that *quod principi placuit legis habet vigorem* (as in imperial Roman law, where it was said that 'what pleases the Emperor has the force of law'; in a more modern idiom, it might be that whatever pleases The Party or The Parliament has the force of law), there would hardly be any requirements of constitutionality to place limits on the exercise of power.

Historically, indeed, ideas such as those of constitutionalism or the *Rechtsstaat* developed precisely as doctrines about the limitation of potentially unrestricted despotic power. The despotism of a benevolent despot was, or at least might tend to become, not monarchical absolutism, but constitutional rule. The state, by autonomously restricting its exercise of its own powers, might become a *Rechtsstaat*. The demand that the state be a *Rechtsstaat* or that the monarchy be or become a constitutional monarchy, amounted to a demand, not merely that a constitution, however skeletal, be respected, but that a certain sort of constitutional framework and constraint be accepted in the state. The limits in question are well-known (MacCormick, 1984; O'Hagan, 1984).

First, there must be a differentiation of governmental powers into those of legislation, adjudication and execution, and different persons should be empowered (even, perhaps, by delegation from a single monarch) to exercise the legislative, adjudicative and executive powers of the state. This is a viable distinction only if it is acknowledged that legislation comprises exclusively the determination of general rather than individual norms and their issuance *prospectively* as guides to the conduct of the subjects (Vile, 1967). The 'issuance', naturally, has to be by way of general and open publication, or the notion of 'guidance' will lose all force. (It was a matter of subsequent elaboration of corrollaries to the basic doctrine which resulted in the addition of such notions as that enacted laws ought to remain reasonably constant in time and clear in their terms, and ought to be possible of performance and non-self-contradictory in effect (Fuller, 1969). Conversely, the power of judging ought to be restricted to the passing of judgement in implementation of the general and prospective norms enacted by the legislature. The rights of subjects under such norms ought not to be subject to executive interference or abrogation, either by the exercise of inherent ('prerogative') powers or under enacted law, except where such enactment satisfies the above noted restrictions.

Secondly, there should be adequate 'checks and controls' (to use the original form of the expression we now know as 'checks and balances') among the different branches of government and their separated powers. A state of permanent actual or potential tension between the branches of the state, with each remaining jealously watchful of any encroachment by another into its own proper prerogatives, is the best guarantee the subject can enjoy against the abuse of power. This will be all the more so if, through the institution of the jury, the ordinary subject is made a sharer in the power of judgement. By such means may government approximate to being 'free government'. As David Hume, a relatively early spokesman of this point of view put it:

The government which, in common appellation, receives the appellation of free, is that which admits of a partition of power among several members, whose united authority is no less, or is commonly greater, than that of any monarch; but who, in the usual course of administration, must act by general and equal laws, that are previously known to all the members, and to all their subjects. (Hume, 1963, 46, Book I, Essay 6)

Where such a form of government exists, the legislature

is obliged, for its own preservation, to maintain a watchful jealousy over the magistrates, to remove all discretionary powers, and to secure everyone's life and future by general and inflexible laws. No action must be deemed a crime but what the law has plainly determined to be such; no crime must be imputed to a man but from a legal proof before his judges; and even those judges must be his fellow-subjects, who are obliged, by their own interest, to have a watchful eye over the encroachments and violence of the ministers. (Hume, 1963, 10, Book I, Essay 2)

Finally, to press home the point, let us notice his words on constitutional checks and controls:

[A] republican and free government would be an obvious absurdity, if the particular checks and controls, provided in the constitution, had really no influence, and made it not the interest, even of bad men, to act for the public good. (Hume, 1963, 14, Book I, Essay 3)

Thirdly, as the two foregoing points suggest, there should be security for the subject in the enjoyment of rights, at least against fellow members of 'civil society', and also, indeed, against the supreme governing authority itself. But what rights? Here, there are two sharply opposed views: the first, that the rights whose security is guaranteed are themselves the products of the legal and constitutional order within which they are protected; the second, that the rights in question are in some sense anterior to, or more fundamental than, the constitutional order, with the corollary that a special function of constitutional order is to protect just such fundamental rights. A third, intermediate view, which supposes that constitutions may or must be based on custom and tradition, is that the same custom and tradition can be a source of customary rights as well as of constitutional order. Such customary (or 'common law') rights subsist independently of the exercise of legislative power under the constitution, and, although susceptible to amendment by legislation, ought to be respected under the prohibition on retrospectivity of enactments. Let us adopt the terms 'constitutionally derivative rights', 'fundamental rights' and 'customary rights' respectively to signify these views. Roughly speaking, one might assign the first view to Jeremy Bentham (Bentham, 1948, 1843; compare Twining, 1975), the second to John Locke (Locke, 1924) and the third to David Hume (Hume, 1963, 1975) or, perhaps, to A. V. Dicey (Dicey, 1968, pp. 206–83).

For present purposes, the significance of the difference between these views is that, on the theory of constitutionally derivative rights, there can be no unique set of rights whose secure protection is of the essence of constitutionalism (all that is required is secure enjoyment of those rights which are granted under constitutionally created norms), whereas, on the theory of fundamental rights, there has to be security in the relevant set of rights for constitutionalism to be observed. On the customary rights view, the question of which rights are to be protected is historically contingent, but the matter is not exclusively determined by the prior decision of the legislator (compare MacCormick and Weinberger, 1986, pp. 174–9). Constitutions such as those of the USA or of the Federal Republic of Germany, which entrench certain rights within their own provisions (or at least, in the American case, through foundational amendments of the constitution) are not proof of any particular theory. It is a theoretical question whether or not these rights have to be supposed to exist anterior to, independently of, and more fundamentally than, the constitution which guarantees their enjoyment (even to the point, in the German case, of exempting some of them from all possibility of abrogation by any process of constitutional amendment). That constitutional law requires certain rights to be treated as prior to all other parts of the constitution does not mean that these rights owe their existence to anything other than the constitution.

All things considered, the weakest constitutionalist assumptions are those made by the theory of constitutionally derivative rights. Yet, even on this weakest view, *some* security of rights is a requirement of constitutionalism. To avoid writing too many assumptions into our basic definitions, let us therefore now redefine constitutionalism in terms of this and the other two features above: constitutionalism is the creed according to which political power ought only to be exercised under constitutional provisions and subject to constitutional restrictions, where such restrictions include a separation of powers and its corollaries, effective checks and controls among the branches of government, and security at least of the rights allowed for by the theory of constitutionally derivative rights. As a virtue, it is the virtue of respecting the constitution and its limits in any situation in which a constitution of this kind exists.

Section III

At the beginning of the last section, we contemplated the possibility that there can be constitutions without (perfect) constitutionalism. Political or military or other leaders can use the power they derive from their constitutional authority to act outside, beyond or against the constitution. When this is done, especially when it is done with common knowledge, it is a practical necessity for there to be some legitimising ideology in support of what is done. Even the leader of a military coup has to lead the soldiery by their opinion, though the rest of the polity may be held simply in awe of armed might. Common experience suggests sundry possibilities – an appeal to traditional religious values (as against godless communism, perhaps), an appeal to the true values of the constitution against their corruption by previous ineffectual leaders, or such like. Most interesting for present purposes, however, would be the possibility of an appeal over the head of the constitution (so to speak) to 'the people' as a supreme authority. 'The people' for this purpose could be given a class connotation, as in an appeal to the working class against the oppressors, or an anti-colonialist one as in the case of an appeal to the people against external oppressors, or a nationalist one (and it is difficult to imagine an entire absence of nationalist appeal in any such case).

Such appeals seem always also to involve the use, or perhaps the abuse, of ideological appeals to some form of democratic ideals. When such upheavals occur, they may tend to be represented in some such terms as that the people as a whole are rising up against oppressors, or uniting their will with that of the charismatic leader – but, at the very least, the great majority is associated with what has been done. During the inquiries into the Irangate scandal, which involved illegal dealings between US and Iranian officials, the popular response to Colonel North's testimony before the joint congressional committee in the USA in 1987 for a period suggested that a 'democratic' appeal to 'American values' against myopic constitution-alism might almost have worked. The Bonapartist resort to the referendum as a direct appeal to the people above the bickerings of parliamentarianism and mere party democracy – an appeal used more recently, but once too often, by General de Gaulle – is almost another example, save that in de Gaulle's case a constitution itself authorised the appeal.

What we are here tendentiously referring to as 'democracy' is pure unfettered majority rule. Democracy in this sense of pure majoritarianism is clearly an anticonstitutionalist doctrine. Any doctrine of unlimited political power, indeed, would necessarily be anticonstitutionalist in the present understanding of constitutionalism. For we have defined constitutionalism explicitly in terms of the endorsement of certain sorts of constitutional restrictions on political power. There is no reason to amend this in the case of popular power. For popularly authorised, like any other, exercises of power can either be subjected to limits or not.

Tendentious as the majoritarian assumption may be, one might still suspect that, as ideal types, or, all the more, as political ideals, democracy and constitutionalism are fundamentally in conflict. If the most legitimate mode of political decision-making is by the people as a whole, with each member of the people counting as exactly the equal of every other, then it is not clear what can make legitimate the decision to impose restrictions of any sort on the decisions the people can take – not clear, for example, why their law-making power should be separated from the judicial power exercised in their name, especially given the well-known truth that general rules cannot decide individual cases, and its corollary that the exercise of judicial power inevitably involves at least an interpretative discretion. That being so, why should the people not be its own interpreter, acting by majority decision in problem cases, on the model of the old French *référé législatif*? (This was the provision requiring courts which found themselves facing problems of interpretation of the law codes to refer these back to the legislature for clarification, and thus avoid infringing the legislative power by deciding general points of interpretation for themselves.)

This argument implies a certain approach to the concept of democracy: namely as a system of government in which all the adult persons under the government are also participants in it, each having equal participatory rights with every other, and each having power to vote for, or to be elected as, a representative member of a govern-mental or legislative body. This is indeed a satisfactory initial working definition of the concept at this pre-interpretative stage of the inquiry; for it is reasonably susceptible of further interpretation along the lines of any one of the main contemporary interpretations of democracy in practical politics. (Compare, on the concept of 'interpretative concepts' borrowed here, Dworkin, 1986.) In the case of so hotly contested a concept, one can scarcely hope for more. On that understanding of the concept of democracy, one can certainly say that democracy in and of itself does not require constitutionalism, and probably that pure democracy would be incompatible with it.

Section IV

This view is contestable. It could be seriously counter-argued that the very idea of a constitution is itself intrinsically a democratic one. In 1791, Thomas Paine in *The Rights of Man* argued that there was only one true constitution then in the world, that of the USA, and but one other in the making, that of France. His thesis was that a constitution is that by which a people constitutes itself as a nation, and that such a thing had ever happened only in these two instances, by the revolutionary action of the people, casting off usurpers and oppressors, restoring each person to proper possession of natural rights, and constituting a polity by the united will of the sovereign people. Such a thing had to be done by the proper process of a constitutional convention or conventions brought together for that very purpose. Nothing else could give validity to a social compact as *pactum unionis*. By contrast, so-called constitutions like the British, albeit albeit deriving from the acts of 'convention parliaments' in the so-called 'Glorious Revolution' of 1688/9, were merely the customary terms and conditions for the exercise of a fundamentally usurped power, one imposed upon the people rather than deriving from it (Paine, 1984, pp. 68–109).

Paine's view, needless to say, had its own antecedents, quite apart from its grounding in American precedent – the precedent itself owing more than a little to the same intellectual antecedents. In sixteenth century Scotland, George Buchanan argued the case that the kingship of an unconquered people such as the Scots could only be a kingship by the consent and original election of the people acting through their representatives, their chief men; and, accordingly, the people retained a right of dismissal of kings who abused their constitutional authority descending into the position of tyrants (Buchanan, 1964; MacCormick, 1982, Ch. 4). A century later, and mediated through English republican and constitutionalist thought, a markedly similar doctrine recurs in John Locke's *Second Treatise of Civil Government*. And it is, of course, in Locke that one finds, alongside the doctrine of the original social contract, the doctrines of separation of powers, of checks and controls (in somewhat rudimentary form) and of fundamental rights – natural rights – as setting limits on legitimate governmental action. Locke, if anybody, is surely the first begetter of British constitutionalism (Locke, 1924, 2nd treatise, Chs. 8–13).

There are, however, two difficulties about any appeal to this tradition of thought as a secure foundation for the theory of constitutionalism as inherently and necessarily a *democratic* doctrine or virtue. The first difficulty concerns the essentially egalitarian quality of democracy as ideal and as a practice of government. It is notorious how inegalitarian the Lockean theory of natural rights is. The restrictions on governmental power in favour of every person's right to 'life, liberty and estate' lead to the possibility of a constitutionally required entrenchment of gross inequalities of fortune and thus of opportunity. Robert Nozick's recent re-elaboration of the political consequences of Lockean natural right in *Anarchy, State and Utopia* firmly underlines this point. It is hard indeed to turn the Lockean doctrine into any kind of unqualified democratic theory (MacPherson, 1962; Nozick, 1974).

The second set of difficulties is the formidable set raised by Hume against contractarian theories as such. There is no evidence anywhere, says Hume, of the agreeing of an original contract; even if there were, the binding character of such a contract already presupposes the institutions of civil society such as contract, so cannot explain them; further, the successor generations descending from the original contractors would, under ordinary contractual principles, not be bound by the original contract's terms. In any event, if there were anything in the contractarian theory, one would expect constitutional arrangements to be much more secure at the time of their first establishment than in later periods when the acts of initial consent and establishment had somewhat faded from people's minds. Yet the reverse is the case, he observes. The Hanoverian accession to the British Kingdom (in 1714) was at its most precarious, weak and vulnerable when it had been most recently agreed. Later, once hallowed by custom and long usage, it grew greatly stronger, as Hume pointed out (Hume, 1978, III.2.vii; 1963).

This line of thought was the basis for Edmund Burke's reply to Thomas Paine in the heated debate provoked in Great Britain by the Revolution in France in 1789. Some saw in it events paralleling those in the British kingdoms at the time of the Glorious Revolution − though Paine dismissed this contemptuously as no true precedent for revolution or constitution-making. Burke, for his part, rejected the analogy on the other ground: namely, that the events in Britain in 1688 had been a restoration of a traditional and established constitutional usage, consistent with respect for prior rights. The French, by contrast, were bent on a wholesale abandonment of all prior rights and traditions and a reconstitution initially of society upon *strictly rationalistic* terms. Exactly what Paine saw to celebrate in the French events, Burke saw in them to deplore (Burke, 1986, pp. 95−185).

Much of what Burke has to say is merely and complacently conservative, speaking for conservation of distinctions and inequalities no longer tolerable on any contemporary view, however conservative. Nevertheless, Hume and Burke and contemporary successors such as F. A. Hayek and Martin Krygier do make a very powerful point in urging the essentially traditional or customary quality of viable constitutional arrangements (Hayek, 1973, 1976, 1979; Krygier, 1986). The moment of founding a constitution, often after the trauma of revolutionary upheavals, often by a determined minority acting in the name of the people, rarely, if ever, with the support of anything more than a simple majority (and that often bitterly opposed by some now ousted minority) is rarely a moment of constitutional stability. Even when an agreed process for adopting a constitution through conventions (as in America in 1787−9) exists, the margins of success of the constitutional proposals may be fairly narrow − and, anyway, the accepted theory of constitution-making itself rests in a standing political and intellectual tradition, so the example is an imperfect counter-example to the theory of constitutions as grounded in custom and tradition.

Where, as in Spain in the post-Franco period, a process of constitutional change can be devised which utilises the pre-existing constitutional order, with all its abundant defects, the new order may be all the more secure for its also having roots in a prior one.

This doubtless also accounts for the stabilising effect of the monarchical element in the largely democratic constitutions of the constitutional monarchies of Europe. What is an imperfection from the point of view of a rigorously and purely democratic theory may nevertheless make a substantially democratic mode of government more securely workable in practice than any available alternative. It is the constitutional tradition that creates conditions for the possible florishing of democracy, not democracy that is a prerequisite for constitution-making

Section V

There may be a yet deeper interdependency of democracy and constitutionalism. For democracy, or people-power, to be an enduring feature of political order rather than a momentary and perhaps revolutionary spasm, it may well require the observance of constitutional order and the securing of a *Rechtsstaat* (compare O'Hagan, 1984, Ch. 6). And, conversely, the spirit of democratic government within a *Rechtsstaat* confirmed by standing tradition and custom may be a solid bulwark against the erosion of constitutional safeguards. Let us examine the reasons for this.

It may well be the case that in any political community or state, there can occur revolutionary moments in which, perhaps even without formal voting, there is convincing evidence of an overwhelming popular will for change. It was impossible for any interested observer not to be aware of this in the events of 1989, which saw so dramatically the ending of Communist government in Poland; its declamatory abolition in Wenceslas Square, Prague; its physical termination in East Germany by the bare hands of those who symbolically demolished the Berlin Wall; and other no less dramatic events elsewhere in Central and Eastern Europe. Such relatively unstructured but cumulatively overwhelming exercises of raw people-power were impressive and even moving to observe. Their authenticity as expressions of popular desire for change and of popular will to bring it about seemed indubitable, the clarity and scale of the majority preference for a new order seemed beyond question.

Experience equally teaches us, however, to beware of treating such moments as paradigmatic for the achievement of democratic government over the longer run. The problem is not just to secure that, when all the people (or the vast majority) are determined to bring about change, they can do so. In ordinary circumstances, it is essential that each can contribute equally to the deliberation about change and thereafter to the forming of the majority will. It is not enough that all should decide; it is important that each is the equal of every other when it comes to deliberating and deciding. At least, each adult citizen (or perhaps each adult resident) of a state should have, in principle, an equal opportunity with every other to participate in political processes. The direct democracy of the old Greek city-states or Swiss cantons (or their direct partial democracy, considering all those who were or are in fact excluded from voting and all else) is impossible in the far larger-scale societies which comprise most modern states. So elaborate electoral laws and systems are required to secure fair equality of involvement, or equality of opportunity to get oneself involved if one chooses, in political processes. There have to be elaborate and highly debatable provisions about access to, and absence of undue influence on, media of mass-communication in relation to political debate and electioneering. Even if recourse to the referendum became easier and more common in practice through electronic media, the devising of fair rules for these would be no less problematic and elaborate.

Further, citizens have to have security in their persons and their private relations, and in enjoyment of at least some kinds of property, if they are to have the personal independence which gives them any decent chance of being authentic contributors to public debate and decision-making. They must have those guarantees against improper state interference with their life or liberty that are summed up in such phrases as 'due process of law', and are at the heart of *Rechts-staat* and Rule of Law. They must not be economically destitute, or perhaps even so economically disadvantaged against better-off fellow-citizens as to have no effective public voice. Their rights to form parties and associations with like-minded fellows must be protected by means which ensure that one person's freedom of association does not become another's source of bullying or intimidation.

Even so sketchy a listing of requirements for securing the longer-run durability of democracy, understood as securing political power to the people on terms of fair equality for each of the people, indicates the necessity for securing at least traditional civil and political rights, and most likely also some of the more controversial social and economic rights as well. Just what mix of these is required will plainly be a highly debatable question. How far freedom of speech and other basic freedoms necessitate market arrangements to prevent state abuse of monopoly powers; how far state intervention in the market is required to correct for social and economic inequalities that create gross differentials in the value of the freedoms involved for different individuals and classes – these are among the profoundest questions about the possibility of establishing and guaranteeing democracy (See Dahl, 1989).

Such questions are also fundamental to the construction of constitutions, and essential to the earlier developed conception of constitutionalism, even on the comparatively weak version which admits constitutionally derivative rights to be sufficient for the basic idea. The advantage of insisting on rights as constitutionally derivative is, as we now see, that this leaves them in the end subject to democratic processes. It is by the people's decision that each of its members holds the very rights which are necessary to guaranteeing the authenticity of the popular will and its fair formation. Thus it is to the people as a whole that belongs the decision about the exact specification of those rights, and about the other essential elements of constitutional structure and distribution of constitutional authority. In this way democracy acquires a self-referential character, and determines its own conditions of operation, in determining the adoption or amendment of constitutional provisions.

But what if self-referentiality should self-destruct? What if amendments strip aliens or unpopular minorities of the very rights that in some form are essential to democracy? What if demagogic leaderships or military adventurers lead majorities to cast aside the constraints that make majority rule durable while majorities may change? Entrenchment of constitutional rights (and other provisions) through a constitutional requirement of super-majorities for constitutional amendment is the leading modern compromise on this point. The introduction of international Human Rights covenants and conventions, with (in some areas) tribunals effectively to back them up, has provided in various settings an external guarantee for internal rights.

Thus the requirements of fair and durable majority rule acquire the backing of a wider (if far from perfectly democratic) majority. Reliance to a like end on political tradition and parliamentary-constitutional values has been advocated, especially in the UK, and is no doubt vitally present even where entrenching provisions are also in force. Tradition and custom can reinforce the idea of certain rights as fundamental at least to *our* way of governing ourselves (for any given 'us'), and thus can inhibit rash amendment or unfair minority-baiting, even where the absence of formal entrenchment makes amendment as simple as ordinary law-reform. Rights can thus assume a quasi-fundamental character even where there is controversy (among those who participate at all in theoretical debates) over the possibility or otherwise of grounding rights in any fundamental way in divine or natural law, or in the natural order of things, or in the character of free society, or in human nature or basic human values of an essentially self-evident sort.

It is no doubt paradoxical that the upshot of reflection on the conditions for enduring democracy seem to involve crucial resort to non-majoritarian modes of decision-making on key matters. For the acknowledgment of the possibility of internal or external guarantees for basic rights through constitutional entrenchment or international convention entails resort to judicial tribunals for determination of alleged or threatened infringements of such rights. The amendment power no doubt subjects such decision-making to a final popular appeal in theory; but, in practice, judges have to take some of the fundamental decisions about the interpretation and application of any current (and often, in practice, very long-enduring) charter or bill or convention defining basic rights. To that extent, the conditions for securing democracy require and justify some trade-off against purely or abstractly democratic principles.

But there is another side to this. For the endurance of any con-stitution appears everywhere to depend in the longer run on a popular commitment to it among the citizens of a state as the accepted and acceptable structure of the state's government. The revolutions of 1989 again remind us how even powerful and long-enduring organ-isations of state coercion and ideological hegemony fall before radical popular dissent. Thus democracy may not only require constitution-alism, but may be at the same time the best guarantee of it in the long run. The relationship appears to be one of reciprocal dependency after all.

It was remarked in the opening paragraphs of this chapter that many now regard the UK as seriously anomalous among contem-porary constitutionalist and democratic states. A simple-majority electoral system with first-past-the-post elections to parliamentary constituencies, a Parliament with theoretical power to make or unmake any law it chooses, a parliamentarily based Prime Minister and Cabinet supported by party discipline and efficient whipping in the House of Commons, and an absence of any radical power of judicial review, coupled with a legally backed and stringent tradition of official secrecy, have all combined to generate what a former Conservative Lord Chancellor calls a system of 'elective dictatorship' (Hailsham, 1978). On the other hand, the perils of judicial review and entrenched rights within the British judicial systems have been highlighted by a Scots law lord who formerly held office in a Labour administration (McCluskey, 1987). Reliance on political custom and parliamentary tradition is considered by some the best available safeguard of democracy and constitutional order within a constitutional monarchy enjoying a long record of substantial if never perfect democratic government.

This is not the place to embark upon the substance of the arguments for or against radical change in the UK, much though the present author is personally committed to such change. But current debates and discussions in the local setting may help to give the more abstract issues of constitutionalism and democracy a livelier edge, at least for a British reader.

However that may be, it needs to be acknowledged that democratic government is indeed a difficult mode of government to set up and sustain. The contemporary world reveals a sad plurality of failed experiments, as well as some considerable successes, all well short of perfection. It does seem that democracy works only where there is some form of well-established constitutional order drawing on a constitutional tradition of some serious standing, where the constitutional order utilises the separation of powers (to that extent removing adjudication from the democratic area save to the extent of possible recourse to jury-trials) and where the security at least of constitutionally derivative rights is firmly upheld. In this sense, constitutionalism is a prerequisite for democracy. It may, indeed it does, impose limits on absolute majoritarianism and absolute egalitarianism. In that sense, constitutionalist democracy is perhaps imperfect democracy; it acknowledges fundamental goods only in part derivable from the concept of democracy itself, and insists that the values of democratic decision-making must sometimes yield to these other goods. It is democracy qualified, not democracy pure and simple. It seems, however, to be the only viable conception of democracy.

References

Bähr, O. (1864), *Der Rechtsstaat*, Berlin.

Bentham, J. (1948), *A Fragment on Government*, Ed. W. Harrison, Oxford: Basil Blackwell.

Bentham, J. (1843), *Anarchical Fallacies*, in J. Bowring (Ed.), *Works*, Vol. II, Edinburgh.

Buchanan, G. (1964), *De Iure Regni apud Scotos*, tr. D. H. MacNeill as *The Art and Science of Government among the Scots*, Glasgow: William MacLellan Ltd.

Burke, E. (1986), *Reflections on the Revolution in France*, Ed. Conor Cruise O'Brien, Harmondsworth: Penguin Classics ed.

Dahl, R. (1989), *Democracy and its Critics*, New Haven, Conn.: Yale University Press.

Dicey, A. V. (1968), *Introduction to the Study of the Law of the Constitution*, 10th ed., Ed. E. C. S. Wade, London: Macmillan & Co.

Dworkin, R. (1986), *Law's Empire*, London: Fontana Books, and Cambridge, Mass.: Harvard University Press.

Fuller, L. L. (1969), *The Morality of Law*, revised ed., New Haven, Conn.: Yale University Press.

Hailsham, Lord (1978), *The Dilemma of Democracy: Diagnosis and Prescription*, London: Collins.

Hayek, F. A. (1973, 1976, 1979), *Law, Legislation and Liberty* (3 Vols), London: Routledge and Kegan Paul.

Hume, D. (1963), *Essays Moral, Political, and Literary*, Oxford: Oxford University Press.

Hume, D. (1975), *Enquiries concerning Human Understanding and concerning the Principles of Morals*, 3rd ed., Ed. L. A. Selby-Bigge and P. H. Nidditch, Oxford: Oxford University Press.

Hume, D. (1978), *A Treatise of Human Nature*, 2nd ed., Ed. L. A. Selby-Bigge and P. H. Nidditch, Oxford: Oxford University Press.

Kelsen, H. (1960), *Reine Rechtslehre*, 2nd ed., Vienna: Franz Deuticke.

Krygier, M. (1986), 'Law as Tradition', *Law and Philosophy*, 5: 237.

Locke, J. (1924), *Two Treatises of Civil Government*, Ed. W. Harrison.

McCluskey, J. (1987), *Law, Justice, and Democracy*, London: Sweet and Maxwell, BBC Publications.

MacCormick, N. (1982), *Legal Right and Social Democracy*, Oxford: Oxford University Press.

MacCormick, N. (1984), 'Der Rechtsstaat und die rule of law', *Juristenzeitung*, 39: 65–70.

MacCormick, N. and Weinberger, O. (1986), *An Institutional Theory of Law*, Dordrecht: D. Reidel Publishing Co.

MacPherson, C. B. (1962), *The Political Theory of Possessive Individualism*, Oxford: Oxford University Press.

Marshall, G. (1971), *Constitutional Theory*, Oxford: Oxford University Press (Clarendon Law Series).

Nozick, R. (1974), *Anarchy, State and Utopia*, Oxford: Basil Blackwell.

O'Hagan, T. (1984), *The End of Law?*, Oxford: Basil Blackwell.

Paine, T. (1984), *Rights of Man*, Ed. E. Foner and H. Collins, Harmondsworth: Penguin Classics ed.

Raz, J. (1979), *The Authority of Law: Essays on Law and Morality*, Oxford: Oxford University Press.

Twining, W. (1975), 'The contemporary significance of Bentham's Anarchical Fallacies', *Archiv für Rechts- und Sozialphilosophie*, 61: 325–45.

Vile, M. J. C. (1967), *Constitutionalism and the Separation of Powers*, Oxford: Oxford University Press.

Zippelius, R. (1985), *Allgemeine Staatslehre*, 9th ed., Munich: Verlag C. H. Beck.

Feminism

Feminism is currently dominated by massive intellectual and political realignments focused on the concept of equality. This essay seeks to chart these sea changes from a somewhat critical perspective.

Feminism would not exist without the idea of equality. At all the key moments of feminist eruption in the modern age, equality has been there, a crucial touchstone for the claims of women. In the late eighteenth century, the birth of modernity and liberalism found Mary Wollstonecraft asserting women's claims to equal standing with men as citizens on the basis that they were just as rational as men (Wollstonecraft, 1792/1989). In the late nineteenth century, women's equal status once again appeared on the agenda in a series of legislative campaigns around marriage, property, legal person-hood and the vote. John Stuart Mill (1869/1966) and Harriet Taylor (1850) championed the cause of women in the context of a utilitarian liberalism that deplored the irrational survival of traditional forms of social division. In the second half of the twentieth century − another period of liberal expansion, now highly committed to welfarist governmental policies − the language of equality and inequality once again provided a basic vocabulary and a minimal programme of legal reform adopted by feminists of all political persuasions, liberal, radical, socialist and Marxist.

Yet today, any such feminist reliance on the discourse of equality has been fundamentally called into question, charged with harbouring a fleet of masculinist presumptions. The central theme in these con-demnations is that equality talk accepts man as the measure of all things. Consequently, any theorisation or politics of women framed in terms of redressing inequality will inevitably end up reaffirming and embedding masculinity as the norm. Its rationality is condemned as a male rationality, in some accounts traced back to Aristotle (MacKinnon, 1987; Okin, 1987), while in others characterised as a thoroughly modern masculinity (Naffine, 1990; Smith, 1987). These failings are evidenced in arenas as 'high' as political theory and as 'low' as everyday life – and especially in the routine operations of the courts and tribunals where the equality legislation of the 1960s and 1970s plays out its losing hand.

These critiques of equality talk dominate feminism today. They are not without internal divisions, especially around the question of whether it is acceptable to posit some alternative woman's perspective that is generically different from masculinity. They are not without external critics either: thus, on the one hand, there are feminists who continue to use the equality perspective – and at some level all do – and, on the other hand, there are anti-essentialist feminists who doubt the monolithic masculinity asserted in these critiques. But the fact remains that all feminists now have to address these issues.

To understand these debates, I shall argue that it is necessary to focus on one particular version of equality-talk: *sex discrimination*, precisely the concept of inequality embodied in the now much maligned equality legislation of the 1960s and 1970s, and also in the everyday term 'sexism'. Law and common parlance come together here in a definition of equality/inequality that focuses on comparisons and contrasts, double standards and unfair differentiations. Formally stated, such discrimination thinking is framed in terms of three basic themes. *First*, it defines inequality as an impropriety in the uniform and even application of given rules, standards and norms. The inspiring principle is that correct decision-making consists in treating like cases alike, thus affirming formal justice and the rule-of-law ideal which casts the principle that all persons are equal before the law in terms of abstract rules and standardised 'fact-situations' (see Chapter 3 by Bańkowski in this volume for analysis of this conception of equality). Then, *second*, the cause and origin of biased decision-making is sought in external factors, coming in from the outside to disrupt the otherwise proper and normal pattern of rule-application. The source of these intrusions may be seen simply in terms of sexist motives and attitudes of individual decision-makers, or diagnosed more grandly in terms of the contaminating appearance of social factors. 'Society' is always assumed to belong properly outside (see Kingdom, 1980/1991). Essentially, then, all deviations and departures from the rules are conceptualised as extrinsic contingencies that can therefore be corrected without disrupting the internal logic of any specific context of modern decision-making, whether it be hiring or promoting someone for a job, awarding them academic marks, or working out their status as a DSS claimant. Finally, the *third* element in discrimination thinking is that it is primarily oriented to the public domain loosely defined to include citizenship, more ambiguously the fields of employment and commercial relations ('the market', which can also count as 'private' from the point of view of state regulation) as well as access to public places (see Chapter 5 by Holmwood for a discussion of this issue).

This general framework for conceptualising bias corresponds very closely to the way sex discrimination is defined in law through the legislation that was introduced in the 1960s and 1970s. In the UK, unlawful sex discrimination is the less favourable treatment of a woman than a man where this differentiation is made purely on the grounds of sex and is unjustifiable on those grounds. The test of discrimination is to compare the woman's treatment with the way a man, real or hypothetical, was or would be treated in a comparable situation (the 'male comparator' test). A discriminating intention is required, although it need not be openly manifested but may be inferred from the circumstances. Sex discrimination is legally recognised both in a direct form in which sex-related factors have been directly involved or in an indirect form where some other factor is discriminatory in its effects as tending to privilege one sex at the expense of the other. This legislation, together with equal pay legislation – which for the purposes of this chapter will be grouped together under the general heading of anti-sex-discrimination law – covers employment, education and access to goods and services. It does not apply to interpersonal relationships outside these areas nor to statutory provisions covering welfare and taxation. This legislation was introduced during the same period as anti-race-discrimination legislation, both in Britain and the US. In Britain the Equal Opportunities Commission and the Race Relations Board (now the Commission for Racial Equality) were set up as parallel bodies.

To focus on sex discrimination may seem unduly narrow. As a term of political discourse, it does not exactly have the grandeur of the great principles of Liberty, Equality and Justice but represents these concerns in a highly circumscribed form. As a term of feminism, sex discrimination is remarkably mute on deep causal questions of power and patriarchy, focusing instead on immediate visible differentiations in the treatment of men and women. As the inspiration of reform, sex discrimination thinking seems to have been inscribed almost from the start with a series of set-piece problems – about balancing formal and substantive equality, about the conflict between principles and policies, about the persistence of sexist attitudes and the structures of dual or segmented labour markets, and the wider split between the family and the market. Yet this low-level, practical and pragmatic domain of anti-sex-discrimination analysis and action has undergone a huge transformation in status so that it now stands as the key, if negative, exemplar of equality talk.

One reason for the importance of anti-sex-discrimination discourse is the reaction against years of attempting to use the law itself. There finally comes a point where the quantitative accumulation of known difficulties flips over into a qualitative rejection of the whole approach as not only a failed solution but actually part of the problem. One writer (Smart, 1989) has thus even coined the term 'juridogenic', as a parallel to 'iatrogenic' in the world of medicine (illness caused by medical intervention), to characterise the way that law's remedies actually contribute to furthering women's oppression.

While feminism has always made a special claim to link theory and practice, the current wave of anti-equality critiques forges such connections at a quite exalted level. Thus the names Aristotle, Marx, Weber, Kant and Freud, Habermas and Rawls are regularly coupled with legal terms such as 'the male comparator test', while one of the important internal debates, the 'equality v. difference' debate, does not make sense without a grounding in the legal context of 'special rights'. And, as I hope to show here, it is the specific thematic of anti-sex-discrimination thinking – the even and uniform application of abstract general rules, standards and norms – that is identified as the heartland of embedded masculinity.

However, the significance of these theory–practice links may all too easily be misconstrued through a 'top down' approach that treats the anti-sex-discrimination focus simply as the concrete realisation of a general principle of equality. Such an approach makes no distinction between different versions of equality. The 'practice' associated with anti-sex-discrimination discourse is crudely conceived as the world of 'action'. Often the principle of equality is simply identified with liberalism and feminist use of equality talk is correspondingly labelled 'liberal feminism' and assigned to an era of the 1960s and 1970s to be neatly succeeded by Marxist and radical feminism. Current critiques of equality talk are then understood as arising from a later appreciation of the need to go 'wider' than the sphere of law and government and 'deeper' to look for underlying causes of oppression. The problems of the legislation may even be portrayed in the genre of innocence and experience as starry eyed, naive liberal feminists come to learn the hard lessons of how deeply entrenched masculinity it. I shall be arguing against such foundationalist narratives of positions. They present an overly simplistic picture of both feminism and liberalism and they fail to represent that what is centrally at stake here is as much modernity as liberalism.

Feminism and liberalism

Equality talk is very much associated with the feminism that emerged in the late 1960s and early 1970s. As a simple description of how feminism *used* notions of equality, I cannot do better than to summarise an account by Virginia Held (1989, pp. 215–17). She gives a very good sense of the ethos and manoeuvres involved in equality talk, and thus provides excellent raw material for subsequent discursive analysis. But whether or not this adds up to the picture of an era of liberalism, as Held presents it, is another matter.

Held begins: 'In the early 1970s, women began to be aware of the degree to which they had been excluded from the liberal principles of freedom and equality by which the systems they lived claimed to be guided.' Even in the texts of the 'founding fathers', Locke and Rousseau, these declarations of the Rights of Man turned out to be all too literal in their proclamations of the freedom and equality of all men. In underlining the sex disqualification hidden behind apparent universalism, feminists of the 1970s were in fact showing a third reservation on top of the 'racial exclusions and property qualifications' already noted by previous critiques – yet even these previous critiques, although sensitised to the question of hidden bias, did not note the omission of women in the 'picture drawn by the founding principles of democracy'. Women's exclusion was itself symptomatically excluded from notice.

The term 'democracy' summons up the key issue of the vote and women's suffrage. Feminists in the late 1960s and 1970s were confronted with a double problem. On the one hand, the fact that they had gained the vote was widely taken to mean that all the problems of women's participation in a democracy had been settled at a stroke.

On the other hand, despite this centrality accorded the vote as the sum of democracy, the fact that in Switzerland women in 1970 still were not entitled to vote had not posed any problems for its recognition as a democratic country.

Held turns next to other aspects of public life from which women have been officially excluded. 'As women began to look at all the ways they did not enjoy equality, glaring inequities leapt into view. When women tried to enter the professions, they found the doors to medical school or law school either completely closed to them or open only a sliver.' Advancement in these professions was blocked either by 'blatant hostility or outright barriers'.

Next in Held's list are disparities around pay 'even for the same kind of work when they were permitted to do it', certainly for the kind of employment designated 'women's work' and no pay at all for that great maw of unpaid domestic labour in running the household and bringing up children. She then turns to note women's absence from all positions of power and influence, from political representation at higher levels to all major institutions. 'Women could see how unmistakably and routinely they were denied the equal opportunity proclaimed to be a fundamental value of liberal society.'

Behind this lack of inequality was discovered the inegalitarian background assumption that women had to choose between career or family, but not both – strikingly different from the lives of men who were naturally assumed to be able to combine the two. Indeed, taking this scrutiny further into the 'private' domain other striking inequalities and double standards emerged in expectations about household and family roles and standards of sexual morality. 'And women became increasingly aware that if they really are to enjoy equal opportunities and equal respect, absolutely enormous changes are going to have to be made in the way societies structure occupations, public institutions and the family.'

Indeed, even the principle of liberty could be scrutinised from the point of view of equality, for it suddenly emerged that, in various ways, men's freedoms and women's freedoms were radically different. Freedom as non-interference (Berlin's 'negative liberty' (1969)) on the one hand, licensed domestic tyranny in the name of privacy yet, on the other hand, presupposed substantial resources not available to women.

Clearly feminist use of equality talk did involve a critique of liberalism in its own terms. But which liberalism, and what equality? –

F

and was it only liberal feminists who invoked these terms of reference? There is a key problem in presenting equality as an obvious principle of liberalism. Equality must be, in fact, one of the most contested concepts within liberalism. Or to put the same point a different way, there are many different versions of liberalism and their differences can be seen particularly clearly in relation to how they construe equality. In fact, the very feminist discourse that Held describes invokes two quite different concepts of equality and, correspondingly, two quite different versions of liberalism.

The first is the classic liberalism signified by the texts of the social contract theorists, Locke and Rousseau, the 'founding fathers', as Held locates them, chronologically, philosophically and textually the first. The kind of equality at stake here concerns basic 'membership rights' in the public community of the polity, the right to count as a person or 'unit' in civil society, a citizen and consequently entitled to enjoy all the other recognitions of civil 'personhood' that follow from that, such as the right to enter into contracts or to assign property. These could be called 'ontological' rights, since they concern one's existence as a socially and legally recognised being, a 'bearer of rights and duties'. There is no doubt that this discourse of equality stands on the very threshold of modernity. This notion of equality is set up *against*, and as rejection of, previous modes of defining civil existence through the hierarchy of feudal/traditional orders according to inherited status and property. Thus when Wollstonecraft attacked Edmund Burke in *A Vindication of the Rights of Men* (1790/1989) she sought to promote the equal claim to liberty that each human person enjoyed through participation in the capacity of reason. Any other basis for participation in public political life – and specifically claims based on the partiality of inheritance-based privilege and landed property – was to be rejected. In *A Vindication of the Rights of Women* (1792/1989) Wollstonecraft goes on to articulate what is probably the first feminist critique of liberalism 'in its own terms'. Here her target is her fellow radical, Rousseau, whom she accuses of betraying his own principles in continuing to accept women's 'natural' exclusion – and 'exclusion' is precisely the right word here – in the private domain of the family, so that women had no claims to citizenship rights. Where Rousseau had otherwise recognised the role of society and convention in forming humans, this lesson was somehow forgotten in the case of women for whom, it seemed, all the arguments of tradition could still be accepted.

The focus on women's exclusion from the public domain of rights – in turn equated with the survival of archaic traditions in the midst of the modern world – has long continued to be a feminist theme, developed as recently as 1988 in Carol Pateman's *The Sexual Contract*. But though Mary Wollstonecraft may well be labelled a 'liberal feminist', in the early 1970s the great text continuing these forms of critique was written by the radical feminist, Kate Millett. *Sexual Politics*, published in 1970, could with the advantage of two centuries make even greater play of the archaic survival of tradition in the midst of modernity and even go on to demolish the great myth of Whig history in which, however slowly, the movement of history is consistently going forward in a grand narrative of progress. On the contrary, one of the key points of her book was that progress for women had reached its height in the mid- to late-nineteenth century and had subsequently gone backward, especially in the post-war era of the twentieth century. But Millett also shifted analysis away from the classic texts of political theory to the sociological register. She took the definition of the tradition/modernity distinction not so much from Locke and Rousseau as from Weber. At the same time, she sought to legitimise the nascent women's movement through the leverage of recognition already accorded the civil rights movement:

In America recent events have forced us to acknowledge at last that the relationship between the races is indeed a political one which involves the general control of one collectivity, defined by birth, over another collectivity, also defined by birth. Groups who rule by birthright are fast disappearing, yet there remains one ancient and universal scheme for the domination of one birth group by another – the scheme that prevails in the area of sex. The study of racism has convinced us that a truly political state of affairs operates between the races to perpetuate a series of oppressive circumstances. The subordinated group has inadequate redress through existing political institutions, and is deterred thereby from organizing into conventional struggle and opposition.

Quite in the same manner, a disinterested examination of our system of sexual relationship must point out that the situation between the sexes now, and throughout history, is a case of that phenomenon Max Weber defined as *herrschaft*, a relationship of dominance and subordinance. (Millett, 1970/1976, pp. 24–5)

There is cultural modernity at stake here as well. Millett seeks to show up the embarrassing realities that undermine the self-image of the age as the triumph of science and rational knowledge over superstitious fear and bigotry. It is no accident that desegregation in education became such a civil rights issue, for in education are invested all the values supposedly imparted by 'universal' literacy.

Yet, for all the rhetorical power of this focus on the gap between the foundations and origins of modern society and the anomalous status of women marooned on an island of traditionalism, it needs asking what exact commitment to equality is entailed in recognising women equally as members of civil society in the classic conception? The answer is 'not all that much'. For the classic liberal focus on key membership rights is no more than laissez-faire individualism of freedom of contract and the market. This is a vision perfectly compatible with the most conservative free-market libertarianism. From this perspective, equality is certainly not a goal to be pursued independently from liberty as embodied in individual rights to freedom. Sufficient equality is installed already in removing the impediments to free action by, on the one hand, abolishing traditional status restrictions while, on the other hand, refusing to recognise as free any transactions involving force and coercion, fairly narrowly defined. So long as all individuals are allowed the same access and are not coerced, they are equal. Such equality is thus seen as secondary, a precondition or side-effect of liberty sufficiently embodied in the market principles of fair dealing and 'commutative justice' in individual transactions. In addition, it is sometimes argued that the free market model also involves a faith that the workings of the market will ultimately produce some deserts-oriented form of justice in which input (variously defined as skills, effort, ingenuity) will ultimately realise its just return. But, in all guises, the *direct* pursuit of equality is perceived as in conflict with the principle of liberty and, on this view, must not be recognised separately. Thus any depiction of feminist concerns that describes women's position simply in terms of the anomaly of a traditional partriarchalism to be brought in line with these basic principles of modernity may score high in terms of the scandal of survivals but will not actually advance women's position very far.

It would hardly be surprising if current feminists found this version of liberalism somewhat lacking − indeed it was found deficient in the equality era itself. For the 1960s and 1970s was very much a time when classic individualistic liberalism was under intense scrutiny across the board, very much including from within liberalism itself. The politics of the civil rights movement in the US (in Britain it was the politics of class and poverty) had already underlined very clearly how inadequate it was merely to remove traditional exclusions. This was a period when 'welfarist' concepts of justice were gaining huge ground and the state was increasingly called upon to pursue collective social goals for the betterment of all. The political horizon was shifting away from the past and towards the future — the kind of society one was striving to create.

Many different sorts of text sought to disrupt that endless, back-ward-looking fascination with the classical problem of the 'break' between traditional and modern society and to see the twentieth century as a historical reality rather than a textbook ideal frozen in the image that classical liberalism had made of the 'free market'. Social studies of poverty, housing and education thus emphasised the types of reforms that were needed to produce a truly egalitarian society while legal theorists such as Atiyah (1979) sought to show what a short-lived thing laissez-faire individualism had actually been, undermined since the late nineteenth century both by statutory controls on what employers could ask of employees (the Factories Acts onwards) and by the growth of tort law with its requirements about manufacturers' unwritten duties to consumers (crucially *Donoghue* v. *Stevenson*). In the name of health and safety, it was clear that many inroads had already been made into the classical 'freedoms'.

The conflicts between welfarist and classic liberal individualism are well known — the clash between individual rights with minimal state intervention as against the instrumental pursuit of collective goals and maximalist state planning. The dilemmas are posed nowhere more clearly than in Ronald Dworkin's attempts to reconcile the policy-oriented, welfarist goals of civil rights legislation with the doctrine that individual rights are and should be the 'trump card' of modern legal and political discourse (1977b). Out of such polarisations arose certain 'halfway house' arguments. For example, attention was paid to the hidden conditions of the possibility of exercising rights and, correspondingly, to the development of the notion of 'enabling rights', i.e. rights (such as the right to housing) that would ensure that equal formal rights also meant equal real rights to act as autonomous beings: freedom and equality were reconceptualised in terms of preconditions. Thus the liberalism of this era was very much the middle course represented by the familiar positions of modern political theory, notably Raz (1972), Dworkin (1977a) and

Rawls (1972). In other words, many of the arguments that Held puts at the end of the equality story, were in fact constitutive of the era.

Such is the background to anti-discrimination as a particular version of equality talk. Sex discrimination legislation − like the position of most of the liberal theorists reflecting that era − is best seen as a *compromise formation*. On the one hand, it had the 'policy' goal of seeking to achieve genuine social justice. On the other hand, it also sought to appease classic liberalism by not making social goals so paramount that they overrode individual rights. In fact this legislation clearly did increase state intervention into the (already much eroded) 'privacy' of ongoing market relations between employer and employee, buyer and seller, but it did so in a form that was designed to be acceptable to more classically oriented liberalism. Although it went far beyond the task of removing exclusions, sex disqualifications and formal bars to entry into the market and the 'public' domain − most of which had been done already − discrimination could still be described in the language of exclusion, as an informal bar, thus preserving the language of the classics even while increasing the degree of internal regulation. (This is not mere sophistry: on the contrary, the formation of the EC 'free market' has given fresh life to the question of whether anti-discrimination legislation simply allows classic free access to the market by removing a barrier to entry or, on the contrary, should count as a form of active intervention within it (see Carter, 1993).) But, crucially, the language of formal justice, like treatment and uniform standards, mimicked the classic rule-of-law ideal. The outcome was that the social goal of substantive future equality between the sexes was to be pursued through the means of formal equality.

The 1970s were far from unique or totally novel in using formal justice as the technique for effecting compromise and negotiated consensus. On the contrary, this has been the consistent role that formal justice has played in modern politics and government. Unger describes the rule of law as a power-broking balance curbing the power of the aristocracy and the working classes and hence coming out in net favour of the bourgeoisie (Unger, 1976). In somewhat different terms, writers as diverse as Hayek (1974), Weber (1954) and Fuller (1964) have described how the technique of treating like cases alike produces a neat convergence of instrumentality, public order, efficiency, and predictability, on the one hand, and a certain ethical component of justice as fairness on the other. Formal justice is substantively rational.

Thus it must be obvious that the 'equality era' of feminism cannot be understood simply as a liberal feminist engagement with the liberal individualism of the classic texts of Locke, Hobbes and Rousseau. Emphasis on the classic 'big break' between traditional and modern societies, playing off the images of the modern age, its cultural values and guiding principles, against existing realities, has been a standard ploy adopted by all feminists, of whatever 'branch' or persuasion. If this discourse is superficial and uncommitted then that superficiality has also provided an important mechanism for overcoming rifts within feminism and forging alliances with the politics of race and class. Yet, even more important, there is an enormous difference between this classic liberalism and the revisionist liberalism of the 1970s.

The inauguration of anti-sex-discrimination discourse within feminism also set off a series of internal developments that can best be described as a form of 'split-mindedness'. Thus, at one level, the notion of equal treatment and uniform standards was applied far, far wider than the areas covered by legislation. As Held describes, what began with equal pay and employment was extended to the family and personal life, where even morality was assessed in terms of 'double standards'. Social life in its entirety was relentlessly reduced to the terms of fairness and unfairness where women were not treated identically to men. Sex discrimination also provided the motif for judging academic disciplines, all to be scrutinised in terms of whether the same standards of arguments and scholarship were applied to the study of women and men. Taking off from the literality of law, this immensely proliferated extrapolation of sex-discrimination thinking became the norm, subjecting all apects of human life, and everything from sociology to literature, to the prism of description in terms of bias. Under this levelling gaze, all forms of knowledge and living could be assessed in terms of a generalised legalism that could be applied anywhere.

By contrast, the pragmatics of anti-discrimination legislation in its own, more circumscribed, milieu went in the opposite direction, to a sense of ever more closure. From very early on, it was recognised that the motives behind the legislation were not necessarily high idealism. The origins of the European commitment to equal treatment of the sexes lay in the 1950 Treaty of Rome and was, notoriously, born less of a wish to recognise women's equal status than fear that cheap female labour might undercut the going rate of pay as fought for by trades unions. Marx's thesis of women as a reserve army of labour was very much accepted in the conventional economics of the European Community. Nonetheless there were important advances, especially the development in America of the notion of indirect discrimination, which essentially argued that it was naive to focus on sexist *motives* when what was at stake was discriminatory effects. Age bars, for example, clearly made it more difficult for women to seek jobs if they were, as often happens, coming back to employment after a period of child rearing.

Perhaps the most important set of criticisms developed around the notion of the 'male comparator test'. In order to show discrimination, a woman must begin by demonstrating that she has been treated differently, and less favourably, than a real or hypothetical male. Yet to find such a comparable male is notoriously hard to do basically because men are not in the same position as women in the first place. Such arguments were developed first in relation to 'dual labour markets' and 'occupational ghettos' – referring to the fact that some areas of employment, especially part-time employment, are occupied primarily by women. Such arguments have become far more subtle and complicated today, as have the attempts to remedy the problem through the notion of equal pay not for equal work but for work of equal value. Yet the rudiments have long been recognised by those working with the law: the simple ideal of formal justice, treating like cases alike, plainly will not better the position of women where they are working, as they often are, in labour markets where there simply are no 'like men' doing the same kind of low-paid, often part-time, and very often non-unionised, work. Like treatment simply cannot bear the weight of the demands placed upon it.

Reversing the sex discrimination axis

The anti-equality critique is virtually a mirror image of the key themes of anti-sex-discrimination analysis. Thus the three basic themes mentioned above (pp. 149–50) are simply negated to argue that:
1) The even and uniform application of rules, standards and norms means the entrenching of male norms in a masculinist mode.
2) Maleness and masculinity are not extrinsic biases distorting rule-application from the outside. Rather they are built right in to all the norms, rules and standards and so, however even handedly

applied, this will still produce biased effects for women.

3) The focus on the public domain has been a huge distraction. Not only is law and education incapable of addressing the real causal locus of oppression which lies in the 'private' realm of sexuality but viewing the private world through the prism of the public domain is a misperception.

The fate of anti-sex-discrimination legislation and its 'male comparator' test occupies an exemplary place in these critiques. The key arguments can thus be neatly illustrated by looking at two early cases brought under British anti-sex-discrimination legislation. The first is *Turley* v. *Allders Department Stores* which concerned a woman who was dismissed when she became pregnant. The majority decision in this case was that this dismissal was not discriminatory because a man could not get pregnant and therefore this did not involve an unlike treatment of like cases. There was also an unsuccessful minority opinion expressed and that was that a likeness could be found, namely that a woman falling pregnant was like a man falling ill. This minority view did ultimately succeed in *Hayes* v. *Malleable Working Men's Club*, where it was decided that it was in fact unfair to dismiss a woman for becoming pregnant. These two cases pose a rather stark set of alternatives for any woman seeking 'equal treatment' with a man. In either case, women have to match a standard defined by men's lives, even biology. In the first case, the standard is a literal norm: men cannot get pregnant. (Similarly, the US Supreme Court decided in 1976 that 'an exclusion of pregnancy from a disability benefits plan ... providing general coverage is not a gender-based discrimination at all' (*General Electric* v. *Gilbert*). In the second case, the standard is a normal pathology − an event that is a normal part of many women's lives can only be recognised if it matches on to a standard abnormal part of men's lives − being ill. Such are the alternatives under 'like treatment'. One legal response, developed in America, was to promote a 'special rights' strategy in which women did not have to be the same as men in order to receive equal rights. Women could thus be exempt from certain jobs, such as mining, and could receive equal pay and employment rights without having to be measured by the male standards. In this way women's differences could be recognised without the usual disabling effects.

The current critiques of the masculinity of equality amount to the 'male comparator test' writ large. Such imposition of male standards is not simply a matter of legal drafting nor limited to biology nor even the economics of labour markets. The problems are neither contingent, local nor accidental. Rather such cases typify a generic masculinity entrenched right within the abstract 'objective' standards whose neutral enforcement thus cannot but help coming out in favour of men. To struggle for a neutral application of rules and standards is hopelessly misguided:

When law is most ruthlessly neutral, it will be most male; when it is most sex blind, it will be most blind to the standard that is being applied ... the point of view of male dominance is the standard for point-of-viewlessness. (MacKinnon, 1983, p. 644)

Or, as put by Naffine, any critique of law that focuses simply on its biased *application* has an inherent

tendency to accept, and approve, law's own account of itself when it is not dealing with women. Law is seen therefore to be essentially a rational and fair institution concerned with the arbitration of conflicting rights between citizens. ... the present character and outlook of law are largely left intact. The prevailing idea is accepted that law should be (and can be) impartial and reasoned. The objection is to the failure of law to adhere to its own professed standards when it invokes discriminatory laws and practices. That is, the objection is to bad law. (Naffine, 1990, pp. 3–4)

Crucially, though, it is not only law literally that poses this problem, but the entire array of extrapolations centred around the theme of bias. The whole idea of bias – the very essence of anti-sex-discrimination thinking – does not make sense without the notion of a standard. Bias has to have a grain to go against. Deviations and departures can be demonstrated only against a norm and thus it also follows that the source of these deviations will be conceptualised as fundamentally separate from the norms, standards and rules as such – as accidental and inessential contingencies that disrupt and distort the standards from the outside. Thus all talk framed in terms of bias, whether applied to special relations or academic forms of knowledge, however tactically used simply to interrogate existing paradigms 'in their own terms', nonetheless willy nilly has the effect of installing a helpless commitment to the existing standards. If male youth crime is to be explained in terms of gangs, then young women too must be investigated for their gang behaviour.

In fact, two different versions of this critique of the masculinity of equality talk can be distinguished. These can be labelled: 1) masculinity as hidden content; 2) masculinity as form. Each focuses on law's abstractness but in different ways.

Masculinity as hidden content

This line of argument is about the way that abstraction is an abstraction *from* some specific circumstances, a generalisation from the specific to a universal. What is at stake here is how the concrete origins of general rules still leave their traces in the abstraction. For, if the original concrete situation was also a typically male situation, then all that abstracting from it does is to accomplish what MacKinnon calls an implicit positive discrimination programme for men, yet one that is rendered invisible through the abstract terms in which it is posed.

Men's physiology defines most sports, their needs define auto and health insurance coverage, their socially designed biographies define workplace expectations and successful career patterns, their perspectives and concerns define quality in scholarship, their experiences and obsessions define merit, their objectification of life defines art, their military service defines citizenship, their presence defines the family, their inability to get on with each other – their wars and their rulerships – define history, their image defines god, and their genitals define sex. (MacKinnon, 1987, p. 36)

Thus, in the field of employment the idea of a standard career pattern, predicated notably on the absence of major childcare responsibilities, is often cited as male norm while, even more subtly, the general mode of self-replication (looking for someone who would 'fit in' with 'us') involves many implicit masculinities of culture.

Another topical legal example is the defence of provocation which in criminal law allows a homicide not to count as murder. Notoriously, women who have suffered long periods of background abuse from their male partners find it difficult to succeed in a plea of cumulative provocation if they cannot also show that there was some immediate triggering incident that led to a loss of self-control, the test for this being the 'reasonable man'. These are the standard criteria and, when applied to cases of cumulative provocation – in exactly the same way as they are applied to men in provocation generally – the women's cases simply do not fit the standard criterion. Yet so long as the same criteria are being applied uniformly to men and women, then a critique framed in terms of uniform application of law is helpless in capturing the problem. By contrast, the anti-equality critique would argue, these very concepts and categories are abstracted *from* typically male situations whether reflecting intra-male violence such as men getting into fights in pubs or, in the more distant past, encountering each other as 'strangers at the crossroads' (Gordon, 1978, paras 25.13 –

25.14) when some immediate triggering incident sparks off a reaction, or alternatively the weight given to men discovering their wives in adultery and the sort of reaction this would be expected to produce. The process of abstraction thus both conceals and preserves the masculine perspectives of these originating concrete situations.

Masculinity as form

The second critique also concerns abstraction, neutrality and objectivity but here the concern is not with a hidden masculine content but rather with the form of objectivity as such. It is the very universality and generality of rules and abstract principles that constitute their masculine mode. Here Carol Gilligan's *In a Different Voice* (1982) has provided the main touchstone of argument. Gilligan's work was developed in the psychology of ethics and began as a methodological critique of experiments conducted in terms of the Piaget–Kohlberg schema of moral development in which the highest stage of ethical maturity involves the ability to make decisions in terms of moral universals seen as applying equally to oneself and others. This stage is seen as an advance both over a self-centred egoism that perceives others necessarily as competitive antagonists (early masculinity, as Gilligan comes to see it) and also over an even more psychically primitive mode in which self – other boundaries are unclear (an androgynous beginning for all subjects, as the mother/ child dyad, but a stage that boys move out of by developing their egoism whereas it remains more definitive for girls). The 'normal' path of development thus sketched out in the Piaget–Kohlberg scenario is the masculine one in which the development into egoism is seen as normal and which 'must' normally develop rational general rules applying equally to everyone because of the need to curb competitiveness and get maximum gains for all in the end – always by an implicit reference to an implied hostile external world of the 'general other' (see Benhabib, 1987). Thus, where the masculinity as hidden content still works through contrasting claimed objectivity and neutrality with hidden (but now internalised) partiality, this form of critique finds the very ideals of neutrality and objectivity unacceptably indifferent to the concrete specifics of lived reality.

By contrast, the feminine mode does not begin from a decisive separation of self and other, and thus always retains a sense of empathy and an ability to see the world from the other's point of view. So the abstracting, rationalising, universalising cure for hostile competitiveness is not required and, consequently, the feminine perspective remains more particularistic and context-oriented, not focused on trying to find abstract general rules and a fixed hierarchy of values to decide between competing rules, but rather a more pragmatic and solution-oriented perspective characterised by altruism. As a defence and promotion of femininity, Gilligan's work clearly corresponds not only to the 'special rights' strategy in anti-discrimination legislation, but also to immensely important strands in feminism that have sought to promote women's work, women's art, women's way of doing things, against the dominant norms. Yet this has earned Gilligan's sense of a 'different voice' immense scorn from MacKinnon who can hear only a 'higher voice' that replicates all the ways in which men, having first devalued women, then validate these second-rate values. To celebrate 'caring' and concern for others means merely to replicate precisely what men have valued women for – their capacity for self-sacrifice and subservience to men.

These two versions of the critique of masculinity – and their contrast to the simple equality/bias version – can be illustrated by returning to the sphere of liberal political theory where Rawls' theory of justice has been subject to feminist review.

Rawls reversed

John Rawls' *A Theory of Justice* (1972) is very much an example of a liberal theory forged in an age conscious of the problems of sex, race and class discrimination. He clearly registers the effects of poverty or ignorance as undermining equal opportunities policies. At the same time Rawls' account could almost serve as John Major's election manifesto, for instance with his justification of the principle that high salary differentials paid to managers may, by stimulating efficiency and business initiative, ultimately lead to greater employment in a revitalised world of competitive industry and commerce.

He takes as his starting point a hypothetical original position in which 'we' are to imagine ourselves as abstract, free, rational subjects, neutral beings who are to design a set of principles of justice such that we would be happy to be 'parachuted in' to any of the concrete realisations of subjectivity that could exist. Gender, ethnicity and class are identified as some of the specific social and contingent positionings one might end up inhabiting, and hence the principles of justice devised from the perspective of the original position are intended to avoid any interest-based presuppositions since the entire project is based on the idea that we do not know which form of incarnation we shall end up with. This is an exercise in 'point-of-viewlessness' assuming we all seek to maximise our self-interest but ruling out any hidden advantages. By the same token, no specific forms of social institution are to be presupposed – rather these are to be 'invented' according to how they would be judged from the 'point of view' of a subject that cannot have any vested interest since it cannot be known in advance where its subjectivity will in fact be invested.

However, as many feminist critics have emphasised (see Okin, 1987), the actual text of *A Theory of Justice* does not always live up to these alleged starting points. At the level of linguistic usage, the terms 'men' and 'mankind' are used alongside and interchangeably with more neutral terms such as 'individual'. The intergenerational concern expressed in the 'principle of savings' is posed in terms of 'fathers and sons', so presumptive of typically male power over property. The 'abstract' individuals who are members of the polity, the subjects of political discourse, are often presumed by Rawls to be heads of households and not, apparently, female heads of households. Further, while Rawls claims that all social institutions must be interrogated to see if they live up to principles of justice derived through the 'original position', in fact he not only fails to interrogate the family in this way but actively relies on a presumption that it simply is a just institution in which new potential members of society will be able to learn what justice means. Yet, is the family actually a just institution with respect to the positioning of men and women within it? And, if not, how on earth can children be expected to learn principles of justice in such a tilted milieu?

For equality-based critics, Rawls' failings would be understood as testimony to the persistence of unconscious sexism disrupting the basically egalitarian general principles and presumptions that constitute the 'real' framework of his theory. Rawls should be chastised for failing to follow through his own principles. For all his attempts at abstracted neutrality, he reproduces the way privileged groups have, in effect, managed to exploit the system to make it run in favour of elites of property, privileged ethnicity and gender. Conversely, once the biased inconsistencies are expelled, *A Theory of Justice* might potentially offer a way forward for women. To focus on abuse of the system means that the system could survive once purified of abuse; bias is thus conceived as contingent, external and repairable.

From the point of view of anti-equality critiques, women can never simply be included in and treated according to the same rules. The system would 'blow up'. The 'hidden content' version of the masculinity thesis might thus focus on precisely what would happen if the assumption of male heads of households was 'corrected'. Okin puts this in terms of the obstacles to the gender system that still bar women's path to the true enjoyment of liberty:

One of the most essential liberties [recognised by Rawls] is 'the important liberty of free choice of occupation'. It is not difficult to see that this liberty is compromised by the assumptions and customary expectations, central to our gender system, that women take far greater responsibility than men for housework and childcare, whether or not they also work for wages outside the home. (Okin, 1987, p. 67)

But a much stronger way of making the point is to put it the other way around: how far does men's enjoyment of liberty itself presuppose the continuing existence of women's responsibility for the household? The era of welfarism got us used to the idea of hidden preconditions of property and status underpinning abstract rights, the implicit concrete situation from which such general rights were abstracted. Now the argument gets taken one stage further than inequality: to what extent does men's freedom depend upon women's subordination?

Something of a parallel can be found in the way race discrimination is currently being rethought in America. The equality perspective was represented very much by Gunnar Myrdal's 'anomaly thesis' (1944/1962) in which racism, just like sexism, was characterised in terms of a tension between liberal-democratic theory and liberal-democratic practice and, more widely, as out of keeping with the broad trends of modern society that were perceived to move generically forwards and away from the traditional birth-based forms of exclusion. As against this 'anomaly' conception of racism, Jennifer Hochschild has argued:

Racism is not simply an excrescence on a fundamentally healthy liberal democratic body but is a part of what shapes and exercises that body ... The apparent anomaly is actually a symbiosis. (Hochschild, 1984, p. 5)

She does not constitute racism as an eternal essence, but rather concentrates on the functional role it has played in forming a consensus politics out of America's waves of immigration and consequent diversity of ethnic groupings and, crucially, huge disparities of wealth. Crudely put, a unity of 'white' Americans could be constituted by opposition to the otherness of 'black'. Whatever ethnic, status or wealth differentiations existed among 'us' counted as little against the huge superiority gained simply by not being the 'other'.

A more dramatic parallel could hark back to ask how far the great Athenian principles of citizenship were not only discordant with, but actually *dependent* upon, the fact that this was also a slave society. Are the very concepts of freedom and equality propped up and made possible by a male perspective that entails the unacknowledged existence of a subordinate class – women – who provide the preconditions of autonomy and freedom for men?

The second line of feminist critique of Rawls – the idea of masculinity as form – concentrates instead on the abstracted individual hypothesised behind the veil of ignorance. How can gender, race and class be postulated as mere external 'clothing' that such a subject may come to wear? To be a human subject *is* to be constituted through such differences and specificities. Then, too, with the inspiration of Gilligan it is often asked whether some of the attributes of this supposedly abstract subject are not in fact more typically masculine, such as the egocentric assumption that our overriding concern would be to maximise self-interest. Most damning of all is the argument that the entire project of abstracting from conditions of existence and, indeed, the general universalising mode of the resulting principles, amount to a typically masculine way of looking at the world as separate from context, concreteness and relation to others. What is at issue here is Rawls' Kantian inspiration and, indeed, for Weber too modernity is often characterised precisely in terms of this mode of constructing universals. Similarly, the Piaget–Kohlberg schema, so criticised by Gilligan is also a major plank for Habermas (1984). The universality of general rules is widely taken to be the essential feature of modern ethics, government and organisation. Law's characteristic way of disregarding the complexities of background and context (again as in the problem of recognising cumulative provocation) thus is also dismissed as 'masculine'. Conversely, what is identified as feminine – contextualisation, reference to specifics and pragmatics – also maps neatly on to traditional decision-making, perhaps along with the privileging of obligations and concerns with others over the more modern priority assigned to self and rights.

As against this, it might be argued, Rawls' basic idea of the original position is precisely to foster the 'feminine' mode of 'putting oneself in the other's place', an imaginative exercise that has been recommended not only in the name of feminism but also by such stalwart legal philosophers as Stair who, in order to answer the question of the duties that parents and children respectively owe to each other, recommends that each should imagine what they would expect of the other.

Liberalism or modernity?

There are a number of ways in which these developments in feminism make more sense when posed as debates and developments about modernity than when limited to the problem of a textbook liberalism. One reason is that liberalism itself takes up a very large swathe of the sphere of modern politics – as indicated here, right-wing libertarianism and 'caring capitalism' are just as much framed within liberalism as the more obvious clichéd 'do-gooders'.

Then, in a very broad sense, current feminisms are often posed as challenging the grand dualities of modern value systems that, since Descartes and especially in the Enlightenment, have prized reason over the passions and, more widely, have sought to promote progress, education and science. The central algorithm here is man: woman:: reason: emotions. Mary Wollstonecraft may thus be rapped across the knuckles for her celebration of women's equal claims to rationality and her complicity in not only denying women's sexuality but metaphorically accepting its associations with mob rule and the threat of revolution (Kaplan, 1986). Why value this masculine value of 'rationality' over the feminate opposites? Why split the world in this binary way – is this mind/body duality not itself a masculine mode? Such explorations, however, often tend to dissolve into more universalistic, ahistorical claims that can be traced back to Plato or Psyche.

One crucial feminist use of the concept of modernity discussed here has been the immensely powerful rhetoric focused on the 'big break' between traditional and modern society and the corresponding imagery of an uncompleted transition to modernity, with women and black people marooned on an island of tradition. Nonetheless, this figure of equality talk, ever poised at the brink in the eighteenth century and classical liberalism, has in fact been enormously counter-productive. Analysis is drawn ever backwards to origins and founding fathers with their classic but highly limited focus on exclusions, 'membership rights' and the overweening symbolism of the vote and 'suffrage feminism'. To characterise racism and sexism as essentially survivals of the past fits all too neatly into classic sociology's favourite pigeonhole (next door to entails) of constricting survivals from a bygone world, rather than actually dealing with the modern roles, functions and dynamics involved. Even where these 'traditions' turn out to be of relatively recent invention – such as the development of late nineteenth century notions of the non-working wife – the power of the argument from modernity and progress has served to cast such knowledge under the shadow of the 'great shame' of archaic survivals. Everything unacceptable must be given the label of 'the past' and 'tradition'. By the same token, those other forms of feminism involved in constituting the realm of the social and involved in the complex and messy politics of familialism have only recently been rescued (Brophy and Smart, 1985, pp. 1–20).

However, the central argument here turns on that different mode of modernity that emerges most clearly through isolating the version of equality talk developed in relation to discrimination: the criterion of rationality in the precise sense of general, uniform rules, standards and norms to be applied to extracted, typified 'fact-situations'. Unlike the notion of rationality as the capacity to reason and grasp the truth, this is rationality as a technique, not 'thought' but a particular way of organising thinking. If this describes a distinctive type of human subject, then it is no longer a being for whom the passions are absolutely split from the higher modalities of the soul but one who may conditionally bring body and soul together in a calculation of interest and an instrumental control of the world through the regulation of rules. It is this criterion of the governance (of self and others) through universal, general rules that links together the 'high' targets of current feminist anti-equality talk – Kant, Weber, Habermas, all of whom privilege such universal rule-talk – and it is here that high philosophy links too with the banal practicalities of anti-sex-discrimination legislation as it wends its weary ways through the courts. It is this generalising of the rule standard that is most grippingly at stake in talk of knowledge as power in the sense that being able to predict the future price of grain gives an entrepreneur control over today and tomorrow.

It is precisely this large-scale definition of modernity that feminism now characterises as masculine – and that is precisely why these anti-equality critiques have in turn been dismissed as themselves too much part and parcel of such modernist thinking. For Smart, this is but another form of 'grand theory', merely replacing one universal abstraction with another (1989, p. 68). Also dubious is the essentialism of the enterprise. The problem here is not biology. MacKinnon and Gilligan do not posit any innate gender characteristics. Rather, the problem is assuming a uniform masculinity–femininity taken to be homogeneous and general in form. Even the long-standing taken-for-granted parallels between ethnicity and gender have come to be questioned. Precisely in the period when the great compromises effected around uniformity of standards are now widely perceived to have broken down, this mode is resurrected by anti-equality critiques.

Yet, by perhaps the greatest irony, I have tried to suggest that what these critiques of equality were most responsive to was not necessarily masculinity but rather the immense feminist 'take-off' in the 1970s and 1980s that applied the principle of 'like standards' with precisely the kind of energy and relentless extrapolation that Weber invoked in describing the spread of rationalisation in the modern West. This process of dissemination of sex discrimination talk truly does deserve attack. It instituted an immense levelling process in which the whole of life and social relations and different forms of analysis ultimately came to be seen through the deadening legal spectacles of fairness and unfairness. The anti-equality critiques are thus truly mirror images of what they set out to attack – a process of 'rationalisation' and generalisation instituted by feminism.

References

Atiyah, P. (1979), *The Rise and Fall of Freedom of Contract*, Oxford: Clarendon.
Benhabib, S. (1987), 'The Generalised and Concrete Other: The Kohlberg-Gilligan Controversy and Feminist Theory', in S. Benhabib and D. Cornell (Ed.), *Feminism as Critique*, Cambrige: Polity Press/Blackwell.
Berlin, I. (1969), *Two Concepts of Liberty*, Oxford: Clarendon.
Brophy, J. and Smart, C. (Eds.) (1985), *Women-in Law*, London: Routledge and Kegan Paul.
Carter, C. (1993), 'The Relations between "Economic" and "Social" in EC Discourse', Edinburgh University: PhD thesis (to be completed).
Donoghue v. *Stevenson* (1932) A.C. 562.

Dworkin, R. (1977a/1985), 'Reading the Civil Rights Act', in *A Matter of Principle?*, Cambridge Mass.: Harvard University Press.

Dworkin, R. (1977b), *Taking Rights Seriously*, London: Duckworth.

Fuller, L. (1964), *The Morality of Law*, New Haven: Yale University Press.

Gilbert v. *General Electric Company* (1976) 429 US 125.

Gilligan, C. (1982), *In A Different Voice: Psychological Theory and Women's Development*, Cambridge, Mass. and London: Harvard University Press.

Gordon, G. (1978), *The Criminal Law of Scotland*, Edinburgh: Greens.

Habermas, J. (1984), *Theory of Communicative Action*, Boston: Beacon and Cambridge: Polity.

Hayek, F. A. (1974/1976), *Law, Legislation and Liberty*, London: Routledge.

Hayes v. *Malleable Working Men's Club* (1983) I.C.R. 703.

Held, V. (1989), 'Liberty and Equality from a Feminist Perspective', in N. MacCormick and Z. Bańkowski (Eds.), *Enlightenment, Rights and Revolution: Essays in Legal and Social Philosophy*, Aberdeen: Aberdeen University Press.

Hochschild, J. (1984), *The New American Dilemma: Liberal Democracy and School Desegregation*, New Haven: Yale University Press.

Kaplan, C. (1986), 'Wild Nights: Pleasure/Sexuality/Feminism', in *Sea Changes*, London: Verso.

Kingdom, E. (1980/1991), 'Women in Law', in *What's Wrong with Rights?: Problems for Feminist Politics of Law*, Edinburgh: Edinburgh University Press.

MacKinnon, C. (1982–83/1987/1989), 'On Difference and Dominance', in *Feminism Unmodified: Discourses on Life and Law*, Cambridge Mass.: Harvard University Press.

Mill, J.S. (1869/1966), *The Subjection of Women*, Cambridge Mass.: Massachusetts Institute of Technology Press.

Millett, K. (1970/1976), *Sexual Politics*, London: Virago.

Myrdal, G. (1944/1962), *An American Dilemma*, New York: Harper and Row.

Naffine, N. (1990), *Law and the Sexes*, London: Allen and Unwin.

Okin, S.M. (1987), 'Justice and Gender', *Philosophy and Public Affairs*, Vol. 16.

Pateman, C. (1988), *The Sexual Contract*, Cambridge: Polity.

Rawls, J. (1972), *A Theory of Justice*, Oxford: Oxford University Press.

Raz, J. (1972), 'Legal Principles and the Limits of Law', *Yale Law Journal*, Vol. 81.

Smart, C. (1989), *Feminism and the Power of Law*, London: Routledge.

Smith, D. (1974/1987), 'Women's Perspective as a Radical Critique of Sociology', first printed in *Social Inquiry* (1974), Vol. 44, No. 1; reprinted in Sandra Harding (Ed.), *Feminism and Methodology* (1987), Bloomington: Indiana University Press.

Taylor, H. (1850), *Westminster Review.*

Turley v. *Allders Department Stores Ltd* (1980) I.C.R. 66.

Unger, R.M. (1976), *Law in Modern Society*, New York: Free Press.

Weber, M. (1954), 'Rational and Irrational Administration of Justice', in M. Rheinstein (Ed.), *Max Weber on Law in Economy and Society.*

Wollstonecraft, M. (1790/1989), 'A Vindication of the Rights of Men', in J. Todd (Ed.), *A Wollstonecraft Anthology*, Cambridge: Polity Press/ Blackwell.

Wollstonecraft, M. (1792/1989), 'A Vindication of the Rights of Women', in J. Todd (Ed.), *A Wollstonecraft Anthology*, Cambridge: Polity Press/ Blackwell.

Political obligation

Introduction

Does one have a moral obligation to obey the laws of one's State? This is one of the oldest questions in political philosophy. Since Plato's dialogue the *Crito*, the question has continually engaged reflective citizens (Plato, 1953). Often, it has erupted as a crucial question for large sections of a society. For example, in Britain in the late 1980s many decided that they had no obligation to pay their community charge (or poll tax) because they believed that the law that imposed it was unjust. Although the question is raised most dramatically by injustice, it will be posed more generally here. Consider this simple example. A motorist considers whether to go through a red light at 3 a.m. when she can see that there is no one else around. If there is a moral obligation to obey the law, then there is a reason to say that going through the red light would be morally wrong.

The most fundamental question in this context is: ought one to obey the law? I take that question as a request for reasons why we ought, morally speaking, to obey the laws of the state. It is a question about the grounds of compliance. Since I am interested in reasons which may be regarded as moral reasons, I exclude from consideration the ground of prudence. It is beyond dispute, I think, that we all have prudential reasons for obeying the law; for example, we fear punishment if we disobey. I shall treat the claim that we have an obligation to obey the law as offering one kind of reason why we ought to obey the law. There are different theories about what gives rise to obligations to obey the law. (For the moment, I am not distinguishing obligations and duties.) The most interesting and influential writers have suggested the following accounts of our obligation (or duty) to obey the law:

1) We have consented to obey it.
2) We have a duty of fair play.
3) We have a natural duty to obey the law.

In the following sections, I will examine each of these theories. The conclusion I find most persuasive is that none of these theories satisfactorily demonstrates that citizens in general have a moral obligation to obey all the laws of their State. This conclusion has been ably defended at length by a number of recent writers, notably A. J. Simmons (Simmons, 1979). Much recent writing, including this chapter, owes a great deal to Simmons.

Consent theory

The basic idea of the consent theory is that no person has an obligation to obey the law unless that person consents. So, for example, being born in a State is not a ground for an obligation to obey the laws of the State. The consent theory treats as crucial the individual's freedom to decide whether or not to obey the law. The classical exponent of the consent theory is often taken to be John Locke, in his Second Treatise (Locke, 1967), but that is not uncontroversial. The consent theory is often associated with the political theory known as the social contract theory, and hence with such philosophers as Hobbes and Rousseau, as well as Locke. There are distinctions that need to be drawn here, and I shall mention them later. My argument in this section will be that, in giving a clear account of consent, we must distinguish what counts as consent from the normative consequences of consenting. Since the personal explicit consent of every citizen is too strong a requirement for an obligation to obey the law, the weaker requirement of tacit consent has been advocated. But the notion of tacit consent generates confusion without solving any problems. Moreover, tacit consent would undermine the voluntarist essence of the consent theory.

Simmons defines a consent theory as follows: 'any theory of political obligation which maintains that the political obligations of citizens are grounded in their personal performance of a voluntary act which is the deliberate undertaking of an obligation' (Simmons, 1979, p. 57). Notice his emphasis that the consent must be personal. It cannot be argued that, in the remote past, some ancestor of mine consented to obey the State and his consent still binds me.

Consent theory assumes that, since persons are naturally free, the only way they can acquire an obligation to restrict their freedom according to law is if they voluntarily undertake the obligation. The only way in which a person can undertake an obligation is by giving some clear sign of the desire to do so. The clear sign is the giving of consent. Finally, it is thought to be a virtue of the theory that consent protects the individual from injury by the State. What this means is controversial (Simmons, 1979, p. 65). It may mean that an individual cannot be bound to obey unknowingly. Alternatively, it might mean that an individual who consents to obey the State cannot logically be harmed by the State. But if the latter is what the consent theorists mean, then it is odd that they should also hold that there are limits to what one can consent to. If my consent negates the harm, then why can I not consent to be enslaved?

It should be clear that the consent theory is a liberal theory, a theory committed to the importance of the individual's freedom to choose. It is this central feature which gives rise to an important problem for the theory. Suppose that a State has authority (or is legitimate) only if citizens have an obligation to obey. On the consent theory, citizens have an obligation to obey only if they individually consent to what the State does. In other words, authority or legitimacy require unanimous consent. But this requirement is too strong, since no State would be legitimate.[1] Instead, authority or legitimacy are founded on the consent of the majority. However, the theory is now impaled on the other horn of the dilemma: if a State has authority when the majority consent to its acts, then the minority have an obligation to obey even though they did not consent. Somehow the consent theory has to be weakened. Either something less than individual personal consent is to be required – but that seems unpromising – or it must be argued that the minority have, in some way, consented.

What is consent?

It has obviously become essential to give some account of consent. There is a mistake which it is crucial to avoid. The mistake is to confuse consent with its consequences (Green, 1990, pp. 162ff). There are two questions to distinguish. The first question is, what actions count as the giving of consent? The answer to this question is largely factual. Someone who utters the words 'I promise' is giving one of the conventional signs of consent. The second question is, what are the normative consequences of those actions? The usual normative consequence of consenting is that the consentor is under an obligation. But someone may consent and not be under an obligation because we make the moral judgement that the consent was not valid. If someone is induced to give consent, he nonetheless consents. However, we might hold that the consent is not valid, has not placed the consentor under an obligation, because we hold – and this is a matter of morality – that induced consents do not create obligations. The distinction being drawn is reflected in the distinction between, for example, promises that are void initially and promises that are voidable.

The first question – what actions count as the giving of consent – is problematic. The core of the consent theory is the claim that there is a distinctive way of acquiring obligations, i.e. by consenting. Since the same normative consequence could come about in various ways (my obligation to pay £100 for example), what the consent theory seeks to explain is how consent brings the obligation about.

Simmons has offered an influential account of consent. However, it seems to me that it runs into difficulties because it fails to make with sufficient rigour the distinction I have just made. While recognising that we use the word 'consent' in various ways, Simmons recommends that we adhere to a strict account:

[Consenting] is the according to another by the consentor of a special right to act within areas within which only the consentor is normally free to act; this is accomplished through a suitable expression of the consentor's intention to enter such a transaction and involves the assuming of a special obligation not to interfere with the right accorded. (Simmons, 1979, p. 77)

Let us consider Simmons' answer to the first of my questions: what actions count as the giving of consent? He tells us that consent is a voluntary act which involves a suitable expression of the consentor's intention to undertake an obligation. Leave aside for the moment that 'suitable expression' is too vague. Consider an argument that consent does not require having the intention to undertake an obligation (Green, 1990, pp. 163–4). As Joseph Raz has argued, we say that a diner at a restaurant consents to pay the bill after his meal even if the diner intends to leave before paying (Raz, 1986, pp. 80–8).

I suppose that Simmons would defend his account by arguing that that is a different use of consent; that is, it is not the kind of consent that figures in discussions of political obligation. It might be argued that the diner case invokes a different principle. The diner is regarded as having consented as a way of protecting the interests of those who might be harmed by the subsequent denial of consent. If that is correct, then a reason for not taking the diner case as relevant to our obligation to obey the law is that consent theory is to be a theory about a special way of undertaking obligations. If the core of the consent theory is that consent is a special way of acquiring an obligation, it must tell us what that way is.

I don't think that this is a trivial problem. Of course, we do agree on certain clear cases of consent, such as promising. But it is likely that we don't agree on anything but a few clear cases. If so, then consent theorists may have to accept that there are only a few actions that count as consent. The fewer the actions which count as consent, the fewer the number of people who have consented. Even if consent is a reason why we ought to obey the law, or a ground of our obligation to obey, it is a reason only for a very few (i.e. few will have the obligation). The net has to be spread wider and the device for attempting to do so is the notion of tacit consent.

Tacit consent

Locke is usually regarded as the most vigorous proponent of the view that tacit consent is sufficient for an obligation to obey the law.

> The difficulty is, what ought to be look'd upon as a tacit Consent, and how far it binds, i.e. how far any one shall be looked on to have consented, and thereby submitted to any Government, where he has made no Expression at all. And to this I say, that every Man, that hath any Possession, or Enjoyment, of any part of the Dominions of any Government, doth thereby give his tacit Consent, and is as far forth obliged to Obedience to the Laws of that Government, during such enjoyment, as any one under it; whether his Possession be of Land, to him and his Heirs for ever, or a Lodging only for a week; or whether it be barely travelling freely on the highway; and in Effect, it reaches as far as the very being of any one within the Territories of that Government. (Locke, 1967, Para. 119)

The usual objection to Locke's view is that, according to our previous account of consent, the examples Locke cites are not acts of consent at all, and so are not acts of tacit consent.

In order to explain Locke's mistake, Simmons has attempted to clarify further the distinction between explicit and tacit consent. Explicit consent is the explicit expression of the consentor's intention to undertake an obligation. Simmons illustrates tacit consent with the following example. Suppose that the chairperson concludes a meeting by saying, 'The next meeting will be on Tuesday instead of as usual on Thursday. Any objections?' No one says anything and the meeting adjourns. Have the participants all consented to rescheduling the meeting? Simmons argues that we do sometimes take it that silence, or other forms of inactivity, constitute tacit consent, but only when certain conditions are satisfied. It has to be understood that consent is being sought, that dissent is appropriate only during a specified period, that the means of dissent are reasonable and the consequences of dissent not seriously detrimental to the dissenter (Simmons, 1979, p. 80).

I take it that Simmons' point is that, although any consent requires the expression of an appropriate intention, the expression need not be explicit. Tacit consent is possible because there are circumstances in which doing (or not doing) certain things are recognised as expressions of the appropriate intention. Tacit consent then depends on the fact that there are widely recognised conventions. On this account of the matter, Locke's examples are not examples of tacit consent because it is false that we have the convention that, for example, continuing to reside in a country is an expression of the intention to obey the law.

Simmons' argument is questionable. It may well be true that people have obligations to do things to which they have not explicitly consented, but false that these obligations arise from tacit consent. Suppose that one of the participants at the meeting finds the proposed new time inconvenient. She prefers the meeting to remain on Thursday because she has important things to say at the meeting and does not know whether she can attend a meeting on Tuesday. However, she decides to remain silent. All of Simmons' other conditions are true. If consent requires the expression of an intention to undertake the appropriate obligation, then the participant has not consented.

The problem in Simmons' argument can be brought out by distinguishing the two questions I distinguished before. First, has the participant consented? This is a question about conventions, about whether, as a matter of fact, silence is regarded as the expression of an intention in certain circumstances. Second, what are the normative consequences of what the participant does? Does the participant, by virtue of her silence, have an obligation (or some other non-prudential reason) to turn up at the meeting? This question is about moral principles. For example, it might be argued that some moral principle about fairness requires her to attend the meeting whether or not she has consented.

As to the first question, it seems to me doubtful that we do have the convention that the participant has consented. I return to my earlier point that, except for a few cases, it is just not clear what counts as consent. But Simmons' case seems to be particularly doubtful since the relevant convention would be that, in certain circumstances, anyone who keeps silent thereby expresses her intention to transfer her right even if she has no such intention. Compare with Simmons' example the following: suppose that some person gives clear evidence (such as telling us) that he regards his continued residence within a country as an expression of his intention to undertake the appropriate obligation. In that case, we would regard his continued residence as tacit consent.

As to the second question, we might argue that the participant has an obligation to attend the meeting *whether or not* she consented. We might argue that a moral principle about fairness applies to the case. Thus, the case of the meeting is parallel to the earlier case of the diner in the restaurant. If the latter is not a case of consent, then neither is the former. In my view, in neither case is it clear whether consent is being given. However, in both cases, it is arguable that there is an obligation. But to argue, as perhaps Simmons does in the meeting case, from the normative consequence that there is an obligation to the conclusion that someone has consented is to make the mistake I described earlier.

The argument that Simmons wants to make against Locke – namely that Locke is mistaken about what counts as tacit consent – has not got to the root of the matter. Either genuine tacit consent does not establish a widespread obligation to obey, or, if there is a widespread obligation to obey, it does not follow that the obligation is based on tacit consent. If continued residence is a way of under-taking the obligation, that could be because we have a principle that it is fair to regard people who continue to reside in a country as having an obligation to obey the law. Thus, whether continued residence is consent is not the problem. The real question is whether continued residence should have the normative consequence of an obligation to obey the law. Both Simmons and Locke appear to have made the same mistake of arguing from the normative consequence to the conclusion that consent has been given.

One cannot appeal to tacit consent to ground an obligation for most citizens to obey most laws since tacit consent is almost as rare as explicit consent. Consent is plausible as a basis for a general obligation to obey the law only if consent theory is transformed into some other kind of theory, such as a theory about fairness.[2] Thus, there is a paradox in the theory of tacit consent of which Locke seems unaware. In the attempt to generate a general obligation to obey, Locke appealed to tacit consent. But his account of tacit consent is inconsistent with the spirit of the theory, that a special voluntary act is required to undertake an obligation.

One should mention a modern version of the tacit consent theory. It has been argued by John Plamenatz that voting is tacit consent to obey the laws (Plamenatz, 1968, pp. 168ff). Two replies can now be given. First, there is no evidence that voting is generally tacit consent, although in particular cases it could be. So voting could not ground a general obligation to obey the law. Second, even if it is argued that voting does give rise to an obligation to obey, it does not follow that the obligation arises from tacit consent. If there is an obligation, it may arise because it is unfair to vote and not to obey the law (Singer, 1973, pp. 47–9).[3]

Consent and contract theories

There is a further objection to consent theory that comes from Hume (Hume, 1987). Hume asked, why does consent create obligations? His reply was that we find it useful to have a device by means of which we can create obligations. However, Hume reasoned, since the reason to obey the law was also the utility of doing so, consent dissolves into utility. Thus, no work is being done by the consent theory of obligation: we can dispense with it.

Hume's argument can lead us to another problem. Why would people consent to obey the law? Imagine that I continue to reside in the country of my birth. I comply with all the laws and accept all the benefits of citizenship. What motivation is there for me to consent to obey the law? The answer must be that, unless I consent, I am not going to be able to obtain the benefits I enjoy. Thus, consent theories are also social contracts theories.

Consent theories and social contract theories often go together, but it is best to distinguish them (Green, 1990, p. 122; Rawls, 1972, p. 155). A rough distinction is this: whereas a contract usually requires a return, consent does not. If I consent to your camping in my field,

I undertake not to interfere with your doing so. If I contract with you, you have to give me something in return, such as a fee. On its own, a consent theory of political obligation does not explain why anyone would consent to obey the law. So consent theories seem to require to be social contract theories as well. The basic idea of a social contract theory is that one agrees to obey the law in return for certain benefits, such as security (Green, 1990, Ch. 5). There is no need to discuss further consent theories that are also social contract theories. They are vulnerable to the objections that have been made, as well as to the following: it just does not seem plausible to argue that, in general, consent is necessary in order to obtain certain benefits. If I comply with the law without consenting (perhaps for prudential reasons), I can obtain the benefits. Nor can one argue that there has to be some original act of consent in order to set up the society which provides the benefits. Since original consent binds no one but the original consentors, one is returned to the theory of tacit consent.

Finally, a number of problems that have been raised thus far about consent theories received interesting and influential solutions in Rousseau's *Social Contract* (Rousseau, 1958). It was remarked earlier that one of the intuitions of the social contract theory is that consent is important as a device which protects the individual from harm from the State. The assumption is that there is at least the risk of serious antagonism between the individual and the State of which he is a member. Rousseau, famously, refused to make that assumption. Rousseau identified the will of the individual with the will of the State, the 'general will' as he called it. According to Rousseau, a person becomes a moral person only within the State. His particular will is then transformed into the general will. In obeying the laws of the State, he is only obeying himself.[4] The standard criticism of Rousseau is that his theory demands too great an identification of the individual with the State to be plausible as a contract theory. In practice, agreement on the general will can only be achieved by coercive socialisation.

Duty of fair play

There is a view that the obligation to obey the law is based on a duty of fair play. The central intuition of those who hold this view is that receiving benefits can, in certain circumstances, create obligations for those who receive them. Consider the following example. Smith is joint owner of a plot of ground in the front of the building in which he lives. His neighbours, the other joint owners, decide to turn it into a garden. Smith is unwilling to co-operate, but does not refuse his permission for the others to do what they like. When the garden comes into being, Smith is often there, enjoying the flowers. He is asked to contribute to its upkeep, but refuses. Smith is what some people would call a free-rider. He receives benefits but makes no contribution. If Smith is a free-rider, what he does is wrong because it is unfair. The duty of fair play makes free-riding wrong. The duty of fair play, it is argued, creates an obligation on Smith to contribute to the garden if he receives benefit from it. According to the duty of fair play theory, the obligation to obey the law is a special case of the duty of fair play. The main fair play theorists are H. L. A. Hart (Hart, 1955) and John Rawls (Rawls, 1964). Let us consider Rawls' argument.

Rawls argued that the duty of fair play arises when the following conditions are satisfied:

1) There is a mutually beneficial and just scheme of social co-operation. The benefits of the scheme are obtained only if nearly everyone co-operates.
2) Co-operation requires certain sacrifices.
3) Free-riding is possible.
4) If 1, 2 and 3 are satisfied, and if one has *accepted* benefits, then one is bound by the duty of fair play not to be a free-rider.

Rawls holds that the duty of fair play creates an obligation to obey only if the scheme is just. It may seem intuitively obvious that a slave cannot have a moral obligation to obey the system that enslaves him. However, a number of writers have argued that that is false (Greenawalt, 1989, pp. 129–33; Simmons, 1979, pp. 109ff). Their objection, if correct, is important. If a duty of fair play could create obligations in respect of a scheme which is unjust, then one could have an obligation to obey the law when the legal system is very unjust.[5]

Consider the following counter-example (Greenawalt, 1989, p. 130). Constance lives in a village occupied by an invading army. To deal with the village's severe water shortage, the army's commander sets strict limits on the use of water and requires every villager to transport a certain amount of water each day from a distant stream. The water to be hauled by the villagers is to be consumed only by the army. If insufficient water is hauled, villagers will be shot at random. Many villagers, including Constance, haul water not only to save themselves but to protect their neighbours.

This looks like a counter-example because it satisfies all of Rawls' conditions except the condition that the scheme is just, and it is arguable that Constance has a duty to her neighbours to obey the invader's law which arises from the duty of fair play.

Now it might seem that Rawls needs a distinction here. He needs to distinguish two kinds of just scheme: (a) schemes which come about in just ways; (b) schemes which distribute goods justly. The counter-example only shows that it is false that schemes have to be just in the first way, that is, coming about in a just way. Perhaps Rawls should have said that the scheme must be just in the sense that it distributes goods justly among the participants?

Suppose, instead of requiring a just scheme, Rawls had required a scheme in which each participant was allocated a fair share of benefits of the scheme. In that case, we could claim that Constance has a duty to her neighbours arising from the duty of fair play. But this amendment will not work because it requires too much. It requires that for *anyone* to have an obligation based on fair play, then *everyone* must be allocated a fair share of the benefits. However, all that is required for some person to have a duty of fair play is that *that* person receive a fair share (Simmons, 1979, pp. 111–12).

Instead of Rawls' condition that the scheme is just, he probably needs a condition that each is bound to co-operate with the scheme to the extent that he receives benefits from it. Rawls may have considered this condition and rejected it because he may have thought that it has unacceptable consequences. Suppose a scheme in which some participants benefit a great deal more than others. If each has an obligation to support the scheme to the extent that he or she has benefited from the scheme, then those who benefit most from an unfair scheme have the strongest obligation to support it. Is this an acceptable consequence or not? Simmons thinks it is (Simmons, 1979, p. 113). His argument is that those who benefit most from an unfair scheme will have the strongest obligation to support it, but that obligation may itself be overridden by a stronger obligation to oppose unfair schemes.

The conclusion thus far is that it is not a necessary condition for a duty of fair play that the relevant scheme is just. If Simmons is correct, the duty of fair play arises even when the scheme is unfair. So it seems that if we use the duty of fair play argument, we have to accept that we have *some* obligation to obey even unjust laws. Thus the crucial feature of the duty of fair play argument is not the justice of the co-operative scheme but the claim that a person has an obligation simply by virtue of receiving benefits from the scheme. That crucial feature has been vigorously attacked by Robert Nozick (Nozick, 1974, pp. 90–101).

Here is Nozick's argument:

Suppose some of the people in your neighbourhood (there are 364 other adults) have found a public address system and decide to institute a system of public entertainment. They post a list of names, one for each day, yours among them. On his assigned day ... a person is to run the public address system, play records over it, give news bulletins, tell amusing stories, and so on. After 138 days on which each person has done his part, your day arrives. Are you obligated to take your turn? You have benefited from it, occasionally opening your window to listen, enjoying some music or chuckling at someone's funny story. The other people have put themselves out. But must you answer the call when it is your turn to do so? As it stands, surely not. Though you benefit from their arrangement, you may know all along that 364 days of entertainment supplied by others will not be worth your giving up one day. You would rather not have any of it than have it all and spend one of your days at it. Given these preferences, how can it be that you are required to participate when your scheduled time comes? (Nozick, 1974, p. 93).

If Nozick's argument is correct, it shows that one does not have a duty just because one has accepted benefits.

Rawls might be defended against Nozick in this way: it should be remembered that Rawls limits his argument to those who accept benefits. The reluctant broadcaster is not an acceptor and that is why he has no duty to participate. But one has to take care that this defence does not collapse into a requirement that consent is necessary for an obligation. So what account of acceptor can we give?

Simmons argues that we need two distinctions. The first distinction is between *accepting* benefits and *receiving* them. One accepts benefits if either (a) one tries to get the benefit and succeeds or (b) one takes benefits willingly and knowingly. Otherwise, one receives benefits. The second distinction is between *open* benefits and *readily accessible* benefits. Open benefits are those which I cannot avoid receiving without considerably altering my lifestyle. Otherwise, benefits are readily accessible. For example, police protection is in general an open benefit. However, if I required special police protection, that would be a readily accessible benefit.

Since I must *accept* readily accessible benefits, in those cases the duty of fair play does give rise to an obligation. Open benefits are more complicated. There are two cases to distinguish. First, I *receive* open benefits. In that case, the duty of fair play is not applicable. Second, I *accept* open benefits in the sense that I take them willingly and knowingly. In that case, the duty of fair play does arise but this is not, Simmons argues, a normal case.

[Accepting open benefits] involves a number of restrictions on our attitudes toward and beliefs about the open benefits which we receive. We cannot, for instance, regard the benefits as having been forced upon us against our will, or think that the benefits are not worth the price we must pay for them. And taking the benefits 'knowingly' seems to involve an understanding of the status of those benefits relative to the party providing them. Thus, in the case of open benefits provided by the co-operative scheme, we must understand that the benefits *are* provided by the co-operative scheme in order to accept them [as opposed to free for the taking]. (Simmons, 1979, p. 132)

Simmons' conclusion is that the duty of fair play arises either when we *accept* readily accessible benefits or when we *accept* open benefits. However, accepting open benefits is unusual. So the duty of fair play will not be an important justification of our obligation to obey the law.

The crucial point in Simmons' argument is the claim that acceptance of open benefits is unusual, and therefore cannot be used as a basis for the claim that there is a general obligation to obey the law. Why does Simmons think that most people do not accept open benefits? He offers two reasons (Simmons, 1979, pp. 138–9). First, many citizens barely notice the benefits they receive. So they do not regard the benefits as the benefits of a co-operative venture. Or if they do notice benefits, they regard the benefits as purchased from government through taxation, rather than as benefits received from a co-operation scheme. Second, many citizens, if they think about the benefits at all, do not consider them worth the price. So they do not accept the benefit willingly.

One might not be convinced by the argument that most citizens don't think about the benefits. Even if true, is it necessary that they do for a duty of fair play to arise? Might it not be enough that either they would think about the benefits in an appropriate context (in which case Simmons' claim that acceptance must be knowing needs qualification) or that they ought to think about the benefits as benefits of a co-operative scheme, that is, they should be blamed if they do not (Greenawalt, 1989, pp. 127–9)? The argument that people regard benefits as purchased through taxation is opaque. Let us distinguish three kinds of benefit:

1) Open. Examples: security, planning controls, environmental health/sanitation controls.
2) Readily accessible. Examples: NHS, special police protection.
3) Contracted. These benefits do not depend on a co-operative scheme but result from exchanges between individuals. Examples include going into a supermarket and buying a loaf of bread; hiring a private security firm.

As I understand it, Simmons' argument is that people view the benefits provided by taxation as contracted benefits and not as open benefits provided by a co-operative scheme (Simmons, 1979, p. 132).

Bear in mind the previous suggestion that the criterion is not what people think, but what they would think if they thought about it. Simmons might argue that the public security provided by the police is a contracted benefit. But that would be to oversimplify. Security is only indirectly a contracted benefit. Taxation purchases the criminal law machinery which encourages self-restraint by punishing the lack of it (Greenawalt, 1989, pp. 135–6). What people benefit from is the co-operative system of self-restraint. Equally, in order to benefit from the criminal justice system, people would realise that the benefits are obtainable only if many do jury service when called, offer to act as witnesses to accidents, and so on. Similar arguments could be made about environmental health. If these points are accepted, then accepting open benefits is not as rare as Simmons thinks.

Notice however that the argument just concluded relies on turning the acceptors into the first kind of Simmons' acceptors: i.e. those who are trying to get the benefit. But these acceptors also have strong prudential reasons to co-operate. They want the benefit and they recognise (or would recognise) that the benefit can be obtained only as the product of a co-operative scheme in which they need to play their part. The conclusion that all and only those who have the required co-operative spirit have an obligation to obey the law is not the most interesting conclusion, since they are precisely those for whom the obligation is least essential as a reason to obey the law.

The interesting case remains those acceptors of the second kind: i.e. those who accept benefits willingly and knowingly. Simmons thinks that such acceptors are rare, but it may be that there cannot be any such acceptors. If I am correct that the second kind of acceptor must be one who would know or ought to know that the benefits are benefits of a co-operative scheme, then it seems that there is no difference between that acceptor and a receiver of benefits. The crucial feature of an open benefit is that it is one that one cannot reject, at least not without great inconvenience. If one cannot reject the benefit, neither can one accept it (Arenson, 1982, p. 619).

To sum up the argument thus far, Nozick argues that receiving open benefits does not give rise to obligations. Simmons agrees but adds: acceptance of open benefits could give rise to obligations; however, acceptance of open benefits is rare. My argument is that acceptance of open benefits may not be so rare, and so it may be possible to justify an obligation to obey the law that is more extensive than Simmons thinks. However, the obligation is on those who least need it as a reason to obey the law. Arguably, Simmons is correct in thinking that accepting open benefits is not going to provide a significant justification for obeying the law; but he has given the wrong reasons. So it may seem that we may draw the conclusion that if receipt of obligations cannot ground obligations (as Nozick claims), then the duty of fair play argument can at best establish obligations for those who least require them as reasons to obey the law (i.e., those acceptors who try successfully to obtain the co-operative benefits). The duty of fair play argument cannot establish that free-riding is wrong because unfair.

However, we should consider an argument that both Nozick and Simmons are wrong in thinking that receipt of benefits cannot generate obligations. Richard J. Arenson (Arenson, 1982) detects a flaw in Nozick's argument. The reluctant broadcaster does *not* think the benefit worth his time as a broadcaster. Suppose, however, that he did. That would make him a different kind of free-rider. He now both wants the benefit and is unwilling to do his part in creating it. (I take it that he is also distinguishable from the first kind of Simmons' acceptor in that this free-rider wants but does not try to obtain the benefit. He is a passive, willing receiver of benefits, distinguishable from Simmons' second kind of acceptor in that he does not satisfy the willing and knowing conditions.) Arenson argues that *this* kind of free-rider does have an obligation generated by fairness. So it is possible to have an obligation to obey the law that is grounded in fairness.

Arenson's intuition is that mere receipt of open benefits (or public goods, as he calls them) does create obligations because many of these open benefits are 'non-excludable', i.e. if the benefit is provided at all, it is provided for all. He proposes the following principle of fairness (Arenson, 1982, p.623):

1) When a scheme of co-operation is established that supplies a collective benefit (i.e. if anyone is consuming the good it is not feasible to prevent anyone else consuming it) that is worth its cost to each participant.
2) Where the burdens of co-operation are fairly divided.
3) Where it is not feasible to attract voluntary compliance to the scheme via supplementary private benefits.
4) Where collective benefit is either voluntarily accepted or such that voluntary acceptance is impossible.
5) Then those who contribute their assigned fair share of the costs of the scheme have a right, against the remaining beneficiaries, that they should also (i.e. have a moral obligation to) pay their fair share.

There is trouble with condition 2. As I argued earlier, that condition appears to be too strong. All that is required for a person to have a duty of fair play is that that person receives a fair share of the benefits. If that earlier argument is correct, then it may be that one has an obligation arising from fair play to obey the law even when the law distributes benefits unfairly.

What are the arguments in favour of this principle of fairness? First, Arenson argues that Nozick cannot consistently reject it, given his views about private property. What underlies the Lockean–Nozickean view about private property is the self-benefit principle: 'moral rules should be so structured that, if the rules are obeyed, the acts of each person benefit or harm only himself, except as he himself chooses to confer or exchange the benefits of his acts' (Arenson, 1982, p.626, quoting Gibbard). Since the principle of self-benefit justifies both Nozick's views on private property and Arenson's principle of fairness, one cannot consistently advocate the former and deny the latter.

Second, Arenson argues that his principle of fairness is consistent with the self-benefit principle extended to include obligations of charity. If obligations of charity exist, then either (a) the principle of fairness does not cover those cases or (b) it does, but it is controversial what a just distribution of benefits requires but uncontroversial that it is not permissible to desire benefits without being willing to reciprocate at all.

In drawing this discussion to a close, we may conclude that if the duty of fair play is an attractive basis for the obligation to obey the law, it is because of the issue of open benefits. A number of positions have been examined: (a) receipt of open benefits cannot create obligations (Nozick); (b) acceptance of open benefits does create obligations but these obligations are not significant because they are either rare (Simmons) or (as I have argued) obligations of those who least need them as a reason to obey the law; (c) receipt of open benefits by a genuine free-rider does create obligations (Arenson).

The natural duty to obey the law

In his *Theory of Justice*, Rawls offers a different account of the duty to obey the law from the account he offered in his earlier paper (Rawls, 1972, Paras. 18–19, Ch. 6). His later argument is that there is no *obligation* to obey the law, but there is a *duty*. It now becomes important to distinguish obligations and duties.

According to Rawls, obligations have four features (Rawls, 1972, p. 113):

1) They arise from voluntary acts, including accepting benefits.
2) Their content is determined by institutions.
3) They are owed to definite individuals, namely those co-operating in maintaining the institution in question.
4) All derive from the principle of fairness. A person has an obligation to do her part as defined by the rules of the institution when:

4a) the institution is just or fair, that is, satisfies Rawls' two principles of justice, which are: that everyone has the maximum liberty compatible with like liberty for all; that social and economic goods be distributed equally unless an unequal distribution would be to the advantage of the least well-off members of the society;

4b) she has voluntarily accepted benefits.

There are two changes from Rawls' earlier account. First, the former *duty* of fair play has become an obligation. Second, Rawls admits that the principle of fairness cannot ground a general obligation to obey the law because there is no relevant voluntary act. However, when there is a relevant voluntary act, such as running for a political office, then an obligation may be created.

Rawls does not tell us as clearly what a duty is. He tells us that none of the four conditions above applies to duties. He tells us that natural duties 'obtain between all as equal moral persons'. He gives us illustrations of natural duties: helping others in distress, not harming another, obeying just laws. His argument is that natural duties are 'derived from a contractarian point of view'. They are 'those that would be acknowledged in the original position. These principles are understood as the outcome of a hypothetical agreement' (Rawls, 1972, p.115).

In order to understand Rawls' account of natural duties, we have to understand his method of arriving at a theory of justice. Rawls thinks that moral and political thinking rests on a contractarian basis. That is, the moral and political principles that are right are those which would be chosen by persons in a carefully described hypothetical situation. This hypothetical situation is what Rawls calls the original position (Rawls, 1972, Ch.3). In the original position, everyone is behind a veil of ignorance. Everyone is required to choose moral and political principles for a society to which all will belong without knowing anything about the society and without knowing what roles they will occupy within that society. All that those in the hypothetical situation know are certain basic facts about human nature. Rawls contends that whatever principles would be chosen by rational, self-interested choosers in the original position are just because the procedure by which they are chosen is fair. Rawls argues that two principles of justice would be chosen first in the original position. People would choose first to have maximum liberty compatible with like liberty for all. Second, they would choose a principle that social and economic goods would be distributed equally unless an unequal distribution would be to the advantage of the least well-off member of the society. These two principles of justice are then used to create the basic institutional structures. Once they have got the basic institutional structures into place, the choosers in the original position can consider principles for individuals. Rawls' claims that certain principles of natural justice would be chosen, such as the principle that we have a duty to support just institutions.

What then is the natural duty of justice that would be chosen in the original position?

From the standpoint of justice as fairness, a fundamental natural duty is the duty of justice. This duty requires us to support and to comply with just institutions that exist and apply to us. It also constrains us to further just arrangements not yet established, at least when this can be done without too much cost to ourselves. (Rawls, 1972, p. 115)

Why would principles of natural justice be chosen in the original position? One of Rawls' arguments is that the previous choice of principles to set up the basic institutions now constrains choosers to choose principles of natural justice. But there is another consideration, which Rawls calls the assurance problem (Rawls, 1972, pp. 336–7). In a well-ordered society, the public knowledge that citizens have an effective sense of justice contributes to the stability of just arrangements. That stability is weakened by the apprehension that others will not obey the laws when it is in their interest not to obey. That apprehension is increased if some voluntary act, like accepting benefits, is required for an obligation to obey the law. Stability seems to require that everyone recognise that everyone has a duty to obey the law independently of the performance of any voluntary act, and that is why the natural duty of justice would be chosen in the original position. To show that we have a duty to obey the laws of just institutions it is sufficient to show that the natural duty of justice would be chosen in the original position.

Obviously, Rawls' claim that there is a natural duty to obey the law depends to a great extent on the soundness of his method, especially the device of the hypothetical contract in the original position. His method has been extensively criticised.[6] It has been frequently argued that we cannot know what choices would be made in the original position, or, if we can know, it is only because the original position has been tailored to produce certain choices. While very important, these are not arguments that can be pursued here.

Simmons argues that an objection can be made to Rawls' theory that does not depend on our taking a view about the soundness of his method. The objection focuses on Rawls' claim that a condition of having a duty to obey the law is that just institutions 'apply to us'. Institutions might apply to us for different reasons. They might apply to us by virtue of some general description (such as 'married') or apply to us by virtue of residing within a given territory. Simmons argues that neither reason for institutions applying to us is a morally relevant reason and thus the application clause is not a necessary condition of our duty to obey (Simmons, 1979, pp. 147ff). For example, he claims that the fact that we are born within a given territory does not give us a relevant reason for obeying the just laws of that territory. Therefore, if we have a duty to obey just institutions, we have a duty to obey all just institutions and not only those which apply to us in either of the ways just mentioned. Of course, if institutions applied to us because we joined in them, then that would be a relevant reason for obeying the laws of *that* institution. But interpreting 'applies to' in that way returns us to an obligation-based account. So the requirement that the institutions must apply to us must be deleted, with the result that we have a natural duty to obey all just institutions. But Simmons argues that this is an unreasonable demand because it requires too much of us.

Suppose that Simmons is correct that we cannot have a natural duty to obey all just laws.[7] The most obvious restriction is to the laws of the individual's own State or that State with which he or she has a significant connection. But Simmons does not have a persuasive argument against the view that one has a natural duty to obey the laws of one's own State. What he offers is an illustration which he claims supports the intuition that someone born into a territory governed by just laws does not thereby have a duty to obey the law. As against that intuition, Rawls could well argue that the principle that he advocates is the one that would be chosen in the original position.[8]

Concluding remarks

We have now examined three influential theories which claim that citizens generally have an obligation or a duty to obey most laws. None of these is convincing, although the duty of fair play theory may be the most promising. There are, then, three conclusions that one needs to consider:

1) There is no obligation (or duty) to obey the law.
2) The obligation is very limited.
3) There is some moral reason other than an obligation why we ought to obey the law.

The arguments that have been discussed in this chapter lend most support to the second conclusion. However, the third should not be entirely overlooked. Even if there were no obligation to obey all or most laws, it does not follow that there is no moral reason to obey. There may be moral reasons to obey which do not essentially involve obligations[9] or natural duties. Utilitarian writers argue that one ought to obey the law of one's State when and only when obedience maximises some desired value, for example, the greatest happiness of the greatest number.[10] Some utilitarians would argue that every act of justified obedience must (for example) promote the greatest happiness of the greatest number. Others argue that all that needs to be justified is a general rule requiring general obedience to the law, and that such a rule can be justified because it does maximise the desired value.

Notes

1   At least one philosopher has grasped this particular nettle and concluded that a committed consent theorist must be a philosophical anarchist. See Wolff, 1970.

2   I think that Simmons may agree with much of this, but he misleads one with his discussion of tacit consent into making Locke's mistake.

3   . Voting may have significance because of an underlying social obligation rather than being itself a source of the obligation to obey. See Waldron, 1990, pp. 169–73.

4   For a modern example of an account of political obligation influenced by Rousseau, see Charvet, 1990.

5   In his later work, Rawls accepts that one may have a duty to obey some unjust laws. See Rawls, 1972, Para. 53.

6   See Daniels, 1975, Parts 1–3. For a recent defence of Rawls, see Kymlicka, 1990, pp. 62–3.

7   But see Waldron, 1990, pp. 169–73 and his Note 13.

8   There is another way of dealing with Simmons' intuition. Natural law theorists also argue that we have a natural duty to obey just laws. According to traditional natural law theory, laws are rules for the common good. Because individuals have a duty to promote the common good, they have a duty to obey just laws. For a fuller account, see Greenawalt, 1989, Ch. 8.

9   Narrowly construed as, for example, by Simmons, 1979, Ch. 1.

10   Utilitarianism was developed by Bentham, 1948 and J.S. Mill, 1962. For examples of modern utilitarian work on political obligation, see Hare, 1976 and Brandt, 1964. Utilitarian theories of political obligation are criticised by Greenawalt, 1989, Ch. 6.

References

Arenson, R. J. (1982), 'The Principle of Fairness and Free-Rider Problems', *Ethics*, 616.

Bentham, J. (1948), *A Fragment on Government with An Introduction to the Principles of Morals and Legislation*, Ed. W. Harrison, Oxford: Blackwell.

Brandt, R. (1964), 'Utility and the Obligation to Obey the Law', in S. Hook, *Law and Philosophy*, New York: New York University Press.

Charvet, J. (1990), 'Political Obligation: Individualism and Communitarianism', in P. Harris, *Political Obligation*, London: Routledge.

Daniels, N. (1975), *Reading Rawls*, Oxford: Blackwell.

Green, L. (1990), *The Authority of the State*, Oxford: Clarendon Press.

Greenawalt, K. (1989), *Conflicts of Law and Morality*, Oxford: Oxford University Press.

Hare, R. M. (1976), 'Political Obligation', in T. Honderich, *Social Ends and Political Means*, London: Routledge and Kegan Paul.

Hart, H. L. A. (1955), 'Are There Any Natural Rights?', *Philosophical Review*, 175.

Hume, D. (1987), 'Of The Original Contract', in E. F. Miller (Ed.), *David Hume: Essays: Moral, Political and Literary*, Indianapolis: Indiana, Liberty Classics.

Kymlicka, W. (1990), *Contemporary Political Philosophy*, Oxford: Clarendon Press.

Locke, J. (1967), *An Essay Concerning the True and Original Extent of Civil Government* [the Second Treatise] in P. Laslett, *Locke's Two Treatises of Government*, Cambridge: Cambridge University Press.

Mill, J. S. (1962), *Utilitarianism*, Ed. M. Warnock, London: Fontana.

Nozick, R. (1974), *Anarchy, State and Utopia*, New York: Basic Books.

Plamenatz, J. P. (1968), *Consent, Freedom and Political Obligation*, Oxford: Oxford University Press.

Plato (1953), *Crito*, in B. Jowett, *The Dialogues of Plato*, Vol. 1, Oxford: Clarendon Press.

Rawls, J. (1964), 'Legal Obligation and the Duty of Fair Play', in S. Hook, *Law and Philosophy*, New York: New York University Press.

Rawls, J. (1972), *A Theory of Justice*, Oxford: Clarendon Press.

Raz, J. (1986), *The Morality of Freedom*, Oxford: Clarendon Press.

Rousseau, J. J. (1958), *The Social Contract*, Everyman edition, London: J. M. Dent.

Simmons, A. J. (1979), *Moral Principles and Political Obligations*, Princeton, New Jersey: Princeton University Press.

Singer, P. (1973), *Democracy and Disobedience*, Oxford: Clarendon Press.
Waldron, J. (1990), *The Law*, London: Routledge.
Wolff, R.P. (1970), *In Defense of Anarchism*, New York: Harper and
    Row.

9 *Barry Barnes*

Power

Conceptions of power

The concept of power in social and political theory is a development of that which we use in everyday life, so let us begin with the everyday notion. Standard dictionary definitions of 'power' include 'ability to do anything' and 'capacity for producing an effect', and we do indeed generally conceive of power as an ability, capacity or potentiality of some kind. In everyday life we attribute powers to agents or things as a reminder of what they might perhaps do at some future time, regardless of whether they are doing it now. By attributing powers we map the possibilities of things. We need to do this because future possibilities are every bit as important as present actualities in planning our actions and co-ordinating them with the actions of others.

In everyday life we are interested in every aspect of the future, and consequently we identify powers of many kinds. We recognise the powers of objects, like magnets; natural processes, like the fall of water; artefacts, like the engines in our motor cars; as well as the powers of the human body, the will, and of the groups, institutions and organisations which human beings collectively constitute. In social and political theory, however, 'power' refers to *social power*; a narrowing of the everyday notion is presumed. A corresponding narrowing of the dictionary definition allows us to describe social power as an ability to do things, a capacity to produce effects, which specifically derives from the existence of social relationships and organised social interactions.

'Power' is a readily intelligible notion which we use without difficulty in everyday life. 'Social power', being more narrowly defined, ought to give rise to even fewer difficulties in use. Yet 'social power' is in fact one of the most problematic and controversial of all the key concepts of social and political theory. Many social theorists offer wonderful insights into the nature and basis of power: Weber, Dahl, Arendt, Parsons, Lukes, Foucault and many others are indispensable reading on the subject. Yet all these writers are in radical disagreement with each other, about what power is, where it is, how we can tell what and where it is, what follows from its being what and where it is. To look at the basic position of any one of them will serve to identify not what the field is agreed upon, but the central topics of dispute and debate.[1]

Let us take Dahl, a marvellously lucid writer whose account of power was for a time widely accepted by political theorists, and the source of the most frequently cited definition of the concept: '(individual) A has power over (individual) B to the extent that A can get B to do something which B would not otherwise do' (Dahl, 1957, pp. 202–3). For all its apparent simplicity this definition embodies a specific view of the *nature* of power, the *social location* of power, and the *effects of the exercise* of power. And in each case this view represents one side of an ongoing controversy.

First of all power is defined entirely in terms of its effects and can be *any* kind of capacity which produces these effects: power is not a capacity of a particular kind or nature, or one with any particular intrinsic characteristics. But others insist that social power does indeed have a specific nature, and that its particular intrinsic characteristics must be taken into account if we are to grasp the role and significance of power in social contexts. Secondly, power is an attribute of *individuals* and is exercised in their relationships with other individuals. But others locate power at the *collective* level, and attribute it to groups or networks or institutions or even entire societies. Finally, by attributing it only to individuals and identifying it as that which secures compliance, power is equated with *domination* or *power over*, and the effects of its exercise become, almost by definition, *exploitative* and *unproductive*. B is forced to further A's interests at the expense of his/her own; A's profits are offset by B's losses. Here is the *zero-sum conception* of power, according to which the powerful gain only to the extent that others lose, and no overall benefit or advantage can accrue from the existence of power. But if power is attributed to collectives and understood as their capacity to do things, then the effects of its exercise will appear in a very different light. Now power can be understood as *power to*, as an enhanced capacity for action produced by and for a membership through the alignment and systematic organisation of its practices. Where *power over* implies domination, constraint and the *zero-sum conception*, *power to* may emerge from co-operation and co-ordination, and denote the *extra* capabilities consequent upon them.

Any attempt to formulate the 'best' way of thinking about social power will imply a particular way of resolving these various controversies. But before we set out upon that road let us pause to contemplate the controversies themselves. Anyone who has read the previous chapters of this book will be well aware that every major concept in social and political theory is surrounded by perpetual controversy. They will know too that writers define and use these concepts for moral and political purposes, and that as these purposes are both variable and conflicting, so too are definitions and modes of use. Nonetheless, it can be argued that controversies about power have a peculiar intensity for quite specific reasons. First of all, while we assume that power really exists, that it is incarnate in the world and not an unrealised ideal like 'freedom' or 'equality', even so power is by its nature *invisible*, and reality can never tell us directly which version of power is the correct one. Secondly, we are nonetheless obliged to employ some specific conception of power, and whichever conception is fastened upon will have a fundamental role in our moral life.

Steven Lukes (1974) is the political theorist who has most insistently and influentially argued that the choice between different conceptions of power is ineluctably a moral and evaluative one. He arrived at this view whilst analysing the way that power affects political decision-making. There are, says Lukes, three *dimensions* of political power, three ways in which it may be used to influence the decision-making process. Most straightforwardly, power may be exercised to ensure that one set of interests prevails over another, and that a contested political decision is made in the way in which the more powerful party prefers: here is the first dimension in which power operates. Less obviously, power may be used to ensure that policy issues are initially framed and formulated in the interests of its possessors, and that formulations which would serve other interests are never made available for debate: this second dimension of power affects not just the immediate process of decision-making, but behind-the-scenes activities like agenda-setting; and it may involve not just visible actions but also failures to act, which failures may prove to be just as significant in their consequences. Finally, power may be a means of shaping the perceptions and cognitions of others, so that what they consider to be in their interests is radically transformed: through this third dimension of power, its possessors may secure their interests not by winning a contest, or even by avoiding a contest, but by transforming the consciousness of their political opponents, and weakening their grasp upon the nature of their real interests so much that no contest threatens.

Lukes argues that any genuinely radical understanding of the operation of power must recognise that it takes place in all these three dimensions, but he stresses that only the first dimension of power is clearly and obviously manifest in visible behaviour. In the other two dimensions, power operates invisibly: what people *fail* to do, and what they *fail* to think of or perceive, is the only evidence for their existence, and negative evidence of this kind may be persuasive but not conclusive. Every actual choice between one-, two- or three-dimensional conceptions of power will in some degree be a moral choice, one which takes account of the moral and political significance of the alternative accounts. Since people invariably differ in morally based choices, Lukes characterises power as an *essentially contested concept.* Rational human beings will always disagree about how power operates, and about what power is and how it should be defined. Nor need a rational human being feel any particular anxiety about cleaving to that particular conception of power which best fits with his/her moral or political convictions.

Lukes must surely be right when he claims that no amount of evidence can force the theorist to just one precise conception of social power. What is *potential* can never be decisively inferred from what is *actual*, so that, even if holes are found in the specific arguments he offers, his conclusion here is still likely to stand. Lukes is also correct to emphasise the profound moral and evaluative importance of how we conceive of power. But he is not quite correct, I shall argue, to think of the selection of a conception of power as a value-laden choice with which an individual is faced. This view actually puts us in danger of underestimating the role of the concept in our moral life. How we should address the issues here may best be perceived if first we look at the central role of the concept of power as a component of the institution of responsible action.

Power and responsibility

The institution of responsible action is curiously neglected by social theorists, and there is little literature in our field which deals with its ramifications and complexities. However, only its most rudimentary features need concern us here. Suppose we seek to establish that a particular individual is responsible for an event or occurrence Z, so that he or she may legitimately be praised or blamed for that event. Normally, we must show that an action X (or a refusal to act) on the part of the individual is what led to or brought about the event in question: X → Z. And we must show at least three further things about the individual and his/her action.

1) That the individual had knowledge of what would ensue from his/her act, had knowledge that X was likely to lead to Z, and was acting in the light of that knowledge.
2) That X → Z was a natural causal sequence, preferably involving the intervention of no other human being, certainly involving no free action by another human being.
3) That when the individual did X he/she could have chosen instead to do something other than X, so that the individual was not *powerless* to act otherwise at this point. Only if an individual has the *power* to do something else instead of X can he/she be *responsible* for doing X.

These are familiar features of the institution of responsible action, and since we are all expert in employing the resources of that institution it is easy to find instances of them in our everyday discourse. Notice then how the imputation of power is an essential prelude to the imputation of responsibility, and hence, in many cases, the assignation of blame and opprobrium. Recall also the opposite tendency, which seeks to exculpate individuals by insisting that they lacked the power to act other than as they did. The behaviour of those identified as powerless is usually described with the discourse of the institution of causal connection, and, lacking responsibility, they escape blame for what they did. Thus, references to genetic abnormality or mental illness offer the possibility of exculpation, since these are putative determinants of behaviour which might perhaps fix it along a set path. References to violence and physical coercion may serve similarly, since we are generally willing to accept that a person in a state of extreme fear may be unable to do anything but comply, whatever 'willpower' he or she puts into resistance.

Whether the threat of more modest sanctions may render the individual powerless is a less settled matter. In the case of those accused of military atrocities, 'having to obey orders' fails as a defence only in the case of the vanquished, or so it would seem. And it apparently remains an open question how far the ordinary concentration camp guard, grade three, with family to support, should be held responsible for his or her actions.

The intimate connection between theories of power and conceptions of blame and responsibility, as well as the immense practical significance of that connection, can be graphically illustrated by reference to events associated with the growth of AIDS in Edinburgh through the 1980s. The unusually large increase of HIV/AIDS in Edinburgh has mainly been due to its transmission between injecting drug-users sharing needles. Persistence in needle-sharing has in turn been the consequence of restrictions placed on their availability. The continuation of the restrictions over a long period was itself the consequence of decisions taken by just a few individuals, all well-informed on the connections between needle supply, needle-sharing and HIV transmission. Indeed some accounts refer to a single 'powerful' individual in this case, a member of the British Government and the Scottish Office, able to restrict or expedite the supply of needles as he chose, who chose to do the former.

Let us say now that the drug-users subsequently to suffer HIV/AIDS were addicts, powerless to do other than they did, physiologically constrained and determined, coerced by dependency. Then there would be a secure causal link from the action of the powerful individual to a number of cases of suffering and death. That individual could legitimately be confronted with the responsibility for these directly engendered consequences of his action (not to mention the, possibly spectacular, second- and third-order consequences). Indeed it would not stretch language unduly to say that what we have here are cases of manslaughter, or worse. But suppose we hold instead that the drug-users were free agents with the power to do other than they did, that their physiological urges were resistible, that if they wished to risk infection for a shot it was their choice. Now the causal chain is broken and our powerful politician escapes without reproach. Those with the virus are responsible for their own tragedy and can blame themselves.

Needless to say, these simple accounts of where there is power and where there is external causation may be varied or embellished in innumerable ways. Stress may be placed on the role not of a single individual, but of a 'powerful' bureaucracy, or political faction, or class or stratum of society, which would then be set up to take the blame for what occurred. Instead of citing individual decisions to restrict needle supply, a 'two-dimensional' account could cite the *failure* of individuals or organisations to act against misguided decision-makers. Or a three-dimensional account could refer to the subtle conditioning which prevented the generality of people from perceiving an identity of interest with the victims of the tragedy, and suppressed their natural inclination to help them. Responsibility might perhaps in this way be lain at the door of whatever powers had successfully induced the cigarette-smoking, alcohol-guzzling, pill-popping population of the country to withdraw its sympathy from 'drug-users'.

Clearly there is enormous scope for choice in constructing accounts of the role of power in episodes of this kind. Any number of different social units may be referred to. Different dimensions for the operation of power may be emphasised. Above all, different assignations of responsible and caused action may be made, implying different invisible distributions of capacities and potentials for action – that is, of power. But there is no indefeasible account of where power really lies, nor of the units with which it is really associated or the dimensions in which it really operates. The details of any actual account will always be contestable. And every set of claims is liable to have a certain moral and political utility. All this is merely to follow Steven Lukes' seminal account.

Nor, having come so far with Lukes, should we dismiss his final claim: there is indeed a certain sense in which any given general conception of power is going to be 'inextricably tied to further background assumptions which are methodological and epistemological but also moral and political assumptions' (Lukes, 1979, p.262). To understand the sense in which this may be correct, however, two key points must be borne in mind. The first is that power does not imply blame, but allows praise or blame: in the context of our institutionalised discourse, where there is power there is responsibility. The second is that the 'choice' of a general conception of power is not a paradigmatic case of individual choice at all. To advance such a conception is to propose the adoption of an institution, by which I mean a routine way of accounting not just for one episode in the context of our social life, but for a vast range of such episodes.

Thus, it may be that oppressed groups in society (like injecting drug-users) are routinely identifiable as powerless on one conception of power, but not on others. As we have seen, such a conception may serve to defend these groups and cause their enemies discomfort – at times. What needs to be recognised, however, is that the same conception may facilitate oppression at other times: it may, for example, provide a credible pretext for withdrawing rights from group members on the grounds that they are not responsible agents.[2] The assumption that oppression is wrong has no evident relevance to the choice between alternative conceptions of power. And indeed it is hard to understand how any set of specific general moral and political assumptions might bear upon people's reasoning when they make choices of this kind. For the role of a shared conception of power cannot be merely that of providing assistance to one or other side in a specific political or moral debate; rather it must be to provide part of the framework within which such debates can occur. We should think of a conception of power as a (potential) constituent of an overall form of life, wherein it may provide the kind of agreement in language essential to the articulation of disagreement in opinion (or assumption). It is only in this sense that a shared conception of power may be understood as having a moral significance.[3] And this is why in everyday life we do manage to sustain a shared basic conception of power despite the many moral and evaluative convictions which divide us.

One of the two great objectives of social and political theory is quite explicitly moral. Political theorists analyse the inadequacies of our current political understanding and organisation with the aim of advancing us towards the good life. Accordingly, there is much for them to say, at the level of detail, about our everyday understanding of power. But the *basic form* of the existing everyday conception of power seems eminently compatible with most existing 'moral and political assumptions'. At least, it is hard to see how effective criticism of that basic form might be straightforwardly derived from 'conservative' or 'liberal' or 'radical' assumptions. Our existing routine conception of power is incarnate in our institution of responsible action, and its basic form may be identified by studying how we assign responsibility. First of all, we account people responsible for their actions in so far as they have the power to act otherwise. Secondly, we employ our knowledge of where power lies, of what engenders it and what dissipates it, to attribute powers in particular cases and hence responsibility. Thirdly, in default of knowledge, and lacking reasons to believe the contrary, we presume that action is responsible action. On this basis we identify responsible agents, those whose actions might perhaps be modified by persuasion or reasoned argument, those who are sanctionable in discourse. And, in so far as we err in our attributions of responsibility, we err by according dignity and especially human qualities where perhaps we should not, rather than by refusing to accord them where perhaps we should. And all this is as it should be.

But to sustain the institution of responsible action we have to deploy knowledge of power, and power is invisible. What then, ideally, should be the basis of this knowledge? The answer is that the knowledge we use here should be *empirically based* knowledge. We should seek to *find out* as much as we can about power, and the more we can find out the better will (may) be our moral and political life. But, again, what of the fact that power and so many of the processes through which it operates are *invisible*? No matter. We may seek empirically based knowledge of power, just as natural scientists seek empirically based knowledge of forces and fields and waves and particles, and the many other invisible entities which are central to their activities. Indeed, to seek to extend our knowledge in this way is a part of the second great objective of social and political theory, which is to advance our knowledge and theoretical understanding of social life as it actually exists. It is now time to consider power in relation to this second objective.

Describing and explaining power

There is no single way of characterising and identifying social power; indeed, there are innumerable ways. If not actually contested, the concept of social power will nonetheless always be contestable. Precisely this can be said, however, of *all* our concepts, including the concepts of the natural sciences. The natural world, like the social world, can be conceptualised and described in innumerable ways, all perfectly reasonable and consistent with evidence. The natural world is silent: it enters no protest whichever of these innumerable descriptions are used. Natural scientists seek to agree in their use of just a few descriptions, consonant with their practical concerns and technical interests. It is open to us in the social sciences to proceed in much the same way, to speak of power without definite evaluative concerns, simply as a part of the business of trying to work out how societies operate, and hence how some kinds of future states of society may perhaps be avoided and others encouraged. If we take this as our project, then we may legitimately develop and evaluate theoretical conceptions of power in terms of their utility in description and/or explanation.[4]

Many social and political theorists have developed classifications of the different kinds of social power. Such taxonomies provide a framework and vocabulary for the systematic description of the relevant phenomena, and sensitise us to aspects of those phenomena which we might otherwise overlook, similarities and differences between states of affairs not routinely marked in our common-sense understanding. One important taxonomy worth detailed attention for this reason is that of Dennis Wrong (1979), who identifies *force, manipulation, persuasion* and *authority* as the four basic forms of power (pp. 21ff). Even more important in the context of social and political theory, however, is the widely accepted identification of *political, economic* and *ideological* power as the basic forms. This traditional taxonomy derives from Max Weber's celebrated account of the distribution of power in terms of *status, class* and *party* (1968, p. 926), an account which every student of social theory reads at some point. However, the original Weberian scheme includes no reference to the power of armed force and physical coercion, to 'condign power' (Galbraith, 1984, p. 22), or 'destructive power' (Boulding, 1989, p. 23). Jessop (1972, p. 58) deals with this problem by treating 'political power' as a composite of two fundamental forms, one based on force and one on status. This leads him to identify *four* kinds of power: *political–military, economic, social (status-based)* and *cultural*. Michael Mann uses a very similar scheme, in which *military, economic, political* and *ideological* power are the basic forms, as the framework for a vast history of the growth of networks of power 'from earliest times to the present' (Mann, 1986, pp. 22ff). This is an invaluable resource for anyone who seeks an empirically based understanding of power.

Classifications and taxonomies have two important kinds of use. They may assist in a clear and systematic description of empirical states of affairs, and they may prepare the ground for attempts at explanation and understanding. All of the theorists cited above make good use of their favoured taxonomies for purposes of description. All of these theorists, however, are also concerned to advance our understanding of power by identifying its *sources* or *bases*, and here they are everywhere muddled and inconsistent. And indeed it is true in social and political theory generally that whilst there is no problem at all in perceiving that power is 'there', and in accounting for all kinds of actions as the consequences of its being there, the problem of explaining how or why the power comes to be there, and why it remains there, is one of extraordinary difficulty.

Consider Michael Mann's account of the four *sources* of social power. Ideological power derives, according to Mann, from the monopolisation of meaning, of norms, or of ritual and aesthetic practices. Economic power derives from control of the means of production, distribution and exchange, and is possessed by those able to monopolise such control. Military force is a source of power for the military elites who monopolise it. The source of political power is usually the State: 'Those who control the state, the state elite, can obtain both collective and distributive power ...' (1986, pp. 22–7). In all these cases the *source* of a form of power is said to be control and monopolisation of a form of power. Power derives from power. And those who derive power from power are those who 'control' or 'monopolise' or 'monopolise control of' the power – which raises the question of what 'control' and 'monopolisation' are based on, if not on power.

This tendency to presume what needs to be explained is no idiosyncrasy of Mann's: his work merely illustrates a lapse encountered again and again throughout the entire literature of the field. Thus, for Jessop (1972, p. 58) 'the ultimate basis of economic power is control over the means of production, distribution and exchange ...'; that of political power is 'control over the means of coercion'; and so on. For Dahl, the ability to exercise power may derive from 'control over information', and, more strikingly yet, from 'legal powers' (1961, p. 226). Galbraith (1984) identifies property and organisation as two basic sources of power; but is not what is required to defend the institution of property, and to constitute and reconstitute organisation, precisely power?

How is this spectacular circularity possible? Why have so many participants in this field remained content with such inadequate accounts? One reason is that when evaluated only in a narrow context there is often some truth in the accounts. A may have power over B because A has power over C. It may be A's capacity to do one thing which accounts for A's capacity to do another. One power may indeed, to an extent, account for another. And if one's concern is entirely with single connections and immediate explanations, one may indeed be satisfied with such an account, even though it leaves the system of power relations in the main problematic and unexplained. But social and political theorists do not suffer from such blinkered vision; indeed their brief is precisely to describe and appraise social relationships on a large scale. Some further explanation of their failures of perception is accordingly necessary. It is to be found in their general acceptance of a conception of power as *power over*.

Theorists who are solely interested in *power over*, in domination and subordination, see other kinds of power as interesting only in so far as they help to explain domination. They explain *power over* in terms of *power to*, and their curiosity switches off when that immediate objective has been achieved. Chains of power are never followed over their full extent, so that a proper appreciation of the pervasive, systemic character of power is never achieved, and the entire repertoire of powers and capacities which constitute our ability to do things is left out of account. Thus, in Michael Mann's account of power its four *sources* are what military organisations can do, what economic organisations can do, what political organisations can do – especially the State, and what ideology and its institutional and organisational expressions can do. Vast capacities for action, immense *powers to* do things, are treated as *sources* of power; they are referred to, not as manifestations of *power to*, the basis of which needs to be understood and explained, but as sources of *power over*, sources which raise no problems of understanding and explanation in themselves. To this extent Mann's book is not an investigation of sources of power at all: its value lies in its provision of an encyclopaedic history of the growth of social organisations and social networks with ever-increasing capacities for action, and in its insights into the consequences of that growth. In this respect it continues the work of Max Weber, the social theorist who initiated the project of analysing history as rationalisation and bureaucratisation.

If our concern is to understand and account for social power, then we should accept, first of all, that *power to* is prior to *power over*, and secondly that powers of both kinds are linked together in chains and networks, and hence can only be understood as extended, delocalised features of social formations. Even if our initial interest is simply in how A enforces compliance on B, we find ourselves forced to attend to the capacities for action available to A and the countervailing capacities available to B. And to understand these, we have to look beyond A and B at the overall distribution of capacities in the social context, and at the entire pattern of organised social relationships which constitutes that context. Among the major theorists who help in the difficult task of conceptualising power in this way are Talcott Parsons and Michel Foucault.[5]

In so far as power is concerned, Talcott Parsons is indeed the unsung hero of the Anglo-Saxon tradition of social and political theory. In the 1960s he developed an account of political power which treated it in the context of political systems as the analogue of money in economic systems. Just as the possession of money affords a generalised capacity to secure the provision of economic goods and services, so the possession of political power affords a generalised capacity to secure the performance of political obligations. And just as money is a circulating currency in the economic system, so political power is a circulating currency in the political system. The details of this account remain of undiminished interest and have still to receive the attention they deserve,[6] but its general implications were no less significant. By making the analogy with money Parsons emphasised the facilitative dimension of power, its existence as *power to*, and its delocalised, systemic character, which required that it be understood and explained as a property of entire social systems.

Nor does the importance of Parsons' work end here; on the contrary, when we seek to understand entire social systems and their properties, he remains a pre-eminent authority. As is well known, Parsons' extensive *oeuvre* analyses entire social systems at two levels. It gives a functionalist account of such systems as integrated sets of social institutions, related to each other like the organs of a living creature. It also considers them as constituted of myriads of individual actions, and asks why those actions result in the stability and persistence of social systems as a whole. Parsons refers to this as *the problem of social order*, and offers what remains the most extensively developed and widely accepted solution to it in the entire literature of social theory.

Parsons rejects the view that social order may persist as a consequence of self-interested individual calculation. He agrees with Thomas Hobbes that self-interest leads inescapably to strife. Fortunately, self-interest can be overridden, and individuals can be induced to act in conformity with (socially functional) rules or norms, through socialisation. During socialisation, norms are *internalised*, and become part of the moral conscience of the individual. The individual develops a non-rational commitment to the norms. The psychological discomfort which arises from deviation from social norms is then usually sufficient to offset the urges of self-interest, and system-sustaining actions ensue. Powers and power relations are themselves elements of the systems of norms to which people are morally committed. Power is legitimate; power is functional: consequently, power persists. Here is a genuine attempt to provide a theoretical explanation of the nature and basis of power, built upon a general theory of social action and social order. It is a measure of Parsons' greatness as a social theorist that scarcely anyone else has made such an attempt.

Whether or not Parsons is correct is, however, another matter. His fundamental ideas provide one starting point for social theory, one that should continue to be explored, but many in the field, including the present author, nonetheless believe them to be wrong. Parsons relates calculative action to the isolated individual and his/her self-interest; he sees nothing in calculative action which might contribute to the reduction of strife and the maintenance of social order. Accordingly, he is forced to ascribe the persistence of social order to internal moral regulation, to non-calculative, non-rational action prompted by internalised social norms. Against this, it has been argued first that internal moral regulation does not and cannot play the crucial role which Parsons requires of it, and second that calculative action is not intelligible as the action of independent individuals in the way that Parsons assumes.[7]

Calculative action is action based on knowledge. But individuals do not make their own knowledge. They acquire it from the collective and develop and modify it collectively. This raises the possibility that individuals may be bound together by the knowledge which they share – that, far from inducing strife, calculative action on the basis of shared knowledge may be precisely what allows people to co-operate and co-ordinate with each other. If this is so then social order is the achievement of rational, knowledgeable human beings, and power persists as an aspect of the distribution of knowledge. Since this way of conceptualising power has not been systematically expounded and evaluated like that of Parsons, I shall try briefly to indicate what it involves in the final section of the chapter.

Power and knowledge

Suppose we want to specify the powers of a given individual, his/her capacities or capabilities. Clearly, we are never in a position to specify everything that an individual is capable of doing, but suppose we seek the best possible account. Such an account will have to refer to the physiology of the individual, to muscle power for example, and also to the physical environment, to the material resources which lie to hand, and the tools and artefacts to which the individual has access. But reference to the social environment will also be essential: the individual will have powers as a result of being trained and socialised as a member of a collective. These social powers will be learned powers, and the best way of describing them will be to describe what the member *knows*.

What is true of the individual will also be true of the collective. Its powers, what it is capable of over and above the separate physical capabilities of its individual members, will depend upon what the collective knows. But now it is necessary to specify not just what but where something is known. Collectives manifest both a mental and a physical division of labour, and their power as collectives depends upon that division. The social power of a collective is a function of the *distribution of knowledge* over the collective.

The identification of power with the distribution of knowledge is intuitively acceptable as far as *power to* is concerned. The power of the US army clearly has a lot to do with what its soldiers know, about firing weapons and avoiding enemy fire, about maintaining and repairing weapons, about sources of supply of ammunition and spares, and so on. Clearly too, the power of the army depends upon this knowledge being appropriately distributed, so that actions can be properly co-ordinated and performed in concert. But what of those aspects of power traditionally referred to in terms of obedience, domination and the power of A *over* B? Why, for example, do officers command and other ranks obey? How is it that the power of the army is effectively *possessed* by the officers or, conceivably, the commanding officer alone, even though it is *constituted* by the capabilities of everybody? How is it that *discretion* in the use of the powers of the army is so concentrated?

Even this should be understood as an aspect of the overall distribution of knowledge. The difficulty is that we generally think of knowledge solely as an asset. Our knowledge of nature helps us to predict and control nature. Our knowledge of other people helps us to co-operate with other people: it allows us to co-ordinate with each other, to act in concert to further everyone's interests, as when we (nearly) all drive on the left or (nearly) all stop at a red traffic light. But knowledge may also constrain and restrict its possessors, so that they are worse off with it than without it. Possession of knowledge may engender obedience and subordination in a way that ignorance would not. And once this counter-intuitive idea is accepted, it is no longer difficult to understand how *power over* as well as *power to* may be constituted as a distribution of knowledge.

Other ranks in the army obey their officers. The officers thereby possess the capacity to act through the bodies of 'their men'. Throughout the army, bodies are liable to move or remain still, move in this way or that, at this time or that, separately or in unity, at the discretion of the officers. How is this possible? In particular, how is it possible simply as a consequence of what officers and 'men' know of each other? The answer is that obedience will be secured when individuals take obedience to be in their interest, given what they know. Consider Michael Polanyi's account of the basis of the power Stalin came to enjoy over his party comrades and his society as a whole:

It is commonly assumed that power cannot be exercised without some voluntary support, as for example by a faithful praetorian guard. I do not think this is true, for it seems that some dictators were feared by everybody; for example, towards the end of his rule, everybody feared Stalin. It is, in fact, easy to see that a single individual might well exercise command over a multitude of men without any appreciable voluntary support on the part of any of them. If in a group of men each believes that all the others will obey the commands of a person claiming to be their common superior, all will obey this person as their superior. For each will fear that if he disobeyed him, the others would punish his disobedience at the superior's command, and so all are forced to obey by the mere supposition of the others' continued obedience, without any voluntary support being given to the superior by any member of the group (Polanyi, 1958, pp. 224–5)

Never mind the historical complexities. Consider the basic idea of how a single person may command a multitude. Stalin could command only because of what each individual knew about Stalin, about what everyone knew about Stalin, and about what everyone knew about everyone else. Knowing what they did, individuals found it expedient to act as they did, obediently; this served to confirm the continuing validity of their original knowledge, and hence to reconstitute the conditions in which it was expedient to be obedient. Lack of knowledge would have precluded all this: knowledge here was a liability, not an asset.

I want to emphasise two important features of our knowledge of each other: the form of knowledge which constitutes *power over*, such as Stalin's. First, whilst there is a deep equivalence between knowledge and power here, so that the *system* of knowledge is the same thing as the *system* of power, there is no one-to-one correspondence between the power, or discretion, at a specific social location, and a specific item of knowledge. Rather, what appertains at any point as far as power and its possession are concerned is intelligible only by reference to *the entire distribution* of knowledge. Stalin was a point source in Soviet society where discretion in the use of power was concentrated; but in so far as Stalin's *power over* was not willingly conceded to him, it had come to exist because of what had become known to all of those whom he dominated.

This is why the question of the sources and bases of *power over* has always proved so difficult, and why writers have tended to go round in circles as they have struggled with it. Starting with the *power over* clearly visible at a given point, the search for its basis is liable to lead one on an unending journey through the entire extended cognitive order, a journey which may suggest that its basis is obscure and ill-defined.

Yet the basis of *power over* is neither of these things. Its identification as an aspect of the distribution of knowledge is perfectly straightforward, and if this seems a vague formulation it is only because it does not fit nicely with the individualistic and atomistic styles of thought which predominate in the social sciences. It needs to be related to genuinely holistic ways of thinking, like those widely employed in the natural sciences.[8] The account just given of Stalin's power may be likened, for example, to the standard account of why a solid body has a centre of mass (or centre of gravity). The centre of mass is defined by the overall distribution of mass: it exists at a *single* specific point which is fixed by the density of the body at *every* point.

Of course, in all real societies powers are exercised at many and various social locations, not just one: there is a distribution of (possession of) power over the whole. But it remains the case that power at any point is constituted by knowledge everywhere.

The mapping between power and knowledge is difficult to grasp because it is not the familiar mapping of one-to-one correspondence of parts, like that between a photographic print and the image it offers the eye. Instead of taking the *photograph* as our model of information storage we should do better to take the *hologram*. Every point on a hologram plays a part in reconstituting the entire representation which it stores. Cut a hologram in half and you have, not two separate halves of the initial image, as with a photograph, but two complete images, albeit each slightly less detailed in resolution than the original. Conversely, take any point in the overall image and it will connect back to every part of the hologram. If we take a magnifying glass to the surface of a holographic plate it is not at all apparent what image is stored there, unlike a photograph where the information presents itself directly, as it were. The image in the hologram is lost to direct apprehension. This is how power gets lost in the minds (brains) of a collective.

Let me move now to the second key characteristic of our knowledge of each other. It is *self-referring* and *self-validating* knowledge. My knowledge of other people includes knowledge of what those people know of me, of others, of themselves. Their knowledge of me likewise includes knowledge of what I know. Consider then the system of knowledge as a whole, and ask what its referents are — what it is *about*. Part of what it is about is itself and its own distribution. This makes the knowledge self-referring. But what knowledge refers to, what it is about, is what we look to to check if it is valid. Self-referring knowledge is implicated in its own validation: acceptance of the knowledge is part of what makes it correct (when it is correct); its rejection is liable to invalidate it.

There is a fundamentally important difference here between our knowledge of each other and our knowledge of nature, which latter serves as our paradigm of knowledge. Knowledge of nature has independent referents. In the last analysis,[9] we check our knowledge of plants or planets or polymers by looking at plants or planets or polymers, and not by looking at how many people already accept the knowledge we are checking. With what we know of each other this independence of acceptance and validity no longer appertains. Does red mean stop at the traffic light? Just so long as (nearly) everyone knows that it does, it does. If a bare majority knows, then it is no longer clear that they are right in what they know. If just one or two claim to know that red means stop, and nobody else has any idea of it, then 'red means stop' is an invalid knowledge-claim.

Stalin's underlings had knowledge of Stalin and of each other. They knew he was everywhere obeyed. Knowing what they did, they obeyed him. By their obedience they confirmed the validity of what they knew, and continued to accept it as valid. Acceptance of the knowledge generated confirming instances of it. Rejection of the knowledge would have led to disconfirming instances. As a system, knowledge of the power structure was self-referring and self-validating: indeed knowledge of the power structure was the power structure. The overall system of domination and obedience had the character of a vast monumental self-fulfilling prophecy.

If social life is constituted by the actions of responsible knowledgeable agents, then this is how we should understand the basis of such stability and orderliness as it possesses. Not just crude systems of domination and obedience, but all manner of organisations, institutions and hierarchies are constituted as systems of self-referring knowledge, and persist as self-fulfilling prophecies. This gives us an answer to one of the perennial problems of the social sciences. We have, both as social scientists and as ordinary members, knowledge of institutions, organisations and social structures of many kinds. But where are these things we know of? Often claimed to be completely external to individuals, they have proved extremely difficult to find, and indeed no clear instructions have ever been produced as to where to go to take a look at them. The reason is now clear: their existence is constituted by their being known. They are brilliantly concealed, not just by being internal to us – states of mind or brain, as it were – but by being the very elements of our internal awareness that constitute our knowledge of them.

Domination and obedience characterise the relationships between people in hierarchies, organisations and institutions. But these are not 'external' structures with an independent existence; they are entities which must be continually constituted and reconstituted in the minds of their members. The processes in which new members learn about a hierarchy are the processes which create and re-create it as a hierarchy. That is perhaps why there is such obsessive concern, in hierarchies and organisations, with the dissemination of knowledge of how they are constituted, and why mutual learning is constantly reinforced by visible symbols and ritual representations. Without the ongoing processes of learning there is nothing to be learned about.

That powers and discretion in their use are constituted by self-referring knowledge also throws light upon what appertains when organisations are disrupted, and hitherto stable hierarchies collapse. Something along these lines has happened on a significant scale in Eastern Europe, and more recently in the former Soviet Union.[10] Where does power lie in circumstances of this kind? As ever, where it is known to lie. But there have been times when nobody seemed to know where it lay, or at least where supreme power lay, so where did it lie then? As ever, where power was not known to be, it was not: if knowledge of where supreme power lay did not exist, then there was no supreme power.

Consider the state of affairs in the Soviet Union at the time of the coup against Gorbachev. What was the balance of forces? How was (discretion in the use of) power distributed? The members of the society themselves did not know. Not even the senior politicians and bureaucrats knew. Throughout the coup these people were guessing. In a sense, the coup itself was a guess. Did some guess right and others wrong? Only with hindsight. At the time, there was no distribution of power independent of the guessing, in terms of which to evaluate it. At the time, what any one person was capable of doing depended on the guesses which others were making. There was a power structure of guesses. If most people had guessed that the preponderance of power lay with the coup leaders then probably it would have come to lie with them; and not just most people but almost all people would soon after have come to know that there was where power had come to lie. No doubt this was the pattern of guesses that the coup leaders hoped for. But their skill in encouraging that pattern to emerge was evidently lacking, and the situation through the coup was initially lacking in pattern and then took on a pattern adverse to them.

Where power lies, and where it is known to lie, are no more independent in chaotic situations than in stable situations. In a stable situation, knowledge of where political power lies is like knowledge of what the red light means: just as the stopping power of the traffic light consists in its being known to mean stop, so the powers of a political agent consist in their being known. In a chaotic situation, agents are like traffic lights operating in a transport system in the absence of a code. Until there is a code, until there is shared knowledge, there is no stopping power and no political power. Only when some fortunate circumstance brings about a co-ordination of belief will power come to exist: only when red comes to be known to mean stop will the lights come to have stopping power, and only when political agent A comes to be known as more powerful than B or C will political power become structured in that way.

In the midst of chaos, before sufficient co-ordination of belief has occurred and knowledge has become securely established, detailed analysis of 'where power really lies' may be misconceived. Better perhaps to *act* in these conditions, in any way which might conceivably encourage a favourable co-ordination of belief, rather than to waste time gathering information and attempting to calculate one's chances. Better to stand on a tank in front of a TV camera.[11]

Notes

1   Recent accounts of the many and various conceptions of power currently employed in social and political theory include Lukes (1986), Barnes (1988) and Clegg (1989).

2   In practice, of course, political and moral argument is thoroughly inconsistent; people make each other out as powerful or powerless just as suits their immediate interests, and juggle conceptions of power as expediency dictates. But this does not count against the basic point.

3   This way of looking at things derives from Wittgenstein (1968). For a Wittgenstinian account of power, see Clegg (1975).

4   A great deal more needs to be said here, but the issues are too large. Lukes (see especially his 1979 article) assumed that social-scientific concepts differed from natural-scientific ones in being essentially contestable. Opinion has now swung to the view that the two kinds of concept are alike in this respect. Indeed, descriptions of the social sciences initially developed to *contrast* these sciences with the natural sciences are now widely recognised as describing the latter very well – certainly better than the mythology of logical empiricism traditionally accepted as an ideal account of natural science (Barnes, Bloor and Henry, 1993).

5   Foucault (1979, 1980) has to be dealt with at length if at all. Hence, despite his seminal importance and his insight into the close links between power and knowledge, a topic treated in some detail in the final section of this chapter, I omit a discussion of his thinking here. For an interesting attempt to situate his work in the overall tradition of social and political theory, see Clegg (1989).

6   I give a detailed evaluation of Parsons' papers on power (1967) in Barnes (1988). The revival of structural functionalist approaches in the social sciences may well bring the ideas of these papers back to prominence. Another important theorist who deserves to benefit from the same trend is Niklaus Luhmann (1979).

7   Both the arguments referred to and the attempt to understand the nature of social power which follows are elaborated and justified in detail in Barnes (1988).

8   The idea that the natural sciences are characteristically individualistic and atomistic in approach is another part of the myth of those fields (see note 4) which needs to be discarded.

9   A very considerable oversimplification is involved here, as readers conversant with current problems in the sociology of knowledge will recognise.

10   The events of 1989 occurred once it was realised that Soviet armed forces would not act to prevent them. Clearly, the distribution of knowledge that constitutes a stable social order is not wholly and entirely self-referring. What people know is only a part of what their knowledge refers to. Notice too what 1989 implies for the notion of *legitimation*, a process regarded by many theorists as crucial in the maintenance of large-scale social stability. No regimes put greater effort and resources into legitimation than those of Eastern Europe. But how many extra minutes of stability did that effort produce? For my own views on legitimation, see Barnes (1988, 4.3).

11   Yeltsin's *coup de théâtre* is perhaps the most vivid memory remaining from Western news coverage of the events. Whether it was crucial is impossible to say; the argument implicit here is that it could have been.

Bibliography

Barnes, B. (1986), 'On Authority and its Relationship to Power', in J. Law (Ed.), q.v.

Barnes, B. (1988), *The Nature of Power*, Cambridge: Polity Press.

Barnes, B., Bloor, D.C. and Henry, J. (1993), *Scientific Knowledge: a Sociological Analysis*, London: Athlone Press.

Boulding, K. (1989), *Three Faces of Power*, London: Sage.

Brown, S.C. (Ed.) (1979), *Philosophical Disputes in the Social Sciences*, Brighton: Harvester Press.

Clegg, S.R. (1975), *Power, Rule and Domination*, London: Routledge.

Clegg, S.R. (1989), *Frameworks of Power*, London: Sage.

Dahl, R. (1957), 'On the Concept of Power', *Behavioral Science*, 2, pp. 202–3.

Dahl, R. (1961), *Who Governs?*, New Haven: Yale University Press.

Foucault, M. (1979), *Discipline and Punish*, New York: Vintage.

Foucault, M. (1980), *Power/Knowledge*, New York: Pantheon.

Galbraith, J.K. (1984), *The Anatomy of Power*, London: Hamish Hamilton.

Henshel, R.L. (1978), 'Self Altering Predictions', in J. Fowles (Ed.), *Handbook of Futures Research*, Westport: Greenwood Press.

Jessop, R. (1972), *Social Order, Reform and Revolution*, London: Macmillan.

Krishna, D. (1971), ' "The Self-Fulfilling Prophesy" and the Nature of Society', *American Sociological Review*, 36, 4, pp. 1104–7.

Law, J. (Ed.) (1986), *Power, Action and Belief*, London: Routledge.

Lewis, D.K. (1969), *Convention*, Cambridge, Mass.: Harvard University Press.

Luhmann, N. (1979), *Trust and Power*, New York: John Wiley.

Lukes, S. (1974), *Power: A Radical View*, London: Macmillan.

Lukes, S. (1979), 'On the Relativity of Power', in S.C. Brown (Ed.), q.v.

Lukes, S. (Ed.) (1986), *Power*, Oxford: Basil Blackwell.

Mann, M. (1986), *The Sources of Social Power*, Vol.1, Cambridge: Cambridge University Press.

Parsons, T. (1937), *The Structure of Social Action*, New York: MacGraw-Hill.

Parsons, T. (1951), *The Social System*, New York: Free Press.

Parsons, T. (1967), *Sociological Theory and Modern Society*, New York: Free Press.

Polanyi, M. (1958), *Personal Knowledge*, London: Routledge and Kegan Paul.

Weber, M. (1968), *Economy and Society*, New York: Beckminster Press.

Wieder, D.L. (1976), *Language and Social Reality*, The Hague: Mouton.

Wittgenstein, L. (1968), *Philosophical Investigations*, Oxford: Basil Blackwell.

Wrong, D. (1979), *Powers: Its Forms, Bases and Uses*, Oxford: Basil Blackwell.

Realism and international relations

Introduction

International relations have been dominated by the gap between
theory and reality. There are three reasons for this. The first concerns
the problem of definition and uncertainty about the nature of the
subject itself. Some problems of definition include whether it is a
discipline in itself, or a cross-disciplinary field, embracing subjects
such as economics, sociology, law, etc. Other difficulties focus on
parameters of the field, e.g. the type of actor playing in the international arena, and the forms of interaction to be examined. So,
at the outset of discussion about international relations theory, we
confront uncertainty about what it is that we wish to discuss.

The second problem concerns the *assumptions* we use to study
international relations. These affect the kinds of questions we ask,
and the types of answers we give to them. Until the late twentieth
century, it had often been assumed that the *only* important questions
requiring answers concerned wars (why do they happen? how do we
prevent them?). It was often assumed that once we discovered the
answers to these questions, we would know the basis of relations
between states, and the answers would guide statecraft. But any
formulation of the problem − or its solution − is invariably coloured
by the context in which it is placed, our notions of reality, and
our values. The person doing the theorising and the type of theory
used are very much bound together (Holsti, 1985, p. viii). Human
beings, with their different values and viewpoints, theorise differently
about the actions of states and organisations because the states and
organisations are themselves human constructs.

It follows that the circumstances in which individuals find themselves also colour the questions they consider to be important, and
their approaches to problems. For example, is it credible to believe

that the causes and prevention of war are burning questions for people in states which do not feel the direct threat of war (for example, Japan or Switzerland)? Are inter-state wars (remember we are discussing *international* relations) considered important by people in States experiencing civil wars (such as Somalia, the Lebanon and Yugoslavia), or seeking to prevent them (such as the Commonwealth of Independent States – the CIS)? Do the problems of, or the solutions to, war matter to new states and their populations, if they have little or no sense of being a state (Africa and the CIS)? Are the causes and prevention of inter-state war of paramount importance to those states which suffer problems of debt, and mal- or under-development (Africa, Asia, Latin America, Eastern Europe)? Do states (and their leaders) behave *objectively*, or do past experiences help them to interpret the present? What ideology (if any) guides the formulation of solutions?

The final problem concerns the *paradigm* (a general or theoretical model) used to elaborate more specific theories about interaction in international relations. Because paradigms embrace our most general assumptions about the world and the way it works, they are subject to the differing human values and perceptions discussed above. Paradigms help to *organise reality* in a comprehensible manner. The paradigm used will determine the manner in which we view international relations, its burning questions, the solutions to those questions, and the policy prescriptions to be identified. The question for idealists identified the causes of war; the solution identified the prevention of war, etc. For Marxists, the question concerned the causes of economic inequality among people, and the political and economic means for eliminating it. Realists assumed that the question concerned survival and power-lust, and that the answers would involve power management. In international relations, as with all other areas in politics, there is no agreement about the best paradigm to use.

It is evident from this discussion that there is not a *single* central problem in international relations, but many; the possible answers are also many, and depend on the assumptions and the values of the person(s) making them. There is not a single type of actor, but many, which have different roles (and impacts) on the international stage. Nor is there a single *uncontested* paradigm of international relations. However, during this century, one paradigm, *realism*, from which most current international relations theories have arisen, has dominated the Western interpretation of and writing on international relations. It came to prominence because it *appeared* to explain the international situation from 1914 to 1945; then it *appeared* to explain the ideological conflict of the Cold War after 1945, and justified the actions and positions of the superpowers (the USA and the USSR). However, recent history, particularly expressed in the events since 1989, has challenged realism.

This chapter will discuss the assumptions behind realism, their implications, and the fit of this world view to events from its rise to the present day. Realism as an organiser of reality will be discussed. I shall argue that although it provides an initially attractive view to explain how the world works, it is neither an accurate predictor of motivations, actions and outcomes, nor of reality in the society of states. This is because realism cannot account for the increasing complexity of international interaction; it is an inadequate paradigm.

The central assumptions of realism

What aspects of realism command respect? Many of its components – such as the idea that power is the dynamic force in international relations, and that the power positions of states determine their survival – were identified long before this century, and were readily accepted by statesmen such as Prince Metternich, Winston Churchill and Charles de Gaulle. The realist thesis is simple and easy to grasp when put systematically, which partly explains its popularity. The truth of realism, say its advocates, resides in the lessons of history: factual events, rather than ideas, are emphasised – hence the realist label, and its popularity for statesmen and the general public since World War II.

Realism is not a single idea; it is a world view, based on several interrelated assumptions. The paradigm forms the basis of theories on more specific aspects of international relations, i.e. foreign policy decision-making, arms control, deterrence, diplomacy, foreign economic policy, etc. These assumptions cover the basis of human behaviour and motivation, the key actors and the environment in which they behave, and their parameters of action. They are interdependent and establish the truth of the paradigm. In other words, our ability to accept the world view as a true one depends on accepting that its key assumptions are true, on the one hand, and our ability to accept that these assumptions apply to actual events today, on the other. Realism is above all concerned with the struggle for power.

The power element appears to be argued far more strongly than any peace element.

The discussion below establishes the general assumptions of realism. It is important to note that these assumptions are often treated in different ways by individual writers. However, most realists would accept (to varying degrees of importance and varying interpretations) these central tenets. The realist thesis begins with three key assumptions about human behaviour and motivation. They are:

1) That all human behaviour throughout civilised history has been predicated on objective, observable and recordable laws which govern all political and social interaction.

2) A sceptical and pessimistic view of human nature and behaviour, because of the assumption that all people are overwhelmingly concerned with power.[1] This concern is in the name of survival (Kegley and Wittkopf, 1989, p. 16).

3) Interest and security are also defined in terms of survival and power (Morgenthau, 1978, pp. 4–12). Human survival is thus based on the struggle for power, and power is treated as an objective category (which implies that it is a *known quantity*), even though its definition is problematic.[2]

The three assumptions above serve as guides to human behaviour (including the behaviour of political leaders). Five further assumptions about the nature of the international system and its components elaborate the paradigm. They are:

4) Nation-states are and will remain the key actors in a state-centric system.

5) The international arena is anarchic, even hostile, and international politics are therefore characterised by a struggle for power among states.[3] This is sometimes referred to as a condition of *formal anarchy*.

6) There is a hierarchy of power positions and capabilities among states.

7) Apart from this power hierarchy, states are *legally equal*. This is expressed as *sovereign independence*.

8) Foreign and domestic policies are separate and separable (Dougherty and Pfaltzgraff, 1991, p. 81).

The final assumption concerns the parameters of State action:

9) The *balance of power concept* is used as the context within which

states act and use their power. This concept conveys the assumption that *all* states pursue the balance in the anarchical society. The balance of power, like the idea of power itself, is subject to a very broad range of definitions and applications, which often conflict with each other.[4]

These nine points constitute the major assumptions embodied in the paradigm called realism. Let us now examine their implications point by point, in the order presented above.

The first three assertions about human behaviour are negative, pessimistic and deterministic. Firstly, let us examine the idea that *all* human behaviour is governed by the same empirical (that is to say, observable) laws. This idea implies that all people react to particular conditions in the same manner. It implies that we make few or no conscious *choices*, which means that we do not have *free will*. Such determinism is difficult to credit, as it implies that all people are (or may be) automatons. If this assertion were the case, there would be no reason to study human behaviour or international relations (everything would be easily predictable), nor would there be any disagreement about the nature of the field (for the same reasons).

Let us turn to the second assumption, that all people are concerned with power. Some interpret this as an instinctive lust for power and domination, justifying these in the name of survival. This assumption can be broken down into two parts. The first part deals with the power-lust element, which emphasises ceaseless competition at all levels of human interaction. It ignores co-operative behaviour; yet co-operative behaviour exists, alongside its opposite, at all levels of human society.

It is difficult to disagree with the idea that all people seek to survive. However, it is altogether different to imply that the imperatives of survival are perceived in the same way by all people in the world, at all times. These imperatives are not the same for the aborigine living in the bush as for the urban socialite. For the socialite, the image of *survival* contains a different meaning (securing a career and status among peers, perhaps) from the person literally struggling against the elements of nature to live. To the socialite, who lives in an industrial welfare state, life itself is not seriously at risk (although perhaps life*style* is!). For the aborigine, it is. Therefore, the idea of *survival* is likely to acquire different meanings in different settings – it is not an objective category.

A final point, linking *power* to *survival*, can be expressed in the following way. If all human interaction involves ceaseless competition and the use of power for survival, what happens to those whose survival is already assured? The above assumption points to the further accretion of power in order to *dominate* others, whether or not survival is at stake. Writers who emphasise the *structural* logic of power relations and competition take up this point. This tendency is the pessimistic element of human behaviour, which realists believe no one can overlook. Again, this view ignores those whose survival is assured who do *not* seek to dominate others. It fails to account for those who *choose* to co-operate even when survival is assured.

If we do believe that the assertions above about survival and power are plausible, then tying the ideas of interest and security to power and survival is sensible. Interest and security are subordinate to and defined by the ideas of power and survival. If the overriding human interest concerns survival and power, then it follows that states – which are human constructs – should also focus on power, interest and security in the same way. This implies that we have a good idea of precisely what *power* is, and how to deploy it – but there is no single accepted definition of the term.

The fourth proposition, that the international arena exists in a state of anarchy, arises from the fact that realists accept neither that there is a natural value system to which all states adhere nor that any automatic mechanism to preserve order exists in the system.[5] Tools such as diplomacy and international law are weak. There is no automatic order mechanism in the system because there is no single entity or organisation which makes and enforces laws on states. This circumstance means that there is no organisation which can guarantee the survival of states, in an environment which is assumed to be hostile. States are sovereign, and as such make and enforce (international) laws for and upon themselves – a situation which emphasises self-help. For a state to accept decisions or rulings handed down from another authority would imply a *less than sovereign* status.

The lack of an over-arching order being imposed (Leviathan-like) upon individual states makes their first priority the struggle for survival. This then is a very Hobbesian view of the society of states: they are in a state of nature because, realists assume, nothing can override state sovereignty. And because states are human constructs, realists assume that they should struggle to survive in the same manner as individuals. That is, states also struggle for power, peace and domination in order to survive. This implies that states behave in the same way as people – but states are not people; they are created by people.

To assume that states behave in the same way as people implies that states have the same autonomy of action and free will as humans. But, as will be discussed below, states operate under conditions of constraint, and have no will (or goal) other than what individuals give them. Furthermore, the goals of leaders change with changes in leadership. It is therefore unreasonable to assume that both states and people behave in the same way.

If we suppose that order among states can *only* be expressed through a super-sovereign entity, then this assertion is difficult to refute. It is indeed the case that there currently exists no international organisation, nor a transnational actor, which can *impose* order on states in the international arena today. However, it is a very strict interpretation of what constitutes international order. It ignores the elements of order which exist *without* the need of an actor to impose them. It does not account for the imperatives of international order and co-operation between states which have intensified during this century (for example, on issues such as pollution, terrorism, communications, travel, trade, security etc). Nor does it account for the fact that the vast majority of states make, accept and enforce international laws upon themselves *without* the need of a super-sovereign.

As realists cast it, international anarchy is a fearful state – with a constant threat of war in all states and on all continents (the natural result of power politics and power-lust). But the existence of inter-state warfare experienced by some countries on the globe today does not appear to threaten all other states. By emphasising the *threatening* nature of international anarchy, realists emphasise competition between states, and all aspects connected to security and survival. This emphasis is placed at the expense of paying attention to regularised and co-operative behaviour between states, which constitutes the bulk of behaviour between states.

When considering the idea of power in relation to states in an anarchical environment, the concept becomes more complex. The realist interpretation of power is based on security and survival, neither of which are specifically defined. Realism's general moral scepticism and its assumption that *power* is a ubiquitous fact could be taken to imply that there is no point in discussing *legitimate* or *illegitimate* uses of power between states. If this is the case, any state action can be justified − even when, for example, such action threatens the existence of members of the system (i.e., conquest). But this poses an uncomfortable tension in the argument: for the use of power could threaten the survival of states which are the basis of the system. Some realists have attempted to circumvent this tension by distinguishing between the *use of power in order to obtain security to survive* (legitimate in their eyes) and the *use of power for outright imperial conquest* (which they view as illegitimate). In this way realists distinguish *power politics* from *imperialism* (Schumpeter, 1951, p. 7). But, given the pessimistic view of human nature, imperialist drives by some states cannot be ruled out. There is little discussion of the behaviour of states whose survival is assured.

The fifth assumption, that nation-states (and their decision-makers) are the key actors in the international system, is axiomatic to realists (Vasquez, 1983, p. 27). To support this axiom with facts, realists note that the signatories to international laws are states, that nation-states (not universal ideals) are the *source* of international law. States both make and enforce international law. State delegations are represented in international organisations such as the United Nations − and they do not lose their identities inside such organisations, but often further them *within* the organisations. States declare and fight wars. The supremacy of the State (usually called the nation-state by realists) in the international system is often discussed in terms of *sovereignty*.[6] A sovereign, after all, is an ultimate entity which *makes* the rules, but to which *no rules apply except those to which the sovereign itself agrees*.[7]

For these reasons, the state is considered by realists to *wield the significant power* in the international system. The state is (or its decision-makers are) the only units for examination in the international system. The emphasis on the *autonomy* of sovereign states fails to take into account economic and security aspects of the international system which serve to *constrain* states, and the co-operative solutions which states have increasingly found to cope with such constraints.

This state-centric proposition is backed up by a reasonable amount of observable fact − for example, those mentioned above regarding international law and international representation. However, it discounts the possibility of groups or organisations other than the state acquiring *international* positions of influence and power in the arena. This gap will be discussed below, but suffice it to note that, for example, a European Community (much less a European Union) does not have a place in the realist schema, except as a purely inter-governmental organisation, although the European Community seeks to be more than intergovernmental.[8] It also implies that non-state actors cannot have a significant impact on a state's foreign policy (international relations) behaviour. But during the twentieth century, terrorist organisations and transnational corporations (to name only) two have both had major impacts on behaviour between states.

The sixth assumption is that there is a power hierarchy among states. That is, that some states are *stronger* (in power terms) than others. Generally, the realist idea of state power is formulated in terms of *capabilities*, particularly *military capabilities*, which can be measured. As mentioned earlier, there are many possible conceptions of power. The idea of a power hierarchy emphasises continuity.

If we interpret the power hierarchy idea to mean that different states have different capabilities to mobilise their resources *in order to* achieve what they want (power/survival/peace), then again there appears to be little with which to differ. But let us examine the implications. Firstly, this interpretation fails to account for the many different conceptions of power which exist, treating *power* as a single, known and agreed idea. Secondly, although this assumption does not rule out changes in the power status of individual states, if followed to its logical conclusion such changes would be difficult. The logic of power accretion would ensure it. Weak states are by definition vulnerable in an anarchical world. The vulnerable must seek protection from potential (or actual) aggressors. This vulnerability, according to realists, enables alliances to form. This assumption appears to condemn some states always to be at the mercy or behest of others, particularly for military security. It also follows that some states might become perpetual *leaders* (with the implied duties for maintaining order through a balance of power), and others perpetual *followers* (which will have implied duties to keep leaders happy, ensure protection in alliances, etc.). If states are perpetually divided between leaders and followers, with the behaviour associated with inequality, then hierarchy and power politics combined could create conditions reminiscent of imperialism.[9]

It is with this implication that we may quibble, but to do so we must also examine condition seven. That is, that aside from the power hierarchy, all states are legally equal. We have already discussed the idea of sovereignty among states. Clearly there is no constraint with regard to *representation*. However, if weak states are compelled to seek the protection of others, this must necessarily constrain the *sovereignty* of weaker states in so far as their control over their destinies is not wholly in their grasp. Equality does not sit well with dependence (especially dependence arising from the structure of relations between states), and realism does not appear to account for this.[10]

The eighth assumption, that foreign and domestic politics are separate and separable is an attempt to recast international relations (and the foreign policy actions which accompany them) as something *different* from regular politics. It also assumes that actors on the domestic stage cannot or do not act on the international arena also, which ignores large actors such as transnational corporations which can affect both internal state political and economic policies, and also the international environment for policy in the economic area. It ignores the growing evidence of interdependence between foreign and domestic spheres.

The final concept uses the balance of power as the means of attaining peace and security in a threatening, anarchical environment. It is an answer to the *security dilemma* which realism poses.[11] Like the idea of power itself, while treated as an existent fact, the balance of power is a difficult concept to pin down. Both its meaning and the means for achieving it are highly contentious.[12] The concept itself emphasises *stability* and *status quo* in the system. It is a conservative concept. While, intuitively, the concept of a balance of power for power management, security, survival and peace may imply power equality, the concept in fact has nothing to do with equality. It has more to do, by definition, with coercion and, in practice, with domination, as its various interpretations make clear.

If a favourable balance of power is considered to be a state of affairs – the preservation of all units (states) in the existing system, and the system itself – it could imply opposition to any significant change away from the current *status quo*. For, any significant change away from the current *status quo* could become a *systemic* change. While not ruling out the possibility of systemic change, the balance of power idea appears to bias against such change.[13] But who determines what a favourable balance of power is? Clearly, those whom it benefits will favour the *status quo*, and those against whom it discriminates will seek change. If we place the balance of power in the context of the hierarchical system discussed above, we inevitably arrive at the implication that strong states at the top of the power hierarchy will enjoy a favourable balance of power, and will seek to maintain it. Such domination might be interpreted as similar to imperialism. Some realists would defend such a power balance as a fact of the structure of the system. Any attempt to change this *status quo* would be interpreted as an attempt to change the balance and also to alter the system − often seen as a revolutionary effort (Kissinger, 1964, p. 1). Stability means *status quo*, in favour of the existing hierarchy, and it is assumed that such stability is more likely to produce security for all, which strengthens and prolongs peace, than any other mechanism.

The discussion above of realism's core assumptions indicates that, while they appear to be plausible at first sight, their foundation is not so solid on closer examination. Realism relies heavily on key concepts (power, survival, balance of power) whose precise definitions are contestable, and the interpretation of which are essential for the success of the paradigm. It is deterministic, and its pessimistic emphasis on competition between states and persons does not account for co-operative action. It equates the actions of states with the actions of individual people. Finally, it assumes that states have a high degree of autonomy, and do not feel constrained in their behaviour. But it is not clear that states have the same autonomy of action that individuals have; indeed, there is no account of economic, security and other constraints which exist today. However, realism does not only claim that its assumptions are universally correct (for which there is room for doubt), but that the lessons of history bear out the truth of the paradigm. It is to the lessons of twentieth century history that we now turn.

The historical record

As mentioned above, some of realism's central assumptions had existed before this century, but were not put together to produce a single, systematic, coherent *interpretation* of and *guide* to state inter-action. That came after World War I and dominated interpretations of international relations thereafter. Its prominence occurred firstly to provide an alternative explanation to the discredited liberal idealism, and subsequently it was embellished to explain and justify the ideological conflict which emerged after World War II.[14] Its proponents interpreted the global political and economic turbulence between and during two World Wars as proof that the anarchical society existed, and of the need for order to be restored through the balance of power. In other words, the disorder of the period was treated as the rule rather than an exceptional conjuncture of terrible events.

Realism was used in the period after 1945 as a means of ordering reality. It supported the values of the superpowers. It also had the effect of preserving the post-1945 power hierarchy (beyond its natural limits) around two superpowers, which competed for power against each other. As the two superpowers (USA and USSR) were at the pinnacle of their power hierarchy, to support realism (which both did in actions if not ideology) was to support the maintenance of their own power positions. It acted to perpetuate the *status quo* through the balance of power, whether or not the rest of the actors in the system fell into line with this view of reality. As will be seen below, although the gap between realism and actual events grew, it continued to be popular with statesmen, scholars and the general public. The discussion below concentrates mainly on the security aspects of realism, but also discusses the evolution of economic relations as complicating factors for the paradigm.

The devastating impact of World War I caused both statesmen and scholars (e.g., Woodrow Wilson) to seek to eliminate war from inter-state bahaviour. Liberal idealists assumed that if the correct causes of war could be identified, then the correct solutions would be found, and violence between states could be prevented or managed. The *idealist* interpretation of the causes of war, in the wake of World War I, identified excessively self-interested, nationalistic behaviour of states, and imperialism, which acted to the detriment of society at large. Their chosen solution turned away from a concentration on the behaviour of states (assumed to be self-interested) to the creation of international organisations and international laws (assumed to be objective and disinterested), with their associated activities, as the principal means of achieving a peaceful world society.[15] To these ends, idealists emphasised the art of good government on an international scale, rather than the more pragmatic art of the possible in international relations (Couloumbis and Wolfe, 1990, p. 8). Idealists such as Woodrow Wilson sought to change the *traditional* behaviour of states to promote their idea of peaceful coexistence between all states, operating under fair and just international laws, and protecting the weak from the strong. Idealism was normative and naive: it aimed at changing state interaction to create a new collective good.

However laudable these motives (and the theory behind them) were at the time, they were not matched by the actions of governments. The United States never entered the League of Nations (an international organisation created to prevent all international war). Despite international attempts to outlaw inter-state war through the Kellogg-Briand Pact (1928), Italy invaded Abyssinia and the League proved powerless to moderate the aggression. Civil war raged in Spain, yet neither states nor organisations mediated the conflict effectively. In fact, the Spanish Civil War was viewed by some as a likely example of how an impending World War would run, and interested onlookers (other governments) acted accordingly.[16] Lack of economic co-operation coupled with economic warfare and beggar-thy-neighbour tactics resulted in and intensified the Great Depression. As political and economic conditions deteriorated internationally throughout the 1930s, governments increasingly sought self-interested solutions (in the realist sense), rather than looking to international organisations as idealists advocated to resolve inter-state problems collectively. Finally, Nazi Germany pursued what was considered an unbridled quest for power and territory (imperialism). The idealist paradigm of peaceful coexistence and international conflict resolution between states simply failed to fit with the events of the period. By the eve of World War II, idealism was thoroughly discredited. Realism, with its pessimistic interpretation of events, motivations and state behaviour, became the dominant paradigm.[17]

International events after World War II confirmed the realist world view. Europe was in ruins and chaos as the result of war, and physically and economically broken by its ravages. And while exhausted leaders and fledgling governments contemplated reconstruction from the ruins and a new international order, events outpaced them, which realism appeared to characterise accurately.[18] Political unrest, produced by growing ideological cleavages, was interpreted as threatening manifestations of Soviet intentions on the West (or of Western intentions on the East), in violation of agreed spheres of influence. The spectacles through which events were viewed were tinged with the increasing political, ideological and military bitterness of the Allied partners – with the USA and Great Britain on one side and the USSR on the other. The political and military vacuum on the European continent as a whole, constituted an apparent crisis in the newly developing balance of power led by the Soviet Union on one side and Great Britain/USA on the other. The vanquished, the overrun and the exhausted in Eastern and South-eastern Europe had neither the organisation nor the physical capability to expel nor to resist existent or latent Soviet expansion. Thus expansion of communist (or Leninist) influence appeared (to its opponents) to be by design, not default, and provoked fears of domino-style take-overs all over Europe. These events made the pessimist assumptions of human (and state) behaviour seem plausible, as well as the ideas of anarchy and power balances.

Great Britain's inability to embark upon another crusade to rescue states dominated or threatened by others (this time by the USSR), required that another state step into the breach. The United States was the only country with the resources to do so. But, until early 1947, it did not have a foreign policy capable of responding to events (Halle, 1991, pp. 100–3). The belated American response confirmed the hegemony of realist assumptions in that country.[19] The US interpretation of events confirmed the idea that international politics concerned the struggle for power between two superpowers. There was a power hierarchy, with the USA (and the USSR) at the top; the USA had obligations (to preserve the new *status quo* of the balance of power) which its power position at the top of the international hierarchy conferred.[20]

The American assumption – shared by others in the West – was that events before, during and after World War II constituted the norm of state behaviour, rather than the exception. Society was anarchic, international politics were the politics of power, power balances and their deployment (not excluding war). The existing international institutions were not effective mechanisms to promote order and integration over disorder and disintegration. A powerful state such as the USA had obligations to maintain or restore the rightful balance of power, which also happened to be favourable to itself. Furthermore, superpowers, such as the United States (and the Soviet Union) had the resources to expand and propound this thesis at all levels (Olsen and Groom, 1991, pp. 139–40). Thus, by the beginning of the Cold War, a conjunction of conditions and events ensured that realism attained acceptability among scholars and the general public. However, while realism was quietly challenged by some scholars, its essential tenets remained popular in wider public circles (Olsen and Groom, 1991, pp. 140–50).

The superpowers began the Cold War with their ideological differences as the major source of the conflict. But over time the expression of this struggle increasingly reflected the systemic opposition of two opposing powers, in the realist sense, rather than a struggle over beliefs. Both superpowers interpreted order in international society as a condition which only existed under the balance of power mechanisms operated by each in its own sphere of influence. Each superpower found itself *competing for power* against the other in all areas of the world, in order to maintain the balance. A gain for the USSR, say, was interpreted as a loss for the USA, and vice versa. The *survival, security and national interests* of the superpowers were interdependent on this competitive struggle for power.[21] Reality would be organised and events would be interpreted accordingly.

The Cold War did not simply create a new *status quo* in the power hierarchy, with the USA and the USSR at the top. Their *status quo* might have been more easily maintained if the number of states in the new system had remained static. Instead, during the period 1945–65 the number of states in the international system expanded dramatically (from 60 in 1939 to 160 in 1983). This expansion had significant implications for the nature of the state system: there were more autonomous units which made decisions. In fact, while many of these new states were *legally* sovereign, they hardly manifested some of the basic elements of sovereignty (ability to protect and defend their borders, and maintain order within their borders).

Realist assumptions imply that the creation of new states ought to have increased the level of anarchy in the world, as more states would have been competing for power. International anarchy did not increase. It might also have led the new, weak states to seek alliances with the superpowers for protection. But the leaders of the new states did not share the superpowers' values, and sought alternative arrangements. Political leaders in the Third World felt that the new security-oriented *status quo* emphatically did not benefit them. They expressed their dissatisfaction with the *status quo* by creating the Non-Aligned Movement, which sought to avoid the balance of power machinations of the superpowers and their allies. The Non-Aligned also formed the Group of 77 to offset the implications of economic hierarchy in the system, seeking to alter relations between rich and poor countries.[22] Some new states became mavericks in the international system, seeking to upset the *status quo* and produce a newer one. Examples of mavericks are Libya, Cuba, Uganda under Idi Amin, Iraq, etc. Other states (mainly European) retained a status of neutrality, which also tended to place them outside the security balance of power. In sum, states did not behave as realists suggested they would. So, from an early period, the status of realism was challenged in fact, if not in theory.

The proliferation of new states had another unforeseen effect on the international system, and on the superpowers. The superpowers' zero-sum interpretation of the ideological divide and the balance of power encouraged them to conduct their conflict on the territory of third parties. This engagement was generally done in the form of outright intervention (for example, in Czechoslovakia in 1968, in Chile in 1972), or by supporting different sides in civil wars (for example, in Somalia, Angola, Mozambique). However, the domestic reasons for engaging in civil war seldom have much to do with outsiders' ideological views and interpretations. The sources of regional conflict are autonomous of outside control. Placing the bipolar template over the existing problems only complicated the situation, and such a misinterpretation of conflict often led to the failure of military intervention. Their world view emphasised the bipolar conflict and not state-building in new states, so the American intervention in Vietnam failed, because it failed to address the problems of self-determination and state-building. The USSR had a similar experience in its Afghanistan adventure. The idea that a superpower could lose a conflict with a much weaker opponent, as the USA did in Vietnam, and the USSR did in Afghanistan, is not compatible with the hierarchical assumptions of realism, nor with power balances. For, if superpowers cannot themselves achieve their stated balance of power objectives, who can?

Finally, the realist world view did not predict the demise of the Soviet Union and the dissolution of its alliance system. Its assumptions became heavily dependent on the reality of a bipolar system which has now disappeared. And the lone surviving superpower, while possessing a global military reach, shows signs of imperial overstretch – a moribund economy, and a need to scale down its security commitments to satisfy domestic opinion at home (Kennedy, 1988, pp. 447–693). The United States appears to be in decline. At the moment, there is no obvious successor to either superpower.

Nor does realism account for economic developments since World War II. The world economy has evolved from a state-oriented system to a seamless transnational web, in which the domestic and the international economics of states are inextricably intertwined, and in which non-state actors have significant roles to play. New economic actors have emerged during this evolution — some purely economic (such as transnational corporations), others created by states to manage the economy. Transnational organisations are independent actors, many of which have a higher business turnover than the entire economic activities of small states.[23] Because of their economic size and their impact on the states in which they operate, transnational corporations (TNCs) have the ability to alter the behaviour of governments. Furthermore, their complex organisation and activities mean that TNCs do not consistently ally their interests with particular states: they are *autonomous* actors (Kegley and Wittkopf, 1989, pp. 166–73). This is an indication of *significant power* being wielded. But transnational corporations are not states, and realism does not account for this *displacement* of economic (and political) power from states to the corporations. It constitutes a further attack on state-centricity and sovereignty.

The growth of transnational economic interaction and TNCs has also inspired increased co-operative activities between states, which are not based on power balances, but on the mutual interest in stability. These governmental (IGO) and non-governmental (INGO) organisations work together in pursuit of common policies and programmes, and the resolution of common problems.[24] Again, realism does not take account of such a phenomenon, and would tend to discount its significance. Yet if international organisation to produce new forms of order were insignificant, its proliferation, from 580 IGOs/INGOs in 1940 to 4500 IGOs/INGOs in 1987/88, would not have occurred (Kegley and Wittkopf, 1989, pp. 132–3). The existence of these entities further blurs the distinction between the domestic and the foreign policy spheres so essential to realism.

The European Economic Community (EEC) is an important example of how economics and new actors have intruded into international relations, and how inter-state behaviour has changed away from the realist reality. The EEC was created to enhance its members' place in the international economic (and political) arena. Its founders' intentions have succeeded — the EEC is the world's largest market, the most important international trader, and has other countries clamouring to join the club. Other states have imitated the European example by attempting their own regional communities.[25] But realism does not account for the success or the popularity of such clubs. The EEC (and its imitators) is neither a sovereign state nor an inter-governmental organisation. It can (and does) enforce rules on states, which fundamentally attacks the realist conception of sovereignty.

Nor does realism explain the proliferation of treaties, agreements and regimes which have been created by states in order to manage the increasingly international aspects of their economies to mutual advantage – and to stop or limit the damage that individualistic action can bring.[26] These, too, undermine the assumptions of autonomy and sovereignty championed by realists, because their very existence is based on the *constraints* states feel which can only be surmounted collectively. They emphasise the *orderly* interaction of states, to resolve or control problems for mutual benefit.

In sum, realism has been made obsolete by the evolution of the world economy, by the waning of bipolar conflict, by the proliferation of states, and by the implications which flow from these.

Conclusion

Realism appeared to convey the best interpretation of international relations after World Wars I and II because of a unique combination of event, which caused both the economic and security climates of the world to deteriorate. When its assumptions were applied to global events during the period 1918–47, they appeared to provide the best explanation and guide to state action. Moreover, the two hegemones (the USA and USSR) had an interest in adopting and maintaining this interpretation. Realism was accepted without much critical thought.

However, once the Cold War was established, events did not occur as the paradigm suggested. Realist values and assumptions were not shared by all governments in all states. Small states misbehaved. Great powers lost wars against weak states. And the international system evolved in ways which directly contradicted realist assumptions and values. It is the inability of realism to come to terms with the blurring of state/international boundaries, the insidious erosion of classical conceptions of sovereignty and anarchy, and the inter-dependence of states (with its associated co-operation) which indicate its failure as a paradigm. The demise of the bipolar system has now invited the greatest challenge to the realist paradigm, but has also challenged alternatives. Other paradigms are as yet embryonic. Perhaps the new world order will bring with it a new world view.

Notes

1   Some thinkers believe that all people possess an instinctive lust for power, and a desire to dominate others whenever possible. Others stress that competition (for power) forms part of the irreducible logic of the international system.

2   There are no clear *definitions* of power. A useful definition for our purposes is: the ability of an actor on the international stage to use tangible and intangible resources and assets in such a way as to influence the outcomes of international events to its own satisfaction (Jones, 1991, p. 241). But this does not give a concrete idea of power. Therefore, *indicators* of latent or actual power are used to convey the idea. The indicators can be grouped under various categories, and many are used with reference to war-making or war-sustaining capacity. The following are some examples of power indicators: military (military force, technological capacity of military force, training of personnel, military expenditure, etc.); population/psychological factors (numbers, national character, education level, morale); physical (size of territory, terrain, geographic locale, raw materials resources); economic (economic resources, raw materials, dependence on vital imports, technological capacity, industrial productivity, volume of trade, savings and investment); government (type, efficiency of decision-making, ideology, influence, prestige, reputation, authority, legitimacy, leadership).

3   This creates difficulties later with the idea that power is only used for survival, but it does integrate the ideas about power-lust and domination. See also Chapter 8 by Barnes in this volume.

4   In a review of the literature on the topic, Ernst Haas found a total of eight definitions of the balance of power. They are: (1) any distribution of power between states; (2) an equilibrium or balancing process; (3) hegemony; (4) stability and peace in a concert of power; (5) instability and war; (6) power politics generally; (7) a universal law of history; and (8) hegemony, or the search for it (Haas, 1952).

5   That is, no order apart from the 'balance of power', discussed below. The realist position against order and values reflects a branch of international law called *positivism*. An opposing view, developed by advocates of *natural law*, asserts that international society has a set of common values and rules (Kegley and Wittkopf, 1989, p. 462).

6   This notion arises from the Peace of Westphalia of 1648. Critics argue that it is too Eurocentric a term (it was designed to reflect the condition of European states at the time), and as such it does not adequately reflect the position of non-European states (which may not have the attributes normally considered essential to sovereignty).

7   This realist view also does not account for the fact that states over-whelmingly *agree* to the international laws that they make, and *do* enforce international laws upon themselves. The exceptions are a minority, not a majority, of cases. This implies that *order* is more prevalent than realism would admit.

8   An intergovernmental organisation is made up of governments (their decision-makers), but in which each government reserves the right to veto or decide differently (not to go with the others). The point here is that the notion of *sovereignty*, of the state as the ultimate arbiter of its own affairs, is preserved. In an *intergovernmental* organisation, a state cannot be out-voted. But in an enterprise such as the European Community, it is possible for a state to be outvoted – which implies a loss of sovereignty.

9   This is a point made by both dependency theorists, e.g. Johann Galtung, and also structural realists, e.g. Kenneth Waltz.

10   This is one of the weakest arguments in realism. Some realists (for example, Robert Tucker) stress that states are fundamentally unequal, and do not attach any importance to such *formal* attributes of the state system.

11   The security dilemma exists because of the above assumptions regarding anarchy and power-lust. If a state in the system seeks *absolute security*, the result may be absolute security for itself, but also *absolute insecurity* for all others. This situation can lead to security competitions such as arms races, in order that each state might procure absolute security. The solution to the security dilemma is for *all* states to opt for *relative security* (which also means that they opt for *relative insecurity*) within a *balance of power* (McKinlay and Little, 1986, p. 235).

12   The *means of achieving* a balance of power are: (1) divide and rule; (2) territorial compensation after war; (3) create buffer states; (4) form alliances; (5) create spheres of influence; (6) interventions; (7) diplomatic bargaining; (8) legal and peaceful settlement of disputes; (9) arms reductions; (10) arms competition and arms races; (11) war (Dougherty and Pfaltzgraff, 1991, pp. 31–2). The functions of the balance of power are supposed to be to: (1) prevent the establishment of a universal hegemony (imperialism); (2) preserve existing constituents of the system and the existing system itself; (3) ensure stability and mutual security in the international system; (4) strengthen and prolong peace by deterring war, through the threat of a counter-coalition (Dougherty and Pfaltzgraff, 1991, pp. 31–3; Haas, 1952.

13   Thus, balance of power politics may not imply a stable equilibrium; also change, when it happens, may be cataclysmic.

14   This chapter primarily discusses realism and its critique of liberal idealism. It should be noted that elements of both coexisted in a dialectic about the nature of relations between states for centuries before. For a more complete discussion outlining this inter-paradigm debate, see, *inter*

alia, Bennett, 1988, pp. 2–19; Couloumbis and Wolfe, 1990, pp. 6–18; Dougherty and Pfaltzgraff, 1991; Olsen and Groom, 1991.

15 The associated activities are, among others, diplomacy, treaties, conferences, rules of warfare and regulation of the use of force, peaceful settlement of disputes (and provision of good offices to those ends), collective security arrangements, international trade and economic co-operation, creating international agencies to solve technical problems (such as pollution, health, etc.) on an international basis, international social co-operation and cultural relationships, world travel and communications, encouragement of international peace movements, cosmopolitanism and universalism, the formation of leagues and federations, and movements for world government and administration. Again, such ideas have existed at least since the Enlightenment, and represent a substantially different viewpoint from the state-centric realists. It is important to stress that idealism counted on the perfectibility of humankind, through correct (moral) education, in order to alter individual (and thence international) behaviour for the good. It stressed freedom of choice, that states and organisations would behave as *disinterested*, not self-interested actors according to a single obvious set of norms and moral laws.

16 Nazi Germany and Fascist Italy aided Franco's Falangists; the Soviet Union aided the Communists within the Republican ranks. The Republicans were also aided, in an *ad hoc* fashion, by international volunteer brigades from other countries. Apart from the Soviet Union, the governments which would become the Allies during World War II did not offer official aid to the Republicans.

17 For a review of the origins of this change, see Carr, 1989.

18 For example, most prominent resistance organisations in Italy, Greece and France were dominated by communists (also with socialists and anarchists). In all three countries, the communists were among the best organised and most effective resisters, and received the bulk of Allied logistical support. Communist resisters were in a good position to press forward their own ideas on political organisation, and did so – whether or not they received support from the USSR. This situation resulted in labour and political unrest in France and Italy, and in civil war in Greece. When viewed through the realist spectacles, it appeared to conform to the conditions of power politics.

19 Articulated in the Truman Doctrine, 12 March 1947, the Marshall Plan, and in American foreign policy statements thereafter. For a good review of US realists' aims expressed in the context of the emerging Cold War, see Graebner, 1977, Section 2: Documents. Note that the lack of an established international organisation framework (the UN was only embryonic at this time) placed greater emphasis on individual states to solve international problems.

20 US Secretary of State George C. Marshall, in an address at Princeton Univesity, 22 February 1947 (Halle, 1991, pp. 109–10).

21 Although, at some point, once the USSR attained the ability to produce and fire nuclear weapons (in 1953) both parties realised that their struggle for power against one another could produce another devastating – perhaps apocalyptic – war. At that point, the superpowers turned their Cold War attention from aggressive power competition to power competition through surrogates (other states' wars and intervention), and controlled power competition through arms control. A balance of power order was imposed on their behaviour in the interests of mutual survival.

22 The Non-Aligned Movement did not become a highly effective third force, due to factionalism and other factors. But it did serve as an organising force, to push issues important to poor countries onto the international agenda for discussion and debate.

23 In 1985, General Motors' turnover was larger than the GNP of the Republic of Korea; Exxon was larger than Indonesia and Belgium; Royal Dutch Shell was larger than, *inter alia*, Hungary, Nigeria, Austria, Norway and Denmark; British Petroleum, Ford Motor and IBM ranked above Yugoslavia (Kegley and Wittkopf, 1989, pp. 164–5).

24 For example, the World Health Organisation, the UN University, the UN Fund for Population Activities, UNICEF (UN Children's Fund), the International Labour Organisation, the General Agreement on Tariffs and Trade, organisations related to agriculture, development, banking etc.

25 Such as ANCOM, the Andean Common Market; CARICOM, the Caribbean Common Market; ECOWAS, the Economic Community of West African States; ASEAN, the Association of South East Asian Nations.

26 Regimes can be formal or informal, and are implicit or explicit principles, about which norms, rules and decision-making procedures are agreed, and which regularise relations between actors (Kegley and Wittkopf, 1989, pp. 26–7). Examples are the General Agreement on Tariffs and Trade, the G7 summits to agree co-ordinated economic policies between the seven wealthiest states in the world, and agreements about the international monetary system.

Bibliography

Beitz, C. R. (1979), *Political Theory and International Relations*, Princeton: Princeton University Press.

Bennett, A. L. (1988), *International Organisations: Principles and Issues*, 4th ed., Englewood Cliffs, N.J.: Prentice-Hall.

Bull, H. (1977), *The Anarchical Society*, London: Unwin.

Calvocoressi, P. (1982), *World Politics Since 1945*, 4th ed., London: Longman.

Carr, E. H. (1989), *The Twenty Years' Crisis*, London: Macmillan.

Couloumbis, T. A. and Wolfe, J. E. (1990), *Introduction to International Relations: Power and Justice*, 4th ed., Englewood Cliffs: Prentice-Hall.

242 *Theories and concepts of politics*

Dougherty, J.E. and Pfaltzgraff, R.L. (1991), *Contending Theories of International Relations*, 3rd ed., London: Harper and Row.

Fukuyama, F. (Summer 1989), 'The end of history?', *The National Interest*, Washington, DC.

Graebner, N.A. (1977), *Cold War Diplomacy: American Foreign Policy 1945–1975*, 2nd ed., New York: D. Van Nostrand.

Haas, E.B. (1952), 'The balance of power: prescription, concept or propaganda?', *World Politics*, V, pp.442–77.

Haas, E.B. (1953), 'The balance of power as a guide to policy-making', *Journal of Politics*, pp.370–98.

Halle, L.J. (1991), *The Cold War as History*, New York: Harper.

Holsti, K.J. (1985), *The Dividing Discipline: Hegemony and Diversity in International Theory*, London: Unwin Hyman.

Jones, W.S. (1991), *The Logic of International Relations*, 7th ed., London: Harper Collins.

Kegley, C.W., Jr. and Wittkopf, E.R. (1989), *World Politics: Trend and Transformation*, 3rd ed., London: Macmillan.

Kennedy, P. (1988), *The Rise and Fall of the Great Powers*, London: Collins.

Keohane, R.O. (Ed.) (1986), *Neorealism and Its Critics*, Surrey: Columbia University Press.

Kissinger, H.A. (1964), *A World Restored – Europe after Napoleon*, New York: Grosset and Dunlap.

Leroy Bennett, A. (1988), *International Organizations: Principles and Issues*, 4th ed., London: Prentice-Hall.

McKinlay, R.D. and Little, R. (1986), *Global Problems and World Order*, London: Frances Pinter.

Morgenthau, H.J. (1978), *Politics Among Nations*, 5th ed., New York: Alfred A. Knopf.

Olsen, W.C. and Groom, A.J.R. (1991), *International Relations Then and Now*, London: Harper-Collins.

Pfaff, W. (Winter 1991), 'Redefining world power', *Foreign Affairs*, 70(1), pp.34–48.

Schumpeter, J.A. (1951), *Imperialism and Social Classes*, Oxford: Blackwell.

Vagts, A. (1948), 'The balance of power: growth of an idea', *World Politics*, 1, pp.82–101.

Vasquez, J.A. (1983), *The Power of Power Politics: A Critique*, London: Frances Pinter.

11 *Martin Clark*

Environmentalism

Introduction

A spectrum is haunting Europe, the spectrum of environmentalism.

Anon

The term 'environmentalism', like 'Nature' itself, has a wide variety of possible meanings and political implications. At one level it can mean little more than 'resource conservationism', a hard-headed, self-interested approach which sees Nature as essentially a provider of raw materials, and therefore to be husbanded for future economic growth (Kahn, 1978; Kahn and Simon, 1984; Stroup and Baden, 1983; World Resources Institute, 1986). Adherents to this view often have links with business interests, are well financed and influential, and have created significant interest groups both nationally and internationally. It is, of course, entirely 'anthropocentric': Nature is 'useful-to-Man'. It often assumes continuing economic growth and 'progress', with no major shifts in institutions or policies (except perhaps on population issues in underdeveloped countries). And it often has overtones of technocratic, 'environmental management' from above, or indeed from outside; 'resources' are to be defined and conserved by elite expert agencies, which will thwart the efforts of ignorant locals to squander them. It is easy to be ironic about this approach to environmentalism, and there has been much mockery of the Club of Rome's dire predictions of the early 1970s (Meadows *et al.*, 1972). Still, I suppose that the 'resource conservationist' approach is a great improvement on cheerful non-conservation, and it is noticeable that virtually all its critics adopt a 'resource conservationist' line on occasions, for example in discussing the future of fish stocks or the maintenance of biodiversity. Indeed, 'resource conservationism' may perhaps best be seen as the basic

premiss of any 'environmentalist' approach, underlying whatever
wider concerns other environmental groups may adopt.

The second major grouping on our spectrum is that of the 'environmental protectionists' (Brundtland, 1987; Scientific American, 1990).
Of respectable antiquity, and now dominant in the environmental
establishment, they too are 'anthropocentric', but their concerns
are far wider than those of the 'resource conservationists'. Initially
they worried over public health. This led inevitably to a focus on
atmospheric and water pollution, but also led to an interest in more
general environmental issues, for example the need for public parks
('areas of outstanding natural beauty') and for public education (e.g.
on diet). Concern for public health, in fact, has been the mainspring
of environmental protection legislation for at least 150 years, and
still is. It triggered the Alkali Acts of the mid-nineteenth century,
and the Department of Health is arguably still, in Britain, the only
section of the government machinery that is at all effective as an
environmental agency.

Most 'environmental protectionists' do not reject economic
development in itself. Indeed, they adopt the language of welfare
economics, stressing the need for 'trade-offs'; development should
not be permitted if the real (environmental or health) costs are too
great. All this implies sophisticated cost-benefit analyses ('environmental assessments') and, again, government agencies staffed by
experts, who can assess the 'optimum' level of pollution (the point
at which the economic benefits of production most outweigh the
environmental costs), however much fearful locals may protest.
It is normally the world of 'business-as-usual', apart from cleaning
up the occasional excessive discharge. It is also the world of 'politics-
as-usual'. The 'environmental protectionists' act as recognised
pressure groups and lobbyists, with their own (minor) niches in
government. They are consulted on occasions, and allowed to talk
to the powerful. It is not surprising that 'environmental protectionism'
is the most common, and most favoured, approach to environmental
issues in official circles. It satisfies the conscience, it shows that
Something is Being Done, but it does not imply any unwelcome
political or economic upheaval.

Next we move on to greener, and more radical, territory. Here,
among the 'mainstream Greens', we find more varied and quarrel-
some groups, and also more original thinking. The Appropriate
Technologists, for example, busy themselves not only with finding

small-scale technofixes, but with new models of what economic development might mean in backward rural areas (Carr, 1985; McRobie, 1981). Among the 'mainstream Greens' the stress, in general, is on 'sustainability' (Brown, 1981; Daly, 1973; Schumacher, 1973). Sustainability, not pollution in itself, is the essential limit to growth. In fact, 'Green' economists reject the whole traditional concept of growth, preferring a 'steady-state' economy which is as self-sufficient as possible. Hence the stress on renewable energy, on recycling of waste into raw materials, and on meeting 'real human needs' rather than Gross National Product growth targets. Both market capitalism and State socialism are deplored, and seen as essentially exploitative and oppressive. Industry, however, is accepted if on a small scale and for purposes of self-sufficiency; so, too, is agriculture, although a low-input regime is *de rigeur*. There is general agreement that 'small is beautiful' in the economy, and also in technology and politics. Extensive decentralisation, perhaps to natural 'bioregions', is advocated. This strategy is, in part, the politics of community – a community that has been destroyed by modern progress, and needs to be re-created. But it is the environment that is at the centre of attention. All 'mainstream Green' groups recognise the need for major structural change in politics and society in order to protect it. The environment is one and indivisible; but it is also fragile.

Finally, we come to the furthest reaches of deeper Green persuasion, where 'ecocentrism' dominates, where wilderness is prized for its own sake, where 'ecosystem collapse' is seen as imminent, and where the Higher Pagans celebrate the ancient cult of Gaia (Devall and Sessions, 1985; Naess, 1973). For these groups, the industrial system is destroying the planet. It must be stopped, or the earth will wreak revenge. 'Growth' means cancer, nothing more; a cancer that threatens to spread worldwide, and destroy all life. No attempt should be made to 'develop' the Third World; people there are fortunate to have escaped industrial civilisation. Some advocate a return to hunter-gatherer society and a collapse in human population. All regard Nature as the fount of stability, interdependence and co-operation (rather than of conflict, as the Social Darwinists had held). The 'spiritual' dimension is strongly emphasised: Nature is not to be preserved so much as worshipped, and all life should be led in harmony with her laws. 'Anthropocentrism', even in its benign form as 'stewardship', is derided: humans are not, and never have been, in charge of the earth. 'Deeper Green' thinkers, however radical, tend to have little interest in everyday political arrangements. Their ideal human society would consist either of hunter-gatherer tribes or, at most, of self-sufficient communes. But they are very interested in changing attitudes, in combating materialism, in awakening people's spiritual sense and in instilling reverence towards Nature.

In short, there is a large variety of opinions among 'environmentalists'. Whatever may be the case in the rainforests, biodiversity is flourishing among them; indeed, for the more radical, the term 'environmentalism' itself has acquired unpleasant ('light Green', 'anthropocentric') overtones, as opposed to the deeper 'ecocentrism'.

But this familiar spectrum of different approaches to environmental issues is not the only relevant one. Many educated Westerners respond to environmental issues along another spectrum, of a more personal kind. The environment obviously arouses strong aesthetic and ethical feelings. The Romantic poets were arguably among the most important founders of modern environmentalism, teaching mankind to view Nature as beautiful, good and true — indeed, as the very source of truth. As Wordsworth implausibly remarked,

> One impulse from a vernal wood
> May teach you more of man,
> Of moral evil and of good,
> Than all the sages can. (Wordsworth, 1798)

In fact, Nature had always, from ancient Greek times, had an 'ethical' aspect, as the strength of the 'natural law' tradition, and the whole concept of 'natural rights', amply shows. The Romantics made it also the Great Teacher of Mankind — a view confirmed by Kropotkin and those other nineteenth-century biologists who (unlike Darwin) saw Nature as a school of co-operation, not conflict. And certainly today Nature has acquired another, more pressing, 'ethical' imperative, derived from this traditional reverence: despoiling Nature is 'wrong'. Mary Midgley, in an essay on Robinson Crusoe's island, has pointed out that Crusoe had an obligation not to wreck his temporary home. This was not mere prudence; it applied just as forcefully on the day of his departure. If Crusoe had burned his habitat down to celebrate his release, we would certainly think much less of him — and so would Defoe's readers have done in the early eighteenth century, before Romanticism had been invented (Midgley, 1983, p. 166). Of course, one must admit that many people do not seem very reluctant to despoil their 'island'; again, we are faced with a spectrum of possible responses.

However, 'environmentalism' in the West has not only been an emotional, aesthetic or ethical response. It is also 'scientific', or at least it makes scientific claims. It is environmentalism's 'scientific' cachet, not its aesthetic or moral arguments, that forces unsympathetic governments to give it even limited attention. 'Scientific' environmentalism in this sense is surprisingly recent, and surprisingly limited. 'Ecology', as a science concerned with the interdependence of living organisms and their environment, may date from the mid-nineteenth century, but for many years it was overshadowed by the dominant interpretation of Darwinian biology (which certainly stressed the importance of the environment, but portrayed a Nature unpleasantly red in tooth and claw), and it has rarely been 'public-friendly' nor even truly interdisciplinary. Professional ecologists have tended, indeed, to be remarkably cautious on environmental issues, at least in public; they have stressed how little is known and, given the long time-scales needed for adequate research, how little is likely to become known. Modern 'scientific environmentalism' may derive some of its basic concepts from ecology, but its detailed information and arguments have tended to come from biologists and zoologists, not ecologists. It may loosely be dated from 1962, when Rachel Carson's *Silent Spring* was published, demonstrating the effect of pesticides on wildlife in the USA. Other scientists have been noticeably reluctant to join in – even the subsequent debates on nuclear power have owed more to biologists than to physicists. Still, the fact remains that 'environmentalism' is now the only set of political or social ideas that can claim a scientific foundation (Marxism, of course, used to do so, never very convincingly). It has, therefore, an emotional, 'Romantic' appeal, an 'ethical' aspect, and a rational, 'scientific' one – an unbeatable combination. It can appeal to various mentalities and proficiencies, at least among the educated.

Political theories and the environment

Dost thou think, because thou art virtuous, there shall be no more cakes and ale? (Shakespeare, *Twelfth Night*, 2: iii, ll. 125–6)

I have shown that 'environmentalism' means diverse and often incompatible things, and that these different meanings derive from different preoccupations and from different reasons for concern over the environment. But they also derive from different intellectual traditions, and have in turn contributed to them. I will now consider the main relevant traditions.

Perhaps the best known 'environmental political theory' derives from the Hobbesian tradition. In 1968 Garrett Hardin published a famous article on 'The tragedy of the commons' (Hardin, 1968). He imagined a society of shepherds, each owning his own flock, where the sheep graze on common land. This arrangement works well for a long time, but eventually, as the flocks increase, the common land can no longer support all the animals. Each shepherd, by adding extra sheep to his flock, thus contributes to collective disaster. The grass fails to grow, the land becomes degraded, the sheep die and all the shepherds are ruined. A banal episode in today's world. But the situation is more complex than it appears. Hardin argued that the disastrous outcome is implicit in the society's structure. Given individual (and individualistic) shepherds out to maximise personal profit, each shepherd may be fully aware of what he is doing as he adds extra sheep to his flock, but he will continue to do it nonetheless: the extra benefit (personal 'utility') to him of one more sheep is greater than the 'disutility' − which will be in the future, and will be general, borne by all members of the society, not by him alone. And, he will think to himself, if he does not do so, other shepherds will. From the point of view of a rational individual (and of classical economic theory), it makes sense to have as large a flock as possible, and thrust the costs on to the community, or on to the future. No shepherd acts illegally; rustling is not the issue here. Nor do the shepherds act immorally, given the premisses of their atomistic society. They are helpless to avoid their fate; it is a true tragedy.

This sequence of events is, of course, exactly what often happens in the real world, although the best-known example relates to fishing stocks rather than sheep. Environmental issues provide splendid examples of the kind of problems known generically as 'prisoner's dilemmas', in which rational individuals choose less than optimum collective outcomes. Indeed, the argument is valid for most environmental issues; not only for 'natural resources' like grazing land or ocean fisheries, but also for pollution questions ('if I take my car, I'll arrive much quicker, and the costs of my exhaust emissions will be borne by everybody else as well as by myself') and, of course, for human population − the real theme of Hardin's original essay.

An extra child may be 'useful' for the parents, whatever the ultimate effect on limited resources.

These arguments are implicit in Thomas Hobbes' *Leviathan*. If we take environmental issues seriously, and if we also start from individualist premisses, we find again and again that we are in a classic Hobbesian society, in which all are 'rational' but condemned to a life that is 'solitary, poor, nasty, brutish and short' (Hobbes, 1651, p. 65). On the 'commons', for example, one may suppose that when grass becomes scarce the stronger shepherds will drive the sheep of their weaker brethren off the land; open conflict will ensue. The 'tragedy' can be resolved satisfactorily even so, but only – as Hobbes argued – by an authoritarian government. It is actually very simple to resolve it, given strong leadership. The obvious answer is fewer sheep. Leviathan – or rather, in this case, the mayor – could decree a limit to flock size, the same for all flock-owners; or he could allow only his friends and relations to graze their sheep on the commons; or he could sell a limited number of grazing permits to the highest bidder; or he could allocate them by lot. However he chose to proceed, he could rescue the situation, provided he guessed right about the maximum number of sheep the commons could sustain, and provided he could enforce his preferred policy.

In practice, of course, the situation is rarely so simple. Perhaps, after all, the best answer is not fewer sheep. The mayor, if he were well versed in botany, climatology, soil sciences and microbiology, might choose to put fertiliser on the commons, to sow new, improved grass seeds, or to introduce new breeds of sheep. There is usually a whole range of possible 'solutions' to environmental problems, ranging from the quick 'technofix' that is likely to appeal to impatient authoritarians, to subtle long-term methods of biological control, known only to a handful of research ecologists. Given that someone has to decide, how much better if that person (or committee) were fully aware of scientific progress and social complexity. Thus it is that some environmentalists have favoured a variant of the neo-Hobbesian view, which we may term 'enlightened despotism' (Hardin, 1977; Heilbronner, 1974; Ophuls, 1977).

This faith in experts is, of course, an ancient belief, held by many philosophers from Plato onwards: only the qualified, in some body of irrefutable knowledge, should rule. The precise nature of the qualifications have varied over the centuries: they have included philosophy, theology, statecraft, economics (in both the 'Liberal'

and Marxist forms), Darwinism and genetics. In our context, knowledge about the environment simply provides another set of plausible
qualifications. The new 'ecoauthoritarians' argue that correct political
and economic decisions can only be made by people who are:

1) in possession of adequate information about the environment,
preferably on a global scale;
2) rational actors, able to assess information correctly, open to
argument and new interpretations;
3) inspired by disinterested motives; and
4) able to take the long-term view, and legislate for the whole community.

They also assume that political decisions, once taken, should be implemented by appropriate agencies, in turn staffed by officials who
are also informed, rational, disinterested etc. Protests from the
'ignorant and unwashed' would be ignored, for the greater good.
Global agencies, with appropriate powers, would probably be
necessary.

This view also, of course, derives from Western political traditions
themselves. We are used, in fact, to interventionist government of
this type. Faced with new problems, we expect governments to issue
laws and decrees, and to found new ministries and agencies with
ample powers. True, we also expect to be able to influence these
decisions, via Parliament and the press, and in most countries there
are certain basic rights that cannot be infringed, but in general
authoritarianism does not seem to be so new or so disagreeable, either
to Burkeian conservatives or to social democrats. And an environmental policy requires, self-evidently, environmental advisers, experts
and consultants. Obscure professors and scientists are wrenched,
not too reluctantly, from their dingy laboratories, and forced to
sit in palatial government offices, advising the Great and legislating
for the Planet. No wonder it has a certain appeal.

The trouble is, however, that environmental knowledge does not
have the 'scientific' status attributed to it, any more than its predecessors have had. Remarkably little is known about the environment, at microlevel let alone globally. The average scientific Ph.D.
is written in three years; but it might take fifty years to understand
the process of change in a lake or a wood. Such studies tend, therefore, to be carried out, if at all, by enthusiastic amateurs, not by
scientific professionals; and the professionals are often condescending

about the efforts of their amateur colleagues. At national or global level the convincing scientific evidence is even less forthcoming. Many countries are too poor to collect adequate data; national prestige, or tourist industries, may be at stake; in any case the information is not static, but subject to multiple feedback mechanisms that remain obscure. In short, there is little scientific basis for ecoauthoritarianism, nor is there likely to be. Even basic assumptions – for example, 'global warming' – may yet turn out to be unfounded, as did the Club of Rome's original predictions.

As for top-down decision-making, even perfectly informed and disinterested environmentalists would find it as problematic as anyone else. How, for example, should they decide an 'acceptable' level of air pollution? Acceptable to whom? – to a healthy adult? – to an asthmatic child? – to a ninety-year-old with pleurisy? Or are these last two persons to be deemed not 'relevant' in determining pollution levels, and their interests ignored for the common good (perhaps I should say that both examples are taken from my own family)? Nor do the problems end here, with fixing 'levels'. There are two, quite incompatible, policies that may be adopted on pollution issues. One is to adopt legal limits, equal for all polluters, on 'emission levels', the normal policy in Britain on air pollution. The other is to insist on 'environmental levels', where the allowed degree of pollution depends on the local situation; this has normally been the case for water in Britain, because of landowners' 'riparian rights' and the strength of the fishing lobby. For example, if a factory has permission to discharge a tonne of lead per year, should one allow a second factory to be built nearby which will do the same? Or should one allow only half a tonne, and force the first to follow suit? Or should one insist that the second factory be built elsewhere, perhaps at higher cost (and in that case polluting an environment that was previously clean)? It does not seem to me that one procedure is more 'rational' than another, although the 'environmental level' policy certainly encourages holistic thinking.

In any case, authoritarian governments are unlikely to be inspired solely by environmental considerations. They might be run by scientific elites, but to survive they would certainly need the support of other groups – for example, the military – for whom the environment was an issue of minor concern. Furthermore, as argued previously, 'environmentalists' have many different viewpoints – anthropocentric, biocentric or whatever. However disinterested, they are unlikely to agree among themselves, least of all on the most problematic environmental issue, human population.

Implementation, via appropriate agencies, would be their biggest problem. Bureaucracies have their own rules and traditions. Lower officials are concerned about their careers, are anxious to keep out of trouble and to advance up the promotion ladder. Routine conformity is their lot. At the top, one finds cynical, defensive people anxious not to reveal embarrassing or unwelcome information to outsiders, or to cause trouble to political superiors. It is not a recipe for effective action, on environmental issues or anything else. Pollution inspectors are not, on the whole, determined enthusiasts striving to stamp out wickedness. Their job is to prevent the more flagrant abuses, but they have little real authority and it is wise for them to stay on as good terms as possible with the inspected. Of course, the typical tolerant British inspector could always be replaced by an ecozealot, but the result would be predictable: the wholesale closure of firms, imprisonment of managers, collapse of local economies – and an inevitable political backlash.

In short, 'enlightened despotism' would not work, any more than it did in the eighteenth century. There is no adequate body of knowledge to apply, there is no agreement on basic viewpoints, there is no way of choosing the most rational procedure, and there is no likelihood of effective implementation.

Before finally giving way to despair, let us briefly examine another set of preferred solutions, that of the economists (Barkley and Seckler, 1972; Baumol and Oates, 1979; Pearce *et al.*, 1989). In the 'commons' example, the mayor could impose a tough tax on sheep; he could issue, or sell, negotiable grazing permits; or he could privatise the commons outright. Provided he did not tax too lightly, or issue too many permits, overgrazing would cease. The richer owners, with many sheep, would buy permits from their poorer rivals. Thus some, at least, of the implementation problems would be reduced – although policing would still be required, perhaps more than ever. The system would also be reasonably decentralised and flexible: the number of permits could vary year by year, in the light of experience or different weather conditions. Cash would also flow into the communal coffers. Of course, the poorer owners would gradually be squeezed off the commons, but that's market economics for you – a more rational allocation of resources. Similar negotiable permits, or 'entitlements', could be issued to use up other natural resources, to pollute the local environment, and so on. All this is currently much favoured by free-market economists anxious to put a price on everything, including wilderness and human life. It might even work – at least, better than other, more bureaucratic, modes of implementation. However, it does not differ essentially from Hobbes' picture. It is the mayor, not the market, who decides the 'correct' level of tax, the 'right' number of permits, or the saleable quotas of land; it is the mayor who issues or sells them (perhaps to his friends); and it is the mayor who organises the policing thereafter, to prevent non-permit-holders from daring to graze their sheep as of old. The 'market', in fact, is little more than a smoke screen, concealing the reality of sheer power – power which would, all too often, be abused.

There is another issue raised by the 'enlightened despotism' model. In practice, modern 'representative governments' rarely have coherent policies, enlightened or otherwise; they are too subject to lobbying from domestic pressure-groups, to short-term pressures from electorates, and to the need to conciliate other governments and international agencies. They have to buy votes, and cannot afford to alienate powerful groups at home or abroad, however environmentally disreputable. 'Government' is a constant process of bargaining; it usually takes place in a frenetic atmosphere of intrigue and uncertainty. As for the 'public good', it is much invoked but, unlike private goods, has no effective institutional voice. True, environmental lobbies do exist along with the others, but are ill-financed and amateurishly run, except when the odd 'environmental entrepreneur' with a gift for public relations, like Des Wilson, takes a hand. In any case, governments never have time to reflect: Something Always Has to be Done. A week is a long time in this kind of politics.

This is the political jungle from which environmental policy emerges or, more usually, does not emerge. To take one example, the British Department of Transport is a fully fledged Ministry; its Minister has a seat in the Cabinet; it is involved in a great deal of politicking; but it has never had a policy for transport, unless road-building counts as a policy. It mediates among various competing lobbies (the Road Federation, British Rail, the Automobile Association, cyclists' clubs), but it does not co-ordinate. And its senior civil servants tend to join road-building firms the moment they retire. The Department of Energy, now abolished, was slightly different. Occasionally it did have a policy – to close coal mines, or to expand the nuclear industry – but it, too, remained essentially the centre of lobbying by various particular interests (gas, oil, coal, nuclear); the still, sad voice of energy conservation was rarely heard, and that of renewable energy sources was ignored or indeed actively suppressed (House of Lords, 1987–88, pp. 178–206).

Decision-making, in short, emerges from a tortuous, complex and highly competitive game, and it is extremely unlikely that the 'right' decision will ever emerge, or that the 'right' issues will even make it on to the agenda. Governments only get away with it all because the process is secretive and because, in peacetime, few people notice even cases of gross incompetence (military incompetence is far more visible, although not necessarily more common). There may be no despotism in this form of government, but there is not much enlightenment either. Yet are we really willing to forget the last two centuries, and give up 'representative government' altogether?

Green democracy

> Economists argue that all the world lacks is
> A suitable system of effluent taxes.
> They forget that if people pollute with impunity
> This must be a sign of lack of community. (Boulding, 1972, p. 139)

Is there an alternative? If there is, it clearly has to come from a tradition of thought that rejects 'expert' bureaucracies and centralised authority, however enlightened, and rejects 'representative government' as well. In other words, it must come from sources close to the anarchist tradition, with some assistance from various spiritual and religious viewpoints, including (in the West) Christian social thought. It is striking that some of the best 'environmental' political thinking has always come from avowed anarchists, including Kropotkin himself (whose *Fields, Factories and Workshops Tomorrow*, written in 1899, was a marvellously prescient analysis of our present ills). The argument here is that environmental problems cannot be successfully resolved from above, by authority. Many of them are not new problems at all, but constant; and so they are regulated mainly by tradition. This is almost bound to be successful, or the society would have collapsed long ago. In Sardinia, for example, until recently no shepherd had more than 500 sheep; this 'social limit' was enforced, if need be, by rustling. Here was a very effective answer to the 'tragedy of the commons'. If a genuinely new environmental problem does arise, the anarchist argues that it should be amenable to 'reasoned consensus', attained after an open debate in which all may take part, and in which all viewpoints may be expressed. All this implies small, decentralised communities. Faced with environmental degradation, sensible shepherds, who would probably have many social and familial links, could and would agree among themselves to conserve the grazing, and would enforce any limits amicably enough. Any shepherd who was tempted to infringe the new norm would suffer social disgrace, and perhaps lack of co-operation in future. As long as the community remained reasonably small, so that people knew each other personally and knew that they would need each other's help in future, few problems should arise.

This seems to me a strong argument, as far as it goes. One may readily agree that, in real life, tradition, common sense, informal social controls, a need to conform, a sense of shame and fear of gossip do in fact resolve most issues, without any need to have recourse to formal authority. Few people can afford to be selfish individuals in small communities. There are, however, three obvious objections.

Firstly, small communities may be just as greedy or ignorant as large ones: small is not always long-sighted. Furthermore, given larger numbers and/or a worsening climate (through drought or desertification), they may sometimes have little choice but to over-exploit the local environment in the short term, whatever the long-term consequences. The 'tragedy of the commons' is clearly a real, inevitable tragedy in much of Africa, and one which local traditions and practices cannot possibly tackle.

Secondly, large communities and states do exist where people can get away with acting anonymously and selfishly. Indeed, most of the planet is controlled by them. And while it is true that large states sometimes collapse, they are normally soon replaced by other, smaller – but still quite large – states rather than by decentralised self-sufficient communes. If it is the case that environmental problems can only be resolved after the collapse of all existing states, our predicament is worse than we thought.

Thirdly, many environmental issues are global in nature, and not greatly affected by the decisions, however wise, of small communities. At the very least, some co-ordinating mechanism would seem necessary to deal, say, with the greenhouse effect; but how could it co-ordinate what would undoubtedly be hugely varying practices throughout the world? This, of course, is a familiar problem in anarchist theory; environmental issues simply make it more obvious.

John Dryzek, following Jürgen Habermas, has suggested what amounts to a variant of the anarchist position, to mitigate such difficulties (Dryzek, 1987). He points out that a long and open debate is needed before sensible environmental policies can be formulated. The debate, in principle open to all, not merely to scientific elites, may not lead to global consensus but should mean more informed decisions. Moreover, the debate should be constant, even in times of international tension, and open-ended. It should be flexible, decentralised and always open to new information and ideas. If this sounds Utopian, something like it already exists. The 'invisible college' of the worldwide scientific community already conducts such a debate, in its periodicals and its conferences; it even has an input into policy, particularly in the preliminary discussions before international negotiations on environmental conventions and treaties, and in the activities of the (extremely numerous) international agencies and commissions that monitor and report on such conventions and suggest improvements. Sometimes they have been remarkably successful, as on Antarctica or the ozone layer. And information can now be swiftly exchanged around the globe. Here, perhaps, is the model of potentially sensible environmental decision-making by smallish groups. They could have access to the best available scientific opinion, as well as relying on their own traditions. Thus 'environmental policy' requires neither Hobbesian authoritarianism nor a process of group lobbying; it requires, instead, informed debate in a 'public realm': 'enlightened non-despotism'.

However, 'scientific consensus' may not exist, or may be mistaken, or too 'elitist', or too affected by the preoccupations of rich Northern societies. Its data and mentalities might be incompatible with 'prescientific' traditions and beliefs; and, coming from outside, would not have the same impact on individuals as locally induced obligations. In any case, translating informed debate and 'scientific consensus' into actual local decision-making is never likely to be simple, as the complex and tortuous process of negotiating international treaties amply proves. It is difficult to see how a 'debate' would have much influence among the shepherds on the commons, let alone the nomads in the Sahel. Again, small communities might have no option but to ignore the scientists; and the co-ordination problem remains. Nor is it clear who would finance the scientists, or decide on their research objectives. Even so, despite all the problems, the argument is attractive. It looks preferable to other models of decision-making on environmental issues, including those adopted by existing States.

The contribution of environmentalism

Environmentalism's real importance to political theory, however, does not lie in endorsing or enhancing some existing political tradition, but in changing the nature of the debate. Environmentalism, at least in its more radical senses, is 'holistic', all-embracing; it stresses that political problems cannot be analysed down into their component parts. Everything is connected to everything else, probably via ill-understood feedback mechanisms. One consequence of this view is that the political and social world becomes far more complex than we supposed. It is beset by almost total uncertainty; we simply do not know what is going on, let alone the causes or the possible consequences. Another, even more significant, consequence is a vision of the world that attempts to be global, not parochial, 'communitarian' not individualistic.

Above all, environmentalism is concerned with stability, not growth. It therefore restores political theory very firmly to its traditional role, that of exploring how societies cohere, and why they collapse. Indeed, the political theory of environmentalism is essentially concerned with 'sustainability', i.e. with the stability of political regimes and societies as well as ecosystems; the possibility of catastrophe is never far from the centre of environmentalist thought. All this is salutary and, alas, realistic. It may be contested, but it is not likely to be ignored, by other more recent traditions. 'Sustainability' is a concept that has already virtually taken over serious discussion of 'development' in Third World countries; it is now expanding into most other economic fields. The term has both an empirical and a prescriptive content, combining what 'is' with what 'ought' to be; or rather, what 'is not' and what 'ought not' to be – 'sustainability' itself may not be a virtue, but non-sustainability is certainly a vice. It would be difficult to exaggerate the importance and fecundity of this concept. 'Sustainability' is replacing 'progress', the guiding ideal in the West since the seventeenth century. It will force us to look at our own societies, and at recent history, in a completely new light.

Another major achievement in the making is environmentalism's role in demoting, or perhaps replacing, the study of economics. Economics, or the 'forces of production', can no longer plausibly be regarded as the 'base' of society, even by Marxists. The 'environment' has taken over that task – an environment that is global, but also fragile. 'Economic growth' itself is seen as a dubious benefit at best, and certainly no longer as an automatic justification for political decisions – or political systems. Here is a real revolution in thought. For two centuries 'political economy' has been supreme, among both conservatives and revolutionaries; production and consumption have been regarded as goods in themselves. Those days are almost over. Environmentalism has replaced the 'dismal science', indeed has become the new 'dismal science', constraining our choices and limiting our ambitions. It may well prove to be even more dismal than economics was. At any rate, if we take it seriously it makes most of our existing political arrangements and most of the policies of our existing political parties obsolete. The despairing efforts of latter-day 'environmental economists' to analyse environmental issues in familiar economic terms are simply flailing attempts to keep the show on the road. This humbling of economics is not, of course, universally recognised yet; but the writing seems to be on the wall for the invisible hand.

Environmentalism has also been important in other areas of political thought, notably in the literature on ethics and obligation. Many environmentalist thinkers have argued that existing admitted, socially recognised obligations and rights should be extended more widely, in particular to animals, but also to plants and trees, mountains, and to the earth itself (Regan, 1983; Regan and Singer, 1976; Singer, 1976). Debates on 'animal rights', and on the biblical concept of 'stewardship', have dominated much recent philosophical thinking on environmental issues. So, too, has the question of obligation to more nebulous entities that may not even exist, like future (human) generations. All this is clearly the result of a more 'global' mode of thought and, in the case of future generations, of rejecting 'short-term thinking'.

Future generations do, admittedly, present peculiar problems (Attfield, 1983; Barry, 1977; Feinberg, 1974; Sikora and Barry, 1978). If we grant them any moral status at all, should they have less claim than current generations? Should our obligations diminish with time, so that we have a considerable duty to the next generation, but nothing to people alive a thousand (or a million) years hence?

Most economists would argue that the interests of future people should be discounted at some appropriate percentage, so a huge environmental problem today (nuclear waste disposal, say) would become trivial in about 200 years. One can argue the same case on the grounds that their technology should be superior to ours, and so better able to cope. But can we count on this? After all, most of today's complex technologies carry a small but measurable risk; hence, if they are continued for long enough, the risk event will probably occur. Furthermore, much pollution is cumulative; many resources are finite. Future generations may therefore have greater problems to solve than we have; and the further in the future they are, the greater the problems will be.

So should future generations perhaps have a greater claim than people alive today? This seems intuitively distasteful, particularly as some revolutionary politicians in the recent past have clearly thought so, with disastrous consequences. Yet on utilitarian grounds, future people would always win any calculation of felicity, since their numbers are infinite. If we have obligations to future people, does it follow that there is an obligation to have children? (As many children as possible?) Similarly, do people with children have greater obligations to future people than those without descendants? More speculatively, would time travel, if it ever became feasible, create new obligations (perhaps the obligation to remain a purely passive spectator in a different time zone)?

If we do have obligations to future generations, what are they? One real problem here is that we cannot be sure what the interests of future generations will be. Future people will certainly be different from us and, of course, from each other; different generations may have competing and contradictory claims upon us. Global warming, for example, presents us with a real dilemma: will our descendants curse us for it, or bless us for averting an Ice Age? How can we guess their 'best interests' on this issue? Yet in this respect we are simply in the same position as any parent. We have to do our best, knowing that we will probably get it wrong. And we may reasonably assume that all future generations, whatever their diversity, will want to inherit a clean, easily inhabitable, biodiverse planet. For most purposes our obligation is therefore quite simple: not to drop litter. This may seem banal but it is not trivial, nor is it easy to accomplish. We are faced with these problems every day, as the nuclear and chemical waste piles up. Genetic damage already, and genetic engineering in the future, present them in even more acute form.

The most stringent ethical criterion proposed by any environmentalist – and the most extreme version of the 'stewardship' thesis – is that of Aldo Leopold's 'land ethic': 'a thing is right when it tends to preserve the integrity, stability and beauty of the biotic community. It is wrong when it tends otherwise' (Leopold, 1949, pp. 224–5). Note the implications of this apparently inoffensive criterion. Leopold assumes it is possible to know what tends to preserve 'integrity, stability [a term which presumably includes diversity] and beauty'. In fact, as I have already argued, our ecological knowledge is often very limited, much depends on the time-scale one chooses to adopt, and of course no universal consensus on beauty is likely or even desirable. Moreover, the criterion justifies, even insists on, culling excess numbers of a particular species, if they pose a threat to the local environment. To take a local example, Leopold would presumably join today with those urging a wholesale reduction in the red deer population of the Scottish Highlands: the consensus view is that the deer are too numerous, are destroying native woodland and thus the habitat of other species, and so on.

The problem with this argument, it seems to me, is not merely whether our knowledge is adequate (Leopold himself would not have been absolutely certain we knew enough about the deer and the habitat); it is the cheerful acceptance of 'environmental cleansing' as a duty. Needless to say, Leopold's criterion rejects 'animal rights' completely, at least in the generally accepted sense: the individual deer has no right not to be slaughtered if it will help the 'biotic community' (including, to be fair, the deer) in the long run. This has perhaps unfortunate overtones, particularly as the main environmental threat today comes not from excess numbers of deer, but of humans. On Leopold's criterion, human rights are no more valid than animal ones; and it follows that the human population should be drastically and rapidly reduced. This view is tacitly (and sometimes explicitly) urged by prominent environmentalists. Their arguments bring out, as rarely before, the general problems in 'rights' theory. In other words, if we accept the hard-line ecological–ethical criterion, we must give up any lingering 'liberal' attachment to individual or personal rights, for humans as well as animals. The 'biotic community' is all. It might have a place for humans, but it would not necessarily be a big place, nor a dominant one.

It will be clear by now that the more radical forms of environmentalism constitute a profoundly pessimistic doctrine. Rejecting 'progress', they offer no prospect of an earthly paradise, and little hope of averting an earthly hell. True, the Good Life may be available to us if we change our ways, but it requires very major changes. Environmentalism provides, in short, a 'global' critique of existing society, which it regards as doomed. If political theorists, from Plato onwards, have used nautical analogies – the 'ship of state', the 'ruler as helmsman' etc. – the radical environmentalists' symbol is the Titanic. We are all on board this 'unsinkable' vessel, with its extravagant use of fuel, as it rapidly approaches the icebergs. What should we do to be saved? We can, of course, fool ourselves that the Titanic is strong enough to survive impact; we can hope that something will turn up – some new 'technofix' that the helmsman will discover just in time; we might simply decide to eat, drink and be merry. But it would be more sensible to change course, if it is not too late. Yet only a tiny handful of passengers are demanding a change of direction. And so the ship sails on.

This new nautical metaphor, like previous ones, is rather convincing. It is, in fact, now setting the agenda for serious debate in many fields, including history, economics, politics, theology, psychology and anthropology. The great intellectual question is: how did we ever get on board this ship in the first place? The answers are troublingly fundamental. We may be on board because we are programmed to be; in that case there is not much we can do about it, unless genetic engineering provides an unlikely solution. Or else we have bought tickets because the dominant ideologies of the past few hundred (or thousand) years have told us to, in which case we have a hugely challenging intellectual agenda, rewriting all our old assumptions. It may all be the fault of the 'scientific' and 'rationalist' revolutions of the seventeenth century, from which most of our analytic sciences and materialist philosophies are derived. Perhaps we should blame the whole Judaeo-Christian tradition, with its sharp separation of God from Nature and its stress on humanity's mission to dominate the external world. Or it may all stem from the alleged 'patriarchal revolution' of pre-history, or from the original agricultural revolution itself, with all the power conflicts and property divisions that accompanied it. At any rate, we now realise just what a package our old charts were: analytic, reductionist, mechanistic science; bureaucratic, hierarchical, 'masculinist' society; 'market-rational', individualistic economy; rationalist, rights-or utility-based philosophy; even a hierarchical book-based religion, offering an individualist salvation. Western industrial society has had a dominant ideology all right: all of a piece. Now, however, it all has to be rejected and rethought, rather rapidly.

The more radical, 'ecocentric' forms of environmentalism assert, therefore, that society as we know it is doomed, and that the industrial revolution certainly, the agricultural revolution probably, were both disastrous errors. Industrialism, in particular, is seen as simply killing the planet. Sometimes it does this more or less deliberately, as in the overtly 'exterminist' policies of industrial-military-nuclear complexes. At other times it is accidental, as at Bhopal or Chernobyl; yet such accidents are barely more damaging than routine non-accidental procedures, and are mere symptoms of the underlying disease. And this industrial system is based on very deep-seated and long-founded assumptions and theories. If we are ever to change course, the deep assumptions and values will have to change too; perhaps they will have to change first. Environmentalism demands, therefore, a vast intellectual 'perestroika', completely subversive of established modes of thought and behaviour. It tells us, in all seriousness, that modern human society has got it all wrong.

References

Attfield, R. (1983), *Ethics of Environmental Concern*, Oxford: Blackwell, Ch. 6.

Barkley, P. W. and Seckler, D. (1972), *Economic Growth and Environmental Decay*, New York: Harcourt Brace Jovanovich.

Barry, B. (1977), 'Justice between generations', in P. Hacker and J. Raz (Eds.), *Law, Morality and Society*, Oxford: Oxford University Press, pp. 268–84.

Baumol, W. and Oates, W. E. (1979), *Economics, Environmental Policy and the Quality of Life*, Englewood Cliffs, N.J.: Prentice Hall.

Boulding, K. (1972), 'New goals for society', in S. Schurr (Ed.), *Energy, Economic Growth and the Environment*, Baltimore: Johns Hopkins University Press, pp. 139–51.

Brown, L. (1981), *Building a Sustainable Society*, New York: Norton.

Brundtland, G. (1987), *Our Common Future*, Oxford: Oxford University Press.

Carr, M. (Ed.) (1985), *The Appropriate Technology Reader*, London: Intermediate Technology Publications.

Carson, R. (1962), *Silent Spring*, Boston: Houghton Mifflin.

Daly, H. (Ed.) (1973), *Towards a Steady State Economy*, San Francisco: Freeman.

Devall, W. and Sessions, G. (Eds.) (1985), *Deep Ecology*, Salt Lake City: Peregrine Smith.

Dryzek, J. (1987), *Rational Ecology*, Oxford: Blackwell.

Feinberg, J. (1974), 'The rights of animals and unborn generations', in W. T. Blackstone (Ed.), *Environmental Crisis*, University of Georgia Press, pp. 43–67.

Hardin, G. (1968), 'The tragedy of the commons', *Science*, 13 Dec 1968, CLXII, 1243–8.

Hardin, G. (1977), 'Living on a lifeboat', in G. Hardin and J. Baden (Eds.), *Managing the Commons*, San Francisco: Freeman, pp. 261–79.

Heilbronner, R. (1974), *An Inquiry into the Human Prospect*, New York: Harper and Row.

Hobbes, T. (1651), *Leviathan*, London.

House of Lords (1987–88), Select Committee on European Communities, *16th. Report* (June 1988), London.

Kahn, H. (1978), *The Next 200 Years*, New York: Morrow.

Kahn, H. and Simon, J. (1984), *The Resourceful Earth*, Oxford: Blackwell.

Kropotkin, P. (1899), *Fields, Factories and Workshops Tomorrow*, London: Hutchinson.

Leopold, A. (1949), 'The land ethic', in *A Sand County Almanac*, Oxford: Oxford University Press, pp. 201–26.

McRobie, G. (1981), *Small is Possible*, London: Cape.

Meadows, D. *et al.* (1972), *The Limits to Growth*, London: Pan.

Midgley, M. (1983), 'Duties concerning islands', in R. Elliot and A. Gare (Eds.), *Environmental Philosophy*, Oxford: Oxford University Press, pp. 166–81.

Naess, A. (1973), 'The shallow and the deep, long-range ecology movement', *Inquiry*, XVI, 95–100.

Ophuls, W. (1977), *Ecology and the Politics of Scarcity*, San Francisco: Freeman.

Pearce, D. *et al.* (1989), *Blueprint for a Green Economy*, London: Earthscan.

Regan, T. (1983), *The Case for Animal Rights*, Berkeley: University of California Press.

Regan, T. and Singer, P. (1976), *Animal Rights and Human Obligations*, Englewood Cliffs, N.J.: Prentice Hall.

Schumacher, E. (1973), *Small is Beautiful*, London: Blond and Briggs.

Scientific American (1990), *Managing Planet Earth*, San Francisco: Freeman.

Sikora, R. and Barry, B. (Eds.) (1978), *Obligations to Future Generations*, Philadelphia: Temple University Press.

Singer, P. (1976), *Animal Liberation*, London: Cape.
Stroup, R. and Baden, J. (Eds.) (1983), *Natural Resources*, Cambridge, Mass.: Ballinger.
Wordsworth, W. (1798), 'The tables turned', in P. Wayne (Ed.), *Poems*, Dent, 1955, I, 37–8.
World Resources Institute (1986), *World Resources* (annual), New York: Basic Books.

Politics and violence

Within political discussion, whether at the level of journalism or high theory, a common assumption is that violence and politics are opposites: that in some important sense politics ends where violence begins and vice versa. Journalists regularly invite politicians to deplore the use of violence, and politicians themselves urge that eruptions of violence indicate that political processes have broken down.

This assumption, which is as old as ancient Greek thought and as contemporary as last night's television programmes, to a large extent draws its plausibility from two others: namely, that violence is something sheerly instrumental and that politics, for its part, is best thought of as a going concern. The conception of violence as sheerly instrumental supports the politics/violence opposition by suggesting a contrast between individuals addressed merely as manipulable and destructible *objects* and individuals addressed as communicable-with *subjects* (this latter being the unique competence of a 'political' ordering of human affairs). The conception of politics as an ongoing concern supports the violence/politics opposition by bracketing off the question of the origins or constitution of political order: these origins may lie in violence, as theorists so diverse as David Hume and Karl Marx and Jean-Paul Sartre have sought to stress.

It is a moot point whether the first assumption I have identified can be upheld without support from at least one of the other two. Unless we can say *either* that politics is communicative and violence isn't *or* that political agents – in the same movement as they become political agents – leave their guns at the door, a defence of the first assumption would seem not just to qualify politics as being a more-or-less unviolent matter but to *redefine* politics as something closer to philosophy or meditation: it would imply that politicians must needs become unworldly ('unworldliness' being defined as any self-abstraction from a communicative and interactive human realm). Whoever redefined politics in this manner would be involved in a *drastic* redefinition. He or she would have to admit to using the term 'politics' in a sense so wholly alien to traditional usage that it was not in the least clear that opponents and proponents in the unfolding argument were talking about the same thing.

The argument of the present paper is to the effect that the second and third of the assumptions just identified — the, as it were, supporting assumptions — are false and, to that extent, the first assumption collapses. Violence can be not just instrumental but creative; and the question of the (potentially violent) origin of politics returns to haunt politics itself.

In what follows, I attempt to supply (selective) chapter and verse for the theses just presented, drawing on ancient, modern and contemporary political thought. Perhaps one more prefatory note is in order, because I shall have to allow violence to speak in, so to say, its own voice. Anyone who does so invites the charge that he or she is making a cult out of violence for its own sake. In fact the category of 'for its own sake' inheres in the instrumentalist conception of violence which I wish to challenge, and the upshot of my argument will be the closest approximation to a defence of outright pacifism which I think can reasonably be made. I turn now to a preliminary consideration of the three assumptions identified above.

1 Politics and violence as opposites

Hannah Arendt's essay 'On Violence' is of especial value because it makes explicit the assumption that violence and politics are opposites, in a clear-cut way. According to Arendt's argument, politics pertains to 'power' whereas violence is apolitical. Violence and power subtract from one another: 'where the one rules absolutely, the other is absent' (Arendt, 1973a, p. 123). There is a perhaps unfamiliar terminology at work here. Anglophone political theory tends to equate a politics of power with 'power politics', or *Realpolitik* — which is precisely the opposite of Arendt's meaning. Her relating of power to politics relies on a contrast between *potentia (Vermögen)* and *potestas (Herrschaft* or *Macht)* which is more or less invisible in English but common in continental European scholarship (e.g. Foucault, 1979,

p. 27; Negri, 1991). Roughly, the distinction is between power in the senses of ability on the one hand and of domination on the other, and it is power in the former sense which Arendt invokes. Politics for Arendt is linked to power, and vice versa, because power (*potentia*) corresponds to 'the human ability not just to act but to act in concert' (Arendt, 1973a, p. 113). So important does Arendt think this correspondence to be that she reserves the term 'action', itself, for interaction in a political sense (Arendt, 1958, Ch. 5). Nor is our political capacity to 'act in concert' merely something fixed and given: it enhances and further empowers us, much in the way that, say, our capacity to understand a difficult book is enhanced if we read it and discuss it in the company of others instead of poring over it in solitude. In contrast to this conception, power in the sense of *potestas* or domination threatens to approximate itself to violence, and for Arendt − just as for Machiavelli and Gramsci, to mention only two further examples − nothing could be more insecure and precarious than a political order premised on the threat of violence alone. Violence is apolitical because it atomises us, whereas power (*potentia*) is both the condition and the product of politics inasmuch as it throws our capacity for interactive achievement into relief.

Arendt is surely right in her contention that interaction empowers us. But her thought becomes politically eccentric − it risks the danger of what I have called a *drastic* redefinition of politics − inasmuch as it drives too harsh and unequivocal a wedge between violence and politics itself. This is most evident in her book *On Revolution*, where, somewhat contentiously, she contrasts a successful American with an unsuccessful French Revolution on the basis that the former, unlike the latter, did not have to cope with the allegedly violent demands of the poor. The demands of the poor are for Arendt violent as a consequence of their 'urgency': a claim upon others to 'give us our bread' is non-negotiable, and hence apolitical or anti-political; in the very nature of the case, as it were, the threat of violence looms. There is of course the danger of a conceptual slippage here, as though everything which is not political must be violent; and enthusiasts for the British Labour Party might be surprised to learn that a case for welfare programmes cannot be pursued in a polite (a 'political') way. Arendt is led by this argument to such extraordinary claims as that nothing could be more 'futile and dangerous' than 'to attempt to liberate mankind from poverty by political means' (Arendt, 1973b, pp. 112, 114) and that welfare problems, being apolitical 'matters of administration', are best 'put into the hands of experts' (Arendt, 1973b, p. 91). The absurdity of this view derives, I think, not so much from a hostility to welfare programmes *per se*, as from a driving-in of the politics/violence wedge too emphatically and at the wrong angle. Shift the pieces on the board, ever so slightly, and we arrive at an endorsement of the violence/politics opposition which entails none of the eccentricity which pertains to Arendt's thought.

Max Weber, in his classic essay on 'Politics as a Vocation' (Gerth and Mills, 1962), urges that violence is the very stuff and substance of politics – but only in the last resort. Whereas Arendt says that politics becomes corrupted whenever it has to deal with issues of even potential violence, such as poverty, Weber is more robust in insisting that *it is the very task of politics* to deal with violence in order to hold it at bay.

Cynics might claim that Weber was happy to see violence as the source of politics (without violence politics could not exist) but others report, perhaps more faithfully, that an 'economy of violence' (Wolin, 1960, Ch. 7) and hence a minimisation of violence is what Weber sought. In other words, *pace* Arendt, politics can and should deal with violent issues without becoming, thereby, a violent politics. The heroes invoked in this tradition of reflection are Machiavelli (for an alternative interpretation, see Gunn, 1988a) and Hobbes (see discussion below). The tradition mentioned supplies, I think, the most *usual* way of reflecting upon politics. The sense of an opposition between violence and politics stands, even when the Arendtian contention that politics becomes corrupted when it addresses violent issues is dropped. The most unsentimental minds of the nineteenth and twentieth centuries have been willing to address 'politics' in this way.

2 Violence as instrumental

Again, it is Arendt who makes the assumption most explicit: she states that '*violence* ... is distinguished by its instrumental character' (Arendt, 1973a, p. 115). She means that it both *uses* instruments – fists, machine guns, atom bombs and so on – and that it addresses others not as subjects but as objects who (or which) can be manipulated through its use or threat. Thereby violence is the opposite of communicative and interactive politics. It is the opposite of 'power' in the Arendtian sense explained above.

Weber says more or less the same. His 'ethic of responsibility' (Gerth and Mills, 1962) enjoins that we must make instrumental means/ends calculations so as to distil violence (construed instrumentally) to a minimum and hold open a space for communicative political life. Habermas, deriving in part from Arendt (cf. Arendt, 1958 and Habermas 1989 on the notion of a public realm) but in a larger-scale way from Weber, urges in similar fashion that there must needs be instrumental subsystems of social life but that it is the task of politics to prevent these from getting out of control. Politics defends the intersubjective 'lifeworld (*Lebenswelt*)' from its bureaucratic instrumentalisation. In Aristotelian fashion, an intercommunicative 'good life' and not just 'life' − a condition of brute survival, to be addressed instrumentally − is both the medium of politics and the goal (*telos*) towards which politics should aim. In short, politics should seek to maintain itself. It can do so, because it presupposes itself and only itself (see next section).

A balance sheet of the arguments and approaches presented so far looks something like this. Arendt agrees with Weber to the extent that she sees violence (*Gewalt*: sometimes 'force' but more usually 'violence') as instrumental; she disagrees with Weber on the score of whether or not politics can and must (Weber) or cannot and should not, on peril of its corruption (Arendt), deal with issues of a potentially violent kind. Habermas agrees with Arendt in so far as he seeks to prise politics away from instrumentality but disagrees with her inasmuch as he tends to construe power solely as *potestas* (domination, *Herrschaft*) rather than as *potentia* and, hence, as anathema to the condition of politics itself. He agrees with Weber in so far as he wishes to hold the nightmare of a sheerly violent/ instrumentalist politics at bay; but in common with the 'Frankfurt School' tradition from which he derives (e.g. Held, 1984; and, on the relation of the Frankfurt School to Weber, Marcuse, 1968, essay VI) he is worried about the fate of communication should the holding-at-bay of violence become politics' sole theme. If it does become politics' sole theme, then it threatens to overtake and eclipse politics. Although, for Habermas, with Weber and *pace* Arendt, politics has to deal with violent and instrumental issues, it must needs (with Arendt and *pace* Weber) clear its own space: namely a non-violent because a non-instrumental space. Politics is for Arendt 'the space of men's free deeds and living words' (1973b, p. 281). One way of reading Arendt's *Eichmann in Jerusalem* (1977) is to construe it as a declaration against (false) bureaucratic and instrumentalist solutions: once 'the Jews' were assimilated to a difficulty to be dealt with via offices, their fate was sealed.

In short, the three theorists so far discussed agree in construing violence as instrumental and as, in response to violent/instrumentalist horror, attempting to secure the foundations of an autonomous or at least semi-autonomous political realm. The only differences between them lie along a line – politics must and can think about violence (Weber); politics has to police instrumentality into a subsystem status (Habermas); politics cannot and never should entangle itself with violent/instrumental issues (Arendt) – which can be plotted in quantitative terms. The qualitative argument is, however, to the same effect in all cases: politics is communicative whereas violence (*qua* instrumental) is not.

3. Politics as on-going

The assumption that politics is best discussed as an on-going activity, as a sort of maintenance of business as usual, is at least as old as Aristotle's *Politics* where it is said (Book I) that a human individual is a *zoon politikon* or political being. In the twentieth century, two, perhaps related, schools of thought have attempted to follow through Aristotle's contention. *Civic humanism* (Baron, 1966; Pocock, 1971, p. 85, and 1975) has attempted to unfold the early-modern notion of 'republicanism' – the notion, emphatic in writers as diverse as Thomas More and Machiavelli, that public goods should be prioritised over private ones – from Aristotelian premises. Equally (e.g. Skinner, 1986) there have been attempts to restate civic humanism in a manner independent of the teleologism (we fulfil ourselves as human beings when we act as citizens) inherent in Aristotelian thought. Secondly, and with or without teleology, modern *communitarianism* has urged, 'following Aristotle', that 'we cannot conceive our personhood without reference to our role as citizens, and as participants in a common life' (Sandel, 1984, p. 5).

Two points are to be made in connection with civic humanist and communitarian schools of thought. The first is to the effect that they both subscribe to a business-as-usual conception of politics whether or not they become explicitly neo-Aristotelian and endorse teleological views. Their central, and plausible, contention is that we are in and of politics at the very same moment as we begin to speak or think. Politics is our context, and not just an external object upon which we may choose to reflect.

The second point is to the effect that contemporary ('liberal') opponents of civic humanism and/or communitarianism share the same view *to the extent* that they treat Kantian transcendental deduction as a means of identifying an individual's duties and/or rights (e.g. Rawls, 1985). A (transcendental) argument to the effect that *if* we want (for whatever reason) a political order *then* the following rights and duties (of whatever kind) must be ascribed is non-viciously circular only if the notion of political order is presupposed. There could of course be good – say, prudential – reasons for wishing to presuppose it; but we need to know whether (the early Rawls and the later Habermas) a foundation for political order is being supplied or whether (the later Rawls and the early Habermas) the major premiss is political order itself.[1] Inasmuch as we need to know this, two strategies are available. One is to construe rights and political order as complementary: hence communitarian liberalism. The other is to attempt to break out of the circle altogether by, say, projecting a derivation of rights from the conditions of action *per se* (Gewirth, 1982, Ch. 1). In the present connection it is unnecessary to evaluate either of these strategies; the point to be underscored is merely that the business-as-usual conception of politics is shared not merely by contemporary neo-Aristotelians, with or without the teleology, but by (many of) those who resist civic humanist and communitarian views. Politics as a presupposition and politics as an on-going activity mean much the same thing.

Why should discussion of politics tend to presuppose politics, thus courting the dangers of vicious circularity and tautology? It is perhaps too easy to say that it does so because 'strong foundationalism' (cf. Bernstein, 1983) has gone out of fashion, although it certainly has. The deeper reason may lie in the circumstance that politics itself is a so-to-say circular activity. This is nicely caught by Wolin (1960, p. 11) when he urges that 'politics is both a source of conflict and a mode of activity that seeks to resolve conflicts and promote readjustment': if it succeeds in doing so then the circle is complete. Politics is a sort of standing miracle. It is the sole 'mode of activity' which can discover its resources within itself. To this effect Arendt construes 'natality' (1958) and 'new beginnings' (1973b) as inherently political. To the same effect, Aristotle's term for revolution is *stasis*: he means that it is a breakdown or interruption of the circuit in which politics consists. Natality is as it were the acceleration which keeps politics going, despite frictions, and *stasis* (or *stopping*) is the breakdown which happens when the cogwheels of the perpetual-motion machine become fouled up.

Politics, like God in the ontological proof offered by St Anselm (1973, pp. 244–6), can renew itself, but only via a circuit; and so we need to understand how wide this circuit is. Hegel (1988, pp. 181–4) thought it should be sufficiently wide to encompass God, as such, thus bringing God down to earth. Hegel, secularising the ontological proof, goes so far as to report the state as 'manifest (*offenbare*) or clear-to-itself ethical will' (Hegel, 1991, p. 275): his term 'manifest' is cognate with 'public' in the sense of Arendt and Habermas, and also with the sense in which 'revealed' religion is revealed (Hegel, 1977, Ch. VII). So far as I know, no stronger claim has ever been made for the self-renewing and *selbst tragende* capacities of the political realm.

There is of course a danger inherent in all of this: namely, that whilst rightly linking politics to themes of self-renewal and empowerment the circuit of political action is drawn so tightly as to confine it within an implausibly narrow field. The attempt to identify the unique capacities of politics threatens to draw politics away from other, no less lively, sources of human concern. The question that is likely to be begged is what the seventeenth and eighteenth centuries thought of as the *origins* or *constitution* of politics. Arendt, in the same movement as she debars politics from considering matters of welfare (because such matters are potentially violent/instrumental), opens up the question of political origins in a courageous way. She links the *principle* of an on-going politics to the question of its *principium* or beginning (1973b) and asks whether or not (her answer is that is cannot) this beginning may lie in violence.

There are a host of others who say that it can. Marx (1976, p. 916) says that '*Gewalt* is the midwife of every old society pregnant with a new one', but since he left the notion of *Gewalt* undefined we have no idea whether or not he thought of violence in an instrumental or communicative way. Certainly he sought to minimise it.[2] Bataille ('The Notion of Expenditure' in Bataille, 1985; Bataille, 1987, Ch. V) declares violent wastage to be the very condition upon which, inasmuch as it constructs a symbolic order, politics depends. Freud's *Totem and Taboo* (1985), reporting as it does the murder of the primordial father, and linking civilisation to repressed guilt (the 'return of the repressed') says more or less the same thing as does Kojève (1947) when the latter, dwelling upon Hegel's *Phenomenology*, reports a master/slave fight to the beginning of human history itself.

The alternative approach is of course social contract theory, according to which the origins of politics lie not in violence but in a polite mutual promising to obey the law and a reciprocal shaking of hands. Why should not a 'recognition' which is 'mutual' (Hegel, 1977, p. 112) emerge at once? The traditional answer to this is that promising and recognition are, themselves, social institutions so that *if* one's question is that of the origin of politics they cannot be presupposed. A hypothetical rendition of social contract theory assumes a pre-existent and on-going politics. The question is begged *only* if questions of the origins − or for that matter the demise − of politics are in view. Placing them out of view, however, requires that we simply posit politics, practically and epistemologically, as an on-going category of thought. The traditional social contractarians knew better. Locke, Rousseau and Hobbes devoted themselves to the issue of the origin of politics − how can the miracle emerge? − and so wondered about how violence should relate to their schemes. Maybe the circuit of political self-origination includes violence: or maybe not! In the same way as an equation of violence with instrumentality (and a contrast between communication and instrumental reasoning) is too easy, so also is the un-self-reflective conception of an always already on-going conception of political thought. In Marxist terms: there is a 'permanence' of 'primitive accumulation' (Bonefeld, 1988). Holding violence at bay becomes less a programme than an alibi, where it attempts to sever politics from violence on a priori grounds.

In support of this contention we can note that a politics which devolves solely upon itself falls into serious philosophical difficulties. They cluster around the unfashionable but perhaps practically crucial notion of 'sovereignty': A. P. d'Entreves urges (1962, p. 92) that a *legislative* sovereign is that individual or body of persons entitled *legitimately* to pass laws. He is so clear that the potential vicious circularity of politics becomes evident, because would it not require a law-behind-the-law to legitimate law itself? Arendt (1973a) celebrates d'Entreves because he abuts on to the question of the origins of political order; but it is by no means clear that d'Entreves would have chosen to defend himself in this way. Arendt (1973b) locates the origins of politics in a pre-political practice of township meetings, soviets and *rate* and all the rest. She offers a communitarian version of the social contract. Instead of the legalistically atomised individual, she invokes the notion of persons who are (always) already political agents, so that revolution's or indeed political constitution's prospects can unfold in a decent way. In this manner she threatens to beg her own question: that of origins. Politics can result only from a prior politics and *because this is so* the question of an origination of politics in violence can be dismissed.

4 Hobbes

Very evidently the ghost of Hobbes stalks through – indeed haunts – all of the arguments above mentioned. Hobbes is, roughly, famous for having argued that violence is so immediately threatening and horrendous that *any* political order which can protect us against it is better than none. A tyrant would be a preferable option to anarchistic chaos, even though most of us would elect for liberty rather than constraint. The raw edges of the above argument – violence may not be merely instrumental; political origins may indeed lie in violence – pertain very directly to the interpretation of Thomas Hobbes.

At first sight, it seems clear enough that Hobbes thinks of violence, and of power too, in an instrumental way. In the pre-political state of nature we *use* violence as a means of defending ourselves, of ensuring that we continue to survive; and very often attack is the best means of defence. Additionally, our survival chances increase in proportion to the amount of resources (scarce or otherwise) that we control, and these resources are our 'power'. 'Glory' is that 'mental pleasure' which derives from our delight in contemplating our 'powers': the image this suggests is of an individual pleasurably contemplating his/her well stocked larder, or gun-room. The further twist Hobbes gives to all of this is that 'power' consists not just in an absolute magnitude of resources but in 'eminence' (*Leviathan*, Ch. X), that is to say, in our possession of more resources than the other fellow.

This *comparative* definition of power – translating it from the realm of *amour de soi meme* to the realm of *amour propre*, in Rousseau's terminology[3] – renders conflict all but logically inevitable. As it were, and employing the terms of the Galileian 'New Science' which Hobbes was always ready to affect, survival represents a continuation of our 'motion' whereas power represents an acceleration of this motion, in part because it amounts to an accumulation of the means which permit this motion and in part (even more diabolically) because the means are defined comparatively. Chapter XIII of *Leviathan* can be read as a horror story, as a sort of awful warning as to the consequences of not erecting a political order which can either translate violent competition into peaceful competition (MacPherson, 1962) or seek to damp down the always unseasonable passionate gusts (Strauss, 1936).[4] We are like atoms in a void which may bang together, not just coincidentally, but because with malice aforethought we seek one another out. We are accelerated towards others. *Politics* is what is supposed (under the condition of the higher fear or 'awe' of a sovereign) to hold all of this at bay. It is, so to say, the lid clamped upon what Freud once called the seething cauldron of the passions and for Hobbes, roughly, the heavier the lid the better. This at any rate is what I take to have been the *usual* way of reading Thomas Hobbes. From it unfolds the 'traditional' and Straussian and Marxist interpretations.

Against it, we can notice an alternative interpretation and at least one awkward passage in Hobbes. The alternative interpretation is that of Taylor (1938) and Warrender (1957), who seek to prise Hobbes' political theory away from his 'egoistic psychology'. Taylor and Warrender's claim is to the effect that Hobbes sees natural law as moral law and as binding even in the state of nature: the difference is that, in the state of nature, our obligations are commanding only *in foro interno* (we are morally required to obey moral law merely in the sense of being required to want to obey it) whereas in a political state we are required to obey it *in foro externo*, not merely through our intentions but our actions as well. No 'hypocrisy of good intentions' (Hegel, 1991) can get us off the hook.

The elegance of the Taylor and Warrender interpretation derives from the circumstance that it can make sense of Hobbes' dark construal of the notion of a social contract. The most evident, and traditional, objection to social contract theory is to the effect that politics and indeed social existence cannot derive themselves from promising (or contracting) because a promise is an institution of a social and political sort. Social contract theory itself − and not just, for example, Arendt's communitarian deepening of it into township meetings and so forth − begs the question of the *origin* or *constitution* of politics (one-off or on-going) that it was supposed to resolve. Taylor and Warrender clear up this matter wonderfully by urging that the social contract is a promise of a unique kind. It is the *sole* species of promise which can pull itself up by its own bootstraps. To place ourselves beneath the 'awe' of a sovereign is to contract into an arrangement whereby we may be killed should our promises not be maintained. To quote Hobbes, 'Covenants, without the Sword, are but Words' (Ch. XVII) and it requires what Hobbes calls a sovereign to make natural law binding – to make it, to all practical effect, moral – not just *in foro interno* but *in foro externo* as well. In the state of nature we can all promise anything duplicitously, and without any comeback save a potential stab in the back. Political order, by contrast, holds us to our promises, including our promise to obey it, and can do so because a promise of obedience alters the very condition of promising itself. We are henceforth held to the words we may have hitherto spoken in a frivolous or instrumentalist or survival-oriented way.

'Awe', of course, connotes not just instrumentalist fear, say of a rock pounding down towards one across a cliffside, but legitimacy; moral respect as well as physical fear is entailed; and Hobbes for his part was happy enough to throw every prudential and ethical argument he could think of into the pan of the scales which – the Galileian physicalist metaphor once again – weighed on the side of obedience to a *de facto* state. According to Taylor and Warrender he sought to make moral obligations lively, i.e. practically effective. According to Strauss he was a moralist rather than a physicist, thinking of the relation between violence and politics, or between 'vainglory' and glory,⁵ more or less by analogy with Holbein's Dance of Death. For Taylor and Warrender (and Strauss), therefore, the 'traditional' and instrumentalist interpretation of Hobbes is wrong. Hobbes himself contains communitarian resources. Without attempting anything so hubristic as an overall Hobbes-interpretation it is interesting to ask what these resources are.

They are, of course, first of all to be found in the passages (much emphasised by Taylor and Warrender) in which Hobbes equivocates between the notion that a law of nature is a moral and/or divine command and the notion that such laws are instrumental or prudential rules of thumb (e.g. Ch. XV *ad fin.*). Furthermore, *in so far as* Hobbes derives the power of a sovereign from a social contract (an inter-communicative promise) he *cannot* have been thinking about power sheerly instrumentally. And, finally, Hobbes, in his famous peroration in *Leviathan* (Ch. XIII), lists being 'solitary' as amongst the

horrors of a state of nature: solitude is no less an evil than unconstrained violence. Read in abstraction from later Hobbes-commentary,
this passage would encourage us to see Hobbes as just the sort of
neo-Aristotelian who resists Aristotle's teleology (see above). Reading
Hobbes backwards (Ch. XIII is a horror story, and a warning, about
what might happen) instead of forwards (from *violence*, we may be
able to constitute *politics*, itself), is an interesting exercise but still
leaves the centre of gravity of Hobbes' political thought out of
account.

Any identification of this centre of gravity has to reckon with
the circumstance of selective reading: Taylor and Warrender are
enthusiasts for *Leviathan* Chs. XIV–XVI and XXX, whereas 'tradi-
tionalists' have based themselves (in Parts I and II) on almost all the
rest. Were Hobbes to be a traditionalist in the classic mould then it
would have been better if chapters XIV–XVI, dealing as they do with
such non-instrumental topics as political rights and authorisation,
were never written: and it is undoubtedly the case that a *consistent*
traditionalist construal of Hobbes has to treat them as an anomaly,
because how can a discourse on our natural and our ethical powers
dovetail in so convenient a way? Warrender urges that, according
to Hobbes, prudential and moral obligations run in parallel, so that
our propensity to survive entails obedience. This may have been,
so to say, Hobbes' Utopia. But what it leaves aside is the question
of how, with such great confidence, Hobbes can pass (as though it
were only a change of topic) from passion-oriented to ethical modes
of political thought.

What follows is only the merest slight slip of a suggestion. I think
it has seldom been noticed to what extent Hobbes endorsed the
premisses of the English Civil War opponents whom he much loved
to hate. In *Leviathan* (Ch. XIII) he reports that the 'Desires, and
other Passions of Man, are in themselves no Sin': nor are the
'Actions' which may well 'proceed' from them. Any Civil War leftist
or anarchist or 'Ranter' (Davis, 1986; Gunn, 1990; Hill, 1972;
Morton, 1970; Smith, 1984) would have found this familiar territory.
The Ranter argument was broadly to the effect that, the creation of
God being good, and our desires being part of this creation, we can
do pretty much what we like. Hobbes accepts the premiss – our
desires are, if not good, then certainly in no a priori sense sinful or
bad – and yet attempts to derive opposite conclusions. An asocial
passion is for Hobbes an antisocial passion, not in the sense that is,

in itself, malevolent, but in the sense that its consequences are sufficiently random and unpredictable to pose a threat to any settled
order of a socio-political kind. Thus it is *the task* of politics to
constitute our 'Desires' and 'Passions' and the 'Actions' which follow
from them as 'Sin', at any rate in so far as they pose a threat to order:
actions are not sinful − asocial actions cannot count as antisocial −
'till they know a Law that forbids them' (*Leviathan*, Ch. XII: the
continuation of the above-quoted passage). Violence thus *counts as*
instrumental only to the extent that politics, construing it as its
'other', attempts to circumscribe it or hold it at bay. Likewise, power
counts as instrumental *Realpolitik* only to the extent that politics
draws its sting. The horror story told in Chapter XIII, about the
state of nature, describes not so much a pre-political condition, nor
indeed a condition which might emerge should political order break
down, as the area of human experience which lies in the shadow cast
by politics itself. Every heaven needs, as its 'other', a hell. Politics
calls in question the Ranterish assumption of the innocence of the
passions and, hence, must regard the passions *suspiciously* even whilst
conceding that people can do as they like within the confines of such
order as is necessary to the maintenance of politics *per se*. Hobbes
thus leaves open a space for negative liberty, whilst insisting that the
demarcation of this space is a political task.[6]

By way of summary, it may be helpful to map the Hobbes interpretations above discussed on to some of the conceptual questions
raised earlier. The 'traditional' reading of Hobbes, premissed as it is
on the notion of an economy of violence, links up with Weber and
a view of politics as having as its central task the containing or cir-
cumscribing or holding-at-bay of a violence which (*qua* instrumental)
is anathema to any politics of a communicative sort. The Taylor/
Warrender reading abandons this stark contrast. As it were, it is
more Arendtian. Although Hobbes, and Taylor and Warrender,
employ a natural law terminology which Arendt resists, their common contention is that our human condition contains resources of a
communicative/participatory and not just of a violent/instrumental
kind. The two readings agree, however, in eliding violence with
instrumentality and communicative behaviour with politics. The third,
Ranterish, reading of Hobbes challenges this presupposition. It
suggests that violence may itself be a politically constituted category
so that, by implication, what I have called the 'circuit' of politics
and indeed the origination of politics can, and perhaps must, be

linked to communicative resources inherent in violence itself. The notion of a *communitarian conception of violence* is, of course, an ugly one: I explore its plausibility and its implications below. For the present all that need be noted is that the rival interpretations of Hobbes replay *all* of the arguments and tensions and aporias which the first section of this chapter sketched. The *Leviathan* is of value as an encyclopaedia of difficulties, rather than as a dictionary giving solutions.

5 Ancients and Moderns

One way of taking stock of the argument presented so far is to compare ancient and modern understandings of how violence and politics interrelate. Digging in behind Aristotle's conception of revolution as *stasis* – a stopping of politics as business-as-usual – we can discover in the Ancient Greek dramatists a deep concern with the origins of politics as such. In the *Eumenides* of Aeschylus, Athene – protectress of the city of Athens – appeals to 'persuasion' and to the 'guardians of our city wall' (e.g. Aeschylus, 1965, p. 178). Both appeals are of interest. Persuasion is for Athene an inherently political matter, and her idea is that a politics of persuasion should replace both the endless see-saw of violent revenge entailed by an eye-for-an-eye conception of justice and the notion of justice as a precarious balance between warring factions (cf. Heraclitus in Kirk and Raven, 1957, p. 195). The overt violence of feuding tribes must give way – and this is the origin of politics – to the sublimated violence of polite rhetoric. Secondly, the reference to 'guardians of city walls' is important because Athene thinks of politics as an essentially urban matter: the walls demarcate the space of politics from its uncivilised and barbaric 'other'. It is no accident that, in the course of Aeschylus' drama, the pre-political Furies, seeking vengeance, become the political Eumenides in the same movement as the scene of action shifts from the rural stronghold of Mycenae to the Athenian urban realm. What in effect the Greek dramatists offer is a sociology of violence (parallel concerns are to be found in, for example, Sophocles[7]) premissed on the notion that a conceptual distinction between politics and violence can be mapped on to a spatial distinction between urban and non-urban life. Modern sociologies of violence, for example the studies of crowd behaviour by Le Bon (1960) and Canetti (1973), abandon such a mapping. In their interrogation of urban crowd violence, they are forced to think qualitatively rather than spatially or quantitatively. However, they tend to accept the Ancient understanding of violence and politics as mutually exclusive and, if anything, tend to side with Aristotle as against Aeschylus (or Sophocles) in construing inner-city crowd activity as an interruption of politics as civilised business as usual. The question propounded by Aeschylus — how can politics originate from eye-for-an-eye conceptions of justice and violent feuding? — threatens to drop out of sight.

It is an important question, and one which concerned Hobbes, despite his contemptuous characterisation of the Ancients as senti-mental republicans who mistakenly prioritised issues of the species of political rule (democratic? monarchical? tyrannical?) over and above the issue of whether political rule should exist at all. In fact it is an inescapable question, because if politics is the standing miracle of an activity which can renew and refuel itself (cf. Arendt on 'natality', 1958); if it is a self-sustaining circuit which can avoid vicious or tautological circularity (Section 3, above); if therefore it is uniquely entitled to presuppose itself (St Anselm and Modern communitarianism) *then* it has to be able to reflect upon its own origins, these origins (Hume, 1903, for instance[8]) being of a poten-tially violent kind. Politics may have to be seen as deriving from — and subsisting in and through its relation with — the violence which, once it is established, it must henceforth deplore.

Translating now, and briefly, from the Ancient to the Modern world we can note a further issue. In Section 3, above, it was suggested that conceptions of sovereignty threaten to trap themselves in a vicious circle. A sovereign legislative body has to be legitimately sovereign, thus standing in danger of relying upon its own edicts for its entitle-ment to command obedience to these edicts, themselves. In the Ancient world, this was not a serious problem. Sovereignty was — for the Greeks if not the Romans — a matter of interpreting a pre-existent unwritten and commonsensical law rather than of inventing laws afresh (McIlwain, 1962). Plato, for example, can rely upon notions of *mimesis* (*Republic* 500c-e) and of knowledge-as-memory (his *Meno* is a paradigmatic example) in order to make his description of an ideal *polis* or *civitas* or state plausible. In a cosmological world, memory systems could be the order of the political and epistemo-logical day (Yates, 1966). The condition of a cosmology, in contrast to a universe, is that truth is pre-inscribed within it (e.g. Koyré,

1962). Once we acknowledge that we inhabit a universe rather than a cosmos, however, everything changes. Modern *legislative* as opposed to Ancient *interpretive* sovereignty is faced with the task of, so to say, pulling politics up by its own bootstraps; stated in slightly different terms, sovereignty in the Modern world assumes an importance that it never carried before. It concentrates within itself what I have discussed as the self-renewing capacity of politics (Section 3, above) whilst also *in virtue of just this concentration* threatening to assimilate an open or 'hermeneutical' circle (on which see Dilthey in Connerton, 1976, p. 115) to a closed or vicious one. The task confronting Modernity is, therefore, to prise the closed and concentrated category of sovereignty apart, unlocking the logical bind in which it is caught and construing the circle or circuit of politics in a manner which is sufficiently wide to throw the logical and ontological resources of politics as a mode of activity into relief. If politics is indeed 'both a source of conflict and a *mode of activity* that [successfully] seeks to resolve conflicts and promote readjustments' (Wolin, 1960, p. 11) we need to understand how such can be the case. However, it is the category of sovereignty which focuses the most crucial questions. Precisely in so far as sovereignty shoulders the logical burden of vicious circularity it imposes upon us (Moderns) the task of considering the origins of politics, which may well lie in violence, and also the task of reflecting upon the relation of an ongoing politics to its founding or originating moment. For if a circle is to be non-vicious it must be broad and precise enough to arc through the origination that allows it to be drawn.

In a splendid, though also splendidly ambiguous, passage Arendt (1973b, p. 204) reports the condition of Modernity to be as follows: 'it is futile to search for an absolute to break the vicious circle in which all beginning is inevitably caught, because this "absolute" lies in the very act of beginning itself'. Does she mean that all new beginnings – revolutions, in Arendt's terminology – are necessarily viciously circular, or does she mean that an invocation or indeed a remembering (cf. Arendt on 'authority', n.d.,) of a new beginning can break the vicious circle in which politics, once it elides itself with sovereignty in the conventionally Modern way, becomes trapped? The latter appears to be Arendt's central contention. Her pivotal categories are those of 'natality' (1958) and of a revolution as 'an unconnected, new event breaking into the continuous sequence of historical time' (1973b, p. 205).[9] But then she has no business to urge, as she does in her essay 'On Violence', that violence (the potential origin of politics; the 'other' of politics) is inimical to the condition of politics itself. The questions of origination (from what?) and of otherness (in relation to what?) are one and the same. A circle loosens up from viciousness into theoretical and political fecundity only to the extent that its circumference draws into its centre *just that which* the very (originating) act of demarcating the circumference threatened to place outside. In a similar fashion, for Hegel, a true infinite had to be a unity of infinitude and finitude, and a true unity a unity of unity and of difference. Arendt in effect concedes this point when, in contradiction to almost all the rest of her thought, she reports that the 'mighty pressure groups of the poor' can secrete within themselves not just instrumental violence, and 'urgency', but revolutionary new beginnings and the seeds of politics as such (Arendt, 1973b, p. 244). Arendt rivals Hobbes in her devotion to making explicit, whilst refusing easy solutions to, the aporias of Modern thought.

6 Violence as political

A non-viciously circular circuit of politics has to be able to encompass its other: namely, violence. Should it choose not to do so, it begs not just the question of its origins (may not the roots of politics be violent?) but also the question of its continuation (may not violence be the shadow cast by politics itself?). The questions of origination and of continuation are one and the same inasmuch as both are highlighted, as crucial, by a claim to the effect that there is a 'mode of activity' which contains its resources for on-going within itself. They are in fact the same question, posed in different ways (as it were, philo- and ontogenetically). Communitarianism, and the liberalism which derives its legitimacy by a process of Kantian transcendental deduction, both threaten to be question-begging in the way just indicated. They presuppose what they were supposed to show: namely, politics. In the name of an already *political* distinction between politics and violence they set out to constitute politics. The to-be-constituted category is advertised as constituting, which may be fair enough as a phenomenological report of the capacities of politics but which in logical terms merely replays the vicious circularity inherent in Modern conceptions of sovereignty, as reported above.

There would appear to be only one way to break out of, or to expand, the vicious circle in which communitarians and liberals and theorists of sovereignty are trapped. This is to say that politics can indeed be an ongoing and self-renewing process *only because it is a self-constitutive one*. Origins do not have to be remembered, because they are always with us (cf. Bonefeld on 'primitive accumulation', 1988). Politics can be on-going only because, and in so far as, it is that mode of action which consists in calling into question itself. To this effect, Arendt (1973b, Ch. VI) invokes – somewhat in contradiction to her elsewhere emphatic insistence on the virtues of a stable political 'world' – the Jeffersonian tradition of grassroots participation as a means of keeping the issue of political origins alive. Politics needs not just to start as it means to go on, but to go on pretty much in the same fashion as it starts. One can diagnose a sort of tension in Arendt's thought between the notions of political constitution as a one-off event, to be enshrined in memory as the source of subsequent 'authority' (Arendt, n.d.), and of political constitution as co-terminous with politics itself and amounting to something not far removed from 'permanent revolution'. Operating within a very different tradition of political reflection, Negri (in Bonefeld, Gunn and Psychopedis, 1992, Vol. 2, pp. 101–2; cf. Bonefeld and Gunn, 1991) urges that the 'real problem' for politics has never been one of its 'constituent power' (*potentia*) but rather that of 'the modality of its Thermidor'. Despite the world of political difference which separates Arendt from Negri we can perhaps discern, here, a faint echo of what can be called the 'left-Jeffersonian' aspect of Arendt's thought.

Politics can broaden its circle (out of vicious circularity) only in so far as it takes the issue of its potentially violent origin on board, and it can do this latter only in so far as it thinks of itself as *internally* related to the violence which is its 'other' and so continues to place itself at issue at every on-going step it takes. The tension in Arendt's thought may be a consequence of the circumstance that she thinks of violence only in an instrumental/antipolitical and never in a political/communicative way. I close my argument with some brief reflections on theorists who have allowed that (some) violence may be of a political and communitarian kind.

In reverse chronological order, these theorists are Sartre, Bataille and Hegel. They renounce all the equivocations and squeamishness about violence which we have diagnosed in Arendt and Hobbes. Sartre declares bluntly (Sartre, 1976) that violence can be a 'practical bond'. In his introduction to Frantz Fanon's *The Wretched of the*

Earth (1967) he says more or less the same thing whilst muddying the issue by discussing the bonding potential of violence only in terms of a huddling together of comrades in arms who confront an external, and for its part violent, threat. It is as though the responsibility for violence is displaced on to an other. However, Sartre's more systematic and consistent thought, from the sado-masochistic see-saw of *Being and Nothingness* through into the more finely shaded *Critique of Dialectical Reason*, is to the effect that violence *per se* contains communicative and political resources. We need to tread carefully here. Not all violence is communicative, but some can be.

The theorist who agonised most over the matter of distinguishing between communicative and antipolitical dimensions of violence is George Bataille, a sort of existentialist colleague of Sartre's whose work Sartre knew well. According to Bataille, violence broaches communicative and communitarian issues only when it amounts to 'expenditure', or wastage, much in the sense of someone opening a wallet, generously, in order to support a good and drunken night out. (Although Bataille could not have known it, 'getting wasted' is the Scottish idiom signalling just such a night.) The *philosophical* roots of this approach lie in Nietzsche's contention, in for example *Also Sprach Zarathustra*, that – again a play on *potestas* and *potentia* – the truly powerful man is he who, generously, 'expends' (Bataille, 1985, pp. 116–29) or gives things away. Only someone anxious about their *potentia* would want to elide it with *potestas* and devote themselves to controlling and delimiting other human individuals in whatever fashion. The weak rather than the powerful man aspires to tyranny, which is more or less what the closing passages of Plato's *Republic* say. The *sociological* origins of Bataille's thought lie in the Durkheimian reflections of Marcel Mauss who, however, in his *The Gift* (Mauss, 1989), construes just the sort of 'potlatch' expenditure which Bataille celebrates as a neurotic and parasitic excrescence growing on to and into the body of an other-wise healthy practice of symbolic exchange. The difference between Mauss and Bataille is (only) the difference between a welfare-state theorist and a surrealist who defined himself as irresponsible: so irresponsible did Bataille define himself to be that he was thrown out of the surrealist movement for being insufficiently poetic. And yet we forget him at our cost. His contention was to the effect that violence, a 'transgression' (Bataille, 1987, Ch. V) of political limits, is part and parcel of these same limits. His further contention is to the effect that only a *wasting* violence in contrast to an *instrumental* violence is defensible, because whereas the former is bound up with the symbolic and societal constitution of politics − in much the same way as a dinner party helps to cement allegiances amongst friends − the latter atomises individuals and drives them away from one another. An 'economy of violence' is apolitical (Bataille claimed to have been diagnosed by an unnamed psychoanalyst as anal-retentive) and it becomes antipolitical (Hobbes) to the extent, only, that it carries its instrumentalism through. Conserving and minimising and re-serving (Derrida, 1979) the circuit of spiritual (*geistige*) or physical energy is the condition of any society, however defined. The only reasonable question to raise pertains to the matter of this energy's use. According to Bataille we can either stockpile it, as for instance in the instrumental and empowering gloating over powers which Hobbes terms 'glory' (see note 5), or we can expend it, thus keeping the political boat afloat.

Sartre (who read Bataille), and Sartre and Bataille, who had read Hegel, derive their challenge to instrumentalist conceptions of politics *and* of antipolitics from a single, highly dramatic and efflorescent passage of Hegelian thought. Contrary to the most usual view this is not the master-slave dialectic (Hegel, 1977, pp. 111–19; Kojève, 1947, opening chapter; and for critical distance Arthur, 1986). Instead it is Hegel's discussion of the French Revolution (Hegel, 1977, pp. 355–63). Hegel who, as a man, found himself unable to support the notion of revolutionary terror (e.g. Cullen, 1978, p. 31) nonetheless, in the *Phenomenology of Spirit* (1977), in the section headed 'Absolute Freedom and Terror', opened his discourse on to the renovative capacities of violence in a political way. Two and only two readings of the 'Absolute Freedom and Terror' passage are possible, and both derive their provenance from the broad plausibility of a left-Hegelian interpretation (Stepelevich, 1979; Toews, 1980). *Either* we read Hegel as saying that politics becomes a debauch of violence when it seeks to project absolute freedom (Hyppolite, 1969, essay 3; Plant, 1973) *or* we can say, along with Gunn (1988b), that for Hegel the most awful horror, worse still than Hobbes' depiction of existence in a warring state of nature, is the suspicion that *terror itself can sustain politics*, a politics of origination and of grass-roots excitement, albeit in an ephemeral way. Violent terror can not just seem to be, but actually can amount to, the condition upon which a politics wide and broad enough to encompass its origins may rest. Communitarian violence – a revolutionary 'tumult', as Hegel calls it, a rise and fall of factions so swift that none can claim legitimacy and so contingent that we can never declare an allegiance to one or other of them – opens a space for political conversation of the best sort. Over our last glass of wine at the end of an evening, our conversation is likely to be sharpened if neither of us knows which of us may be unlocking the guillotine blade tomorrow.[10] This is just one version of the way in which politics can be expanded towards its origins, whilst – and is it not the same argument, stated differently? – violence (or the threat of it) need not be seen in a sheerly instrumental and antipolitical way.

The upshot of the lines of thought just sketched is a series of questions, and of suggestions, rather than answers. Indeed it is the aim of the present chapter to pose these questions rather than to resolve them. The questions reduce themselves to three.

1) How does politics get going? The suggestion is that it *cannot* get going if it thinks of itself as having a merely external relation to violence, as in Arendt or Weber. Scenarios of a non-violent politics or of a politics whose central task is to hold violence at bay either become sentimental and wish-fulfilling (the charge Weber would undoubtedly have brought against Arendt) or taken over by the instrumentalism they seek to oppose (the charge brought against Weber by Arendt). This being so it is tempting to set the questions of how politics gets going – the question of the *origination* of politics – aside. But then politics threatens to beg its own question; it threatens to construe what I have called its own self-renewing 'circuit' or 'circle' too narrowly; it threatens to tread the vicious circle of 'sovereignty' and to forget that a mode of action promising self-renewal and what Arendt calls 'natality' and 'new beginnings' (Arendt, 1958; 1973b) can make its promise good only by encompassing its own origins. The difficulty, emphasised by Hobbes and Hume, is that these origins may well lie in violence. If therefore we set aside the notion of politics as on-going, and if we think of politics as being able to continue (or 'on-go') only in so far as it continues to thematise its origins and place itself at issue, in relation to violence, the question which remains open is very simple: how should politics think about itself?

2) How does violence take on an instrumental character? One rather obvious suggestion is to the effect that violence is constituted as

(solely) instrumental to the extent that communicative politics construes it as its 'other'. Politics casts violence into a hell of otherness in the same movement as it projects a heaven of a communicative – an authentically political – kind. The communicative voice of violence becomes gagged, for better or for worse, in the same movement as politics, whose self-understanding is to the effect that it is the opposite of violence, reserves (perhaps if need be violently?) all discourse to itself. The open question is, therefore: how should violence think about itself? The force attaching to this question derives from the circumstances that a violence gagged by politics, a politically repressed violence and to this extent a politically constituted violence,[11] threatens to turn nasty in precisely the Hobbesian sense of an 'acceleration'.

A violence constituted *by* politics as the other *of* politics is a purely instrumental violence, a violence stripped of all the symbolic and ritual and communicative dimensions which, as in pre-Modern codes of chivalry and honour, impose controls upon violence that are immanent in violence itself. French Revolutionaries, for example, might guillotine one another without a qualm but could (or could be imagined to) think of murder for private gain as corruption of the worst sort. It is instrumental rather than communicative violence which counts as, so to say, 'raw' violence, as a violence whose 'use' becomes the only matter of consideration; and the legitimate occasions of 'use' can be determined only by external (political) means. Whereas there are no intrinsic limits whatsoever to considerations of potential usefulness, a misguided recourse to violence in, say, a duel or a revolution would be like a mistaken move in a language-game; it could (be imagined to) leave all participants and spectators aghast. Aboriginal violence, it can be suggested, is communicative rather than participatory; instrumental or 'raw' violence is a highly artificial construct, constituted by precisely the Modern states which 'deplore' it and use it and whose 'other' it is. Modern sovereignty and instrumentally stripped-down violence, on this view, come into being together. The latter is the potentially endless shadow which the former casts. *Statist* violence, however liberal the state and however enlightened the argument for its deployment, may be that species of violence concerning which we should have the gravest worries of all. *States* may, therefore, be in part culpable for the violence they claim to hold down, depress and deplore.

3) How can politics maintain itself? It can be done, I think, only by

acknowledging that politics and violence are internally related. Each is the 'other' of its other. As reported in my concluding section, the ontological distinction between instrumental and communicative modes of activity fails to coincide with the ethical or moral distinction between (good) politics and (bad) violence. It would be convenient, not just ethically but epistemologically, if these distinctions did indeed coincide. Inasmuch as they do not we live in a complex world. In such a world, what competence attaches to the political judgements (Arendt, 1982; Beiner, 1983) that we make?

7 Pacifistic implications

One way of reporting the implications of the arguments presented above is to examine, albeit briefly, their relations to views of a pacifistic kind.

The ethical and philosophical difficulties which beset pacifism can, I think, be traced to the circumstance that it relies upon a wholly instrumental conception of violence (on the moral underpinnings of which see Honderich, 1980). A consistent pacifism has not just to prioritise principle-based arguments over and above consequentialist or utilitarian arguments but also to be willing to say that the guilt attaching to the death of a single man or woman is no less, or greater, than the guilt attaching to the massacre of millions. The failure of a principle is an absolute failure, and so numbers are irrelevant. This is a declaration which stands in opposition to every moral intuition that we recognise, or know.

Nonetheless, pacifism corresponds to everyone's moral intuitions in so far as we seek peace. According to Aristotle, peace is the goal of war. Pacifism polices itself out of such consequentialist moral arguments to the extent that it thinks of itself in absolute terms. These absolute terms are precisely the instrumentalist and consequentialist and utilitarian terms it opposes, because an absolute is an end in itself and reference to such an end can have status only in a discourse which weighs ends against means. Pacifism contradicts itself *unless* it draws a distinction between instrumental and communicative violence. Once it does so, and once it castigates the former in the name of the latter, it can both shed its instrumental/ absolutist mantle and reflect upon politics as on-going and self-constitutive more rigorously than can any alternative school of thought. In effect it will have to celebrate the (participatory or communicative) violence which liberals count horrendous, and deplore the (instrumental and statist) violence which liberals reluctantly defend. In doing so, pacifism will be able to deploy instrumentalist arguments against themselves: the partipatory violence of the French Revolutionary terror killed only single numbers of thousands of persons; following the defeat of the Paris Communards in 1871, 20,000 bodies were incarcerated in mass graves; in our own century, the conventionally numbered dead resulting from concentrated political action accelerates into the hundreds of thousands and tens of millions. Pacifism debars such arguments from itself because it thinks absolutely, and it thinks absolutely because it thinks defensively (originating as it does from a project of making a *rapprochement* with a reactionary state which had been victorious in a damaging civil war).[12]

Whether or not the position towards which my argument tends is termed pacifism is of little moment. The logical point is to the effect that the two assumptions I set out from − (1) that violence is instrumental and (2) that politics is on-going − each rise higher on a scale of plausibility to the degree that the other is dropped. Violence advertises itself as more than just instrumental to the extent that politics casts it as its own shadow, and perhaps can derive from it. Politics advertises itself as (potentially) violent inasmuch as it is internally related to violence as light is to shade. Were an ontological distinction between good and bad human capacities to coincide with an ethical distinction between political and barbaric practices, as Arendt most usually claims to think, the world would be a relatively simple place in which to pass judgement. In fact it is sheer wish-fulfilment to imagine such a coincidence, and the world is complex. Violence can be communicative, and politics can reflect on itself and on its on-going self-constitution only in so far as it is willing to reflect upon violence. On this despairing note the present chapter ends. The only theorist to take heart from is, perhaps, Bataille, according to whom no humanistic charity or *caritas* can be authentic if it fails to learn to love the dark side of our lives.

Notes

1   Compare Habermas' early *Knowledge and Human Interests* (1972, p. 314), where it is declared that 'the truth of statements is based on anticipating the realisation of the good life', with his later *Autonomy and*

Solidarity (1986, p. 90) according to which the 'ideal speech situation' is not a 'utopia', i.e. a practically realisable political goal. Compare Rawls' *A Theory of Justice* with, for example, Rawls, 1985. Rawls and Habermas appear to have moved in opposite directions towards one another's starting points, a nice illustration of the circularity in which discussion of politics can be caught.

2   Marx (e.g. Marx and Engels, 1962, p. 494) thought that some revolutions could be peaceful, and reckoned that it would be all the better if they were.

3   In his *Discourse on the Origins of Inequality* (Rousseau, 1973, p. 66).

4   Cf. Strauss, 1936; MacPherson, 1962 and his Introduction to the Penguin Books edition of *Leviathan*.

5   In the Hobbesian lexicon, 'glory' is delight in the powers we possess in fact, whereas 'vainglory' is delight in such powers as we think we possess, but do not. Strauss (1936) tends to elide glory with vainglory, thus assimilating Hobbes to a moralistic discourse according to which we ought not to be pricked up with pride. In the Hobbesian lexicon, 'pride' is vainglorious delight and hence the diametric opposite of glory. Strauss challenges, moralistically, the 'traditional' interpretation of Hobbes, rightly but wrong-headedly, and threatens to go not far enough.

6   For the interpretations of Hobbes alluded to but not so far specifically cited see Taylor in Brown (1965); Warrender (1957); Watkins (1965); and the useful summary in Tuck (1989).

7   In the *Antigone* of Sophocles a crucial question is the location of Antigone's brother's body, which Creon decrees should not be buried. It lies outside the city walls and, roughly, Antigone's claim is that the 'divine' law of the family is more spatially universal than the 'human', or political, law of the city which Creon propounds. *If* there is a moral to be drawn from this highly agonistic and indeed deconstructive play it is to the effect that a human law which severs itself from divine law undermines itself; and so Creon's political rule as well as his very conditions of survival fail. The best commentary is still, I think, the opening sections of Hegel (1977) Ch. VI. On the public and political significance of Ancient Greek drama, see Finley (1985), where it is reported that perhaps more than 10,000 persons attended the dramas of an Aeschylus or a Sophocles as a ritualised civic event.

8   Cf. Hume's essay 'Of the Original Contract' (Hume, 1903, pp. 452–73). Hume concedes that in utterly simple (= primitive) conditions of association the reciprocal promising of a social contract may be sufficient; but he rejects the notion that complex (= civilised) society can be established upon the same foundation because most of such societies result from conquest, revolution, mayhem and so on.

9 Arendt's indebtedness, here, is to the 'Theses on the Philosophy of History' of Benjamin (1973). Young-Bruehl (1982) contains a poignant description of the circumstances under which this text by Benjamin was first read by Arendt and her close associates.

10 Cf. Hegel, 1977, pp. 360, 394, on the communicative possibilities inherent in a drama of 'suspicion'. The root idea is that, in so far as we recognise the freedom of others, we recognise *inter alia* their freedom to break recognitive ranks. Violence is of course the ultimate breaking of ranks, in this sense, but on the other hand − according to the Hegelian argument − the very condition of a reciprocal or 'mutual' recognition is that it must summon the possibility of violence (its own 'other') if it is to exist at all. There is an internal relation between politics (or 'recognition') and violence inasmuch as only a politics which self-reflectively places itself at issue, if need be violently, is a politics worthy of the name. An attempt to justify this interpretation of Hegel is to be found in Gunn (1988b).

11 In other words it is politics which constitutes violence *as instrumental* and therefore as liable to the 'acceleration' or turning-nasty which Hobbes reports. There is an analogy here in Freudian thought, and I make this analogy explicit because (*only* as an analogy, and not at all as a diagnosis or prognosis of the implications of, say, Hobbes and Weber) it underlies the entire argument. In Freud's correspondence with Jung (Freud and Jung, 1974), Jung urges that it is a sense of guilt which constitutes desire, and Freud, responding as an irritated positivist, replies to the effect that unless we had (Oedipal) desires in the first place we would have nothing to feel guilty about. Later on, Lacan (1977) and Foucault (1981) report the 'law of the father' to be the condition of desire − we want what is forbidden to us − in the name of Freudian orthodoxy. The grass on the other side of the fence is always greener. Politics, I want to say, romanticises and constitutes violence in just this sense.

12 Hill (1975) documents the emergence of pacifism in the seventeenth century as a response on the part of radical groups to a reinstated monarchy which threatened to repress them: 'We undertake to confine our opposition to not fighting your wars on condition that you leave us alone.' Regarded in this way, pacifism amounts to a negotiated settlement between radicals and the State rather than to an anti-State or anti-authoritarian argument, as such.

References

Aeschylus (1965), *The Oresteian Trilogy*, Harmondsworth: Penguin Books.
Anselm, St (1973), *The Prayers and Meditations*, Harmondsworth: Penguin Books.
Arendt, H. (1958), *The Human Condition*, Chicago: University of Chicago Press.

Arendt, H. (1973a), *Crises of the Republic*, Harmondsworth: Penguin Books.

Arendt, H. (1973b), *On Revolution*, Harmondsworth: Penguin Books.

Arendt, H. (1977), *Eichmann in Jerusalem*, Harmondsworth: Penguin Books.

Arendt, H. (1982), *Lectures on Kant's Political Philosophy*, Chicago: Chicago University Press.

Arendt, H. (n.d.), *Between Past and Future*, London: Faber and Faber.

Arthur, C. J. (1986), *Dialectics of Labour*, Oxford: Basil Blackwell.

Baron, H. (1966), *The Crisis of the Early Italian Renaissance*, Princeton: Princeton University Press.

Bataille, G. (1985), *Visions of Excess: Selected Writings 1927–1939*, Manchester: Manchester University Press.

Bataille, G. (1987), *Eroticism*, London: Marion Boyars.

Beiner, R. (1983), *Political Judgement*, London: Methuen.

Benjamin, W. (1973), *Illuminations*, Glasgow: Collins/Fontana.

Bernstein, R. (1983), *Beyond Objectivism and Relativism*, Oxford: Basil Blackwell.

Bonefeld, W. (1988), 'Class Struggle and the Permanence of Primitive Accumulation', *Common Sense*, No. 6, Edinburgh.

Bonefeld, W. and Gunn, R. (1991), 'La Constitution et sa signification', *Future Antérieur*, No. 8, Paris: Editions Harmatton.

Bonefeld, W., Gunn, R. and Psychopedis, K. (1992), *Open Marxism*, London: Pluto Press.

Brown, K. C. (1965), *Hobbes Studies*, Oxford: Oxford University Press.

Canetti, E. (1973), *Crowds and Power*, Harmondsworth: Penguin Books.

Connerton, P. (1976), *Critical Sociology*, Harmondsworth: Penguin Books.

Cullen, B. (1978), *Hegel's Social and Political Thought*, London: Gill and Macmillan.

Davis, J. C. (1986), *Fear, Myth and History*, Cambridge: Cambridge University Press.

Derrida, J. (1979), *Writing and Difference*, London: Routledge and Kegan Paul.

d'Entreves, A. P. (1962), *The Notion of the State*, Oxford: Oxford University Press.

Fanon, F. (1967), *The Wretched of the Earth*, Harmondsworth: Penguin Books.

Finley, M. I. (1985), *Democracy Ancient and Modern*, London: Hogarth Press.

Foucault, M. (1979), *Discipline and Punish*, Harmondsworth: Penguin Books.

Foucault, M. (1981), *The History of Sexuality*, Vol. I, Harmondsworth: Penguin Books.

Freud, S. (1985), *Totem and Taboo*, The Origins of Religion, Pelican French Library, Vol. 13, Harmondsworth: Penguin Books.

Freud, S. and Jung, C. G. (1974), *The Freud/Jung Letters*, London: Hogarth Press and Routledge and Kegan Paul.

Gerth, H. and Mills, C. W. (1962), *From Max Weber*, London: Routledge and Kegan Paul.

Gewirth, H. (1982), *Human Rights*, Chicago and London: University of Chicago Press.

Gunn, R. (1988a), *Civic Humanist Themes in Machiavelli*, Edinburgh: Edinburgh University New Waverley Papers.

Gunn, R. (1988b), ' "Recognition" in Hegel's Phenomenology of Spirit', *Common Sense*, No. 4, Edinburgh.

Gunn, R. (1990), 'Coppe and Ranters', *Edinburgh Review*, No. 83, Edinburgh.

Habermas, J. (1972), *Knowledge and Human Interests*, London: Heinemann.

Habermas, J. (1986), *Autonomy and Solidarity*, London: Verso Books.

Habermas, J. (1989), *The Structural Transformation of the Public Sphere*, Oxford: Polity Press.

Hegel, G. W. F. (1977), *Phenomenology of Spirit*, Oxford: Oxford University Press.

Hegel, G. W. F. (1988), *Lectures on the Philosophy of Religion*, Berkeley: University of California Press.

Hegel, G. W. F. (1991), *Elements of the Philosophy of Right*, Cambridge: Cambridge University Press.

Held, D. (1984), *Introduction to Critical Theory*, London: Hutchinson.

Hill, C. (1975), *The World Turned Upside Down*, Harmondsworth: Penguin Books.

Honderich, T. (1980), *Violence for Equality*, Harmondsworth: Penguin Books.

Hume, D. (1903), *Essays: Moral, Political and Literary*, London: Grant Richards.

Hyppolite, J. (1969), *Studies on Marx and Hegel*, London: Heinemann.

Kirk, G. S. and Raven, J. E. (1957), *The Presocratic Philosophers*, Cambridge: Cambridge University Press.

Kojève, A. (1947), *Introduction à la lecture de Hegel*, Paris: Gallimard.

Koyré, A. (1962), *Du Monde clos à l'universe infini*, Paris: Gallimard.

Lacan, J. (1977), *Ecrits: A Selection*, London: Tavistock Publications.

Le Bon, G. (1960), *The Crowd*, New York: Viking Press.

McIlwain, C. H. (1962), *The Growth of Political Thought in the West*, New York: Macmillan.

MacPherson, C. B. (1962), *The Political Theory of Possessive Individualism*, Oxford: Oxford University Press.

Marcuse, H. (1968), *Negations*, London: Allen Lane.

Marx, K. (1976), *Capital*, Vol. I, Harmondsworth: Penguin Books.

Marx, K. and Engels, F. (1962), *On Britain*, Moscow: Progress Publishers.

Mauss, M. (1989), *The Gift*, London: Routledge.

Morton, A. L. (1970), *The World of the Ranters*, London: Lawrence and Wishart.

Negri, A. (1991), *The Savage Anomaly*, Minneapolis and Oxford: University of Minnesota Press.

Plant, R. (1973), *Hegel*, London: Heinemann.

Pocock, J. G. A. (1971), *Politics, Language and Time*, London: Methuen.

Pocock, J. G. A. (1975), *The Machiavellian Moment*, Princeton: Princeton University Press.

Rawls, J. (1971), *A Theory of Justice*, Oxford: Clarendon Press.

Rawls, J. (1985), 'Justice as Fairness: Political Not Metaphysical', *Philosophy and Public Affairs*, Vol. 14, No. 3.

Rousseau, J.-J. (1973), *The Social Contract and Discourses*, London: Dent.

Sandel, M. (1984), *Liberalism and Its Critics*, New York: New York University Press.

Sartre, J.-P. (1976), *Critique of Dialectical Reason*, London: New Left Books.

Skinner, Q. (1986), 'The Paradoxes of Political Liberty', *The Tanner Lectures on Human Values VII*, Cambridge: Cambridge University Press.

Smith, N. (1984), *The Ranters*, London: Junction Books.

Stepelevich, L. S. (1979), *The Young Hegelians: An Anthology*, Cambridge: Cambridge University Press.

Strauss, L. (1936), *The Political Philosophy of Hobbes*, Oxford: Oxford University Press.

Taylor, A. E. (1938), 'The Ethical Decline of Hobbes', in Brown (1965).

Toews, J. E. (1980), *Hegelianism*, Cambridge: Cambridge University Press.

Tuck, R. (1989), *Hobbes*, Oxford: Oxford University Press.

Warrender, H. (1957), *The Political Philosophy of Hobbes*, Oxford: Oxford University Press.

Watkins, T. (1965), *Hobbes's System of Ideas*, London: Hutchinson.

Wolin, S. (1960), *Politics and Vision*, Boston: Little, Brown.

Yates, F. (1966), *The Art of Memory*, London: Routledge and Kegan Paul.

Young-Bruehl, E. (1982), *Hannah Arendt: For Love of the World*, New Haven and London: Yale University Press.

Index